A PROMISE

OF EDEN

A PROMISE

OF EDEN

Life Energy and Personal Growth
In an Age of Transformation

ALAN SILVERMAN

Tiferet Press
Boston, Massachusetts

ISBN 13: 9780978750800.
ISBN 10: 0-9787508-0-2. Library of Congress Control Number 2006906641.
First Edition.

Grateful acknowledgement is made to the following for permission to reprint previously published material:

From *Anatomy of the Spirit* by Caroline Myss, Ph.D., copyright © 1996 by Caroline Myss. Used by permission of Harmony Books, a division of Random House, Inc.

From *Autobiography of a Yogi* by Paramahansa Yogananda, copyright © 1997 by Self Realization Fellowship; and *The Holy Science* by Swami Sri Yukteswar, copyright © 1990 by Self Realization Fellowship. Used by permission of Self Realization Fellowship, Los Angeles, CA.

From *The Centaur* by John Updike, copyright © 1962, 1963 by John Updike. Used by permission of Alfred A. Knopf, a division of Random House, Inc.

From *Energy Medicine* by Donna Eden, copyright © 1998 by Donna Eden. Published by arrangement with the author and Susan Schulman, A Literary Agency, New York, NY.

From *Hands of Light* by Barbara Brennan, copyright © 1987 by Barbara Brennan. Used by permission of Bantam Books, a division of Random House, Inc.

From *Tao te Ching* by Lao Tsu, translated by Gia-Fu Feng and Jane English, copyright © 1997 by Jane English. Copyright © 1972 by Gia-fu Feng and Jane English. Used by permission of Alfred A. Knopf, a division of Random House, Inc.

From *Wheels of Life: A User's Guide to the Chakra System*, by Anodea Judith. Copyright © 1987, 1999 by Anodea Judith. Text used by permission of Llewellyn Worldwide, Woodbury, MN. Diagrams used by permission of Mary Ann Zapalac.

From *Your Life is in Your Chakras* by Guru Rattan Kaur, Ph.D., copyright © 1994 by Guru Rattan Kaur, Ph.D. Used by permission of Guru Rattana, Ph.D.

From *Zen Shiatsu: How to Harmonize Yin and Yang for Better Health,* by Shizuto Masunaga and Wataru Ohashi. Copyright © 1997 by Japan Publications, Inc. Used by permission of Japan Publications, Inc.

To the memory of

my little brother Bobby

who travels with me still

The more we come to understand the universe,
 the less it looks like a great machine,
and the more like a great thought.
                    ——Sir James Jeans

To see a world in a grain of sand
And a heaven in a wild flower,
Hold infinity in the palm of your hand
And eternity in an hour.
                    ——William Blake

Contents

A NOTE TO THE READER

The unifying theme of this book—life energy or *chi*—is an elusive concept that is hard to define or explain. It is far more than energy as we think of it in the West. On the other hand, it behaves in some ways like a simple fuel. It is, in a sense, both a thing and an idea, both abstract and concrete. We know it is tangible because we can feel it flowing in the body; we know it is intangible because it somehow unites mind and body at a level beyond our awareness. We know it is of this world because we can sense and feel it; we know it is of the next world because it is a direct conduit to the realm of Spirit.

Some prefer to think of life energy, not as a thing or even an idea, but as a process. In that sense it embodies the Chinese view that life is not a collection of things or concepts but a series of interacting patterns. In the end, life energy cuts across too many categories and does too many different things to be defined or adequately explained. I see it as a kind of metaphor for the mystery of life itself.

In spite of these difficulties—or possibly because of them—I have chosen to make life energy the centerpiece of this book. It is without doubt the most useful tool available for showing the underlying unity of mind, body and Spirit—the core of the holistic philosophy. Demonstrating that truth is one thing; fleshing it out with real meaning is another. My goal in this book is a relatively modest one: to describe how the human energy blueprint embodies the many interesting, beautiful and sometimes transcendent connections between mind, body, Spirit and the heavens above. Future books will have to deal with the more difficult question of what life energy really is, and how it manages to unite the different aspects of our experience.

Two other terms I use at various times are the New Age and the Age of Aquarius. I hesitate to use them, and have been advised not to, because they have come to represent, for many people, some of the less appealing features of the 1960's and 70's, including a kind of childish self-absorption and a corny, sentimen-talized version of spirituality. I use these terms because I have no choice—they identify an event so central to our lives that, I argue, the energy blueprint itself contains a symbol of it. With time, I hope, the unflattering associations with the late 20th century will gradually fade, and the era we are now entering will no longer have to be, for many people, the Age with No Name.

A final note about the title. For me, there is great beauty and meaning in Biblical images as symbols of a new era. They repre-sent continuity between the teachings of the past and the new and exciting ideas of the present and the future. That continuity, in fact, is an underlying theme of this book. The trend in progressive spiri-tuality today is toward new ideas, new practices—in some cases a whole new language of the Spirit—often with little or no connec-tion to the past. Although many of these ideas may be valid and important, they cannot help with a task that I believe is essential: to build a bridge between traditional religion, with its emphasis on faith, doctrine and prayer, and a more direct kind of spirituality based on meditation and inner experience. Since both Eastern and Western religions have their own rich mystical traditions, those teachings, appropriately updated, may be the most natural way for many people to discover a new kind of spirituality. This book, I hope, will help in a small way with that transition by laying one or two planks in the bridge connecting the old and the new.

INTRODUCTION

Human history is a holistic process. Little by little, as the years, decades and centuries roll by, there is a gradual movement toward wholeness, a slow connecting up—of ideas and, more importantly, of people. For the first we rely on our scientists and technicians, our writers and philosophers; for the second we rely on ourselves and sometimes, when we are very lucky, on our political leaders. The net result, after many a setback, detour and tragic disappointment, is that the race is slowly and gradually evolving toward a higher and better future.

The pace of change, as we know, has been accelerating for some time. When Darwin discovered the laws of evolution 150 years ago, he shattered the cherished belief that humans and animals came from fundamentally different origins. That connecting up of ideas, and of living things, was both humbling and grand. It showed that we are more like the apes, and the worms, than we like to admit. But at the same time it opened up the likelihood of a deeper and more beautiful unity in nature than we had known was there—one that bears the mark, not only of a great Engineer, but of a supremely inspired Artist.

When Einstein developed his theory of relativity 100 years ago, he showed that time and space, two seemingly separate and independent phenomena, are not only dependent on each other but form one unified entity called the Space-Time Continuum. Among other things, this meant that time could slow down or speed up or that space itself could curve. For those few able to fully absorb these mind-bending insights, there was again, as with Darwin, both humility and awe—humility that what we thought were fixed realities of life are actually plastic, moveable and hard to pin down; and awe that there could be such deep connections between things that seem on the surface so separate—again suggesting a Designer whose talents we can only struggle to guess at.

More recently, when 20th century wizards invented the semiconductor and the computer, we thought they had created something new under the sun. Then we began to notice an eerie similarity between the structure of these amazing machines and our own brains. As the century was coming to a close, we were seeing a new, and disconcerting, kind of connecting up—between ourselves and our own creations. I discuss some of the implications of that strange correspondence in Chapter 6.

Leaving aside science and technology, our everyday world has been seeing a quickening holistic process for some time. The impetus has been, not the drive for technical discovery, but the human desire for freedom and reconciliation. The rise of democracies around the world over the last 200 years, beginning with the French and American revolutions in the late 1700's, is the most obvious and important example. For what is democracy, after all, but the breaking down of barriers between ruler and ruled, a coming together of people with their government? Over the last few decades dozens of countries have become newly democratic, and those that haven't are feeling increased pressures in that direction, both from within and without. The United Nations, flawed though it is, continues to serve as a force for freedom and human dignity.

Within individual societies, there are other strong holistic forces at work, gradually breaking down longstanding barriers between different kinds of people. Steady advances in civil rights, women's rights and gay rights, among others, have all been made possible by a sense that differences that seemed important only a short time ago now seem quite minor compared to a growing sense of our common humanity.

Finally, of course, there is globalization, a major world movement toward the integration of national economies, markets, currencies and cultures. Although not without its costs, globalization is another sign of a world that wants to be increasingly interconnected. Even countries with exceptionally rich cultural traditions and fierce national pride—the countries of Western Europe for example—are merging currencies, markets and other institutions even though it means sacrificing important parts of their national identities. Whatever problems these changes may bring, the die has been cast and solutions will have to come through increased cooperation and concerted action across national borders.

Intimations of A New Age

History has a way of repeating itself, or at least of mirroring itself. The 1860's were a decade of mingled tragedy and hope in the United States—a time of war, injustice and racial strife but of new ideals and new beginnings as well. Lincoln's Second Inaugural address, delivered in 1865 at the end of a terrible Civil War, carried a message of compassion and reconciliation that set the tone for a new, more inclusive society and a far greater equality in American life.

Exactly a century later, the 1960's saw a similar period of war, injustice and racial turmoil. As the Vietnam War raged abroad, cities burned at home during the Watts race riots and following the assassination of Dr. Martin Luther King. As had happened 100 years earlier, a president was murdered along with a presidential candidate and a major civil rights leader. The ferment, discord and discontent in American society were like nothing the nation had seen since Civil War days.

But like the 1860's before them, the 1960's were as much a time of hope and new beginnings as they were of tragedy and loss. The idea was born that a new, more enlightened age was dawning in the world—the Age of Aquarius, an era of deep humanitarian values along with undreamed of technological progress. The idea captured the public imagination, particularly among the young, whose ideals of peace, compassion, equality and justice echoed those of Lincoln a century earlier. Those ideals found a home, not only in the struggle for civil rights and against war, but in the beginnings of the women's movement and in the search for a deeper meaning in life. That search included a new interest in Eastern philosophy and meditation and even the excesses of the period, such as psychedelic drug use, hinted at the discovery of a deeper kind of awareness that would be part of a New Age.

In retrospect, the 1960's and 70's saw the high water mark of initial enthusiasm over the coming of a new era. As the years passed, excitement about an imminent revolution gave way to a more realistic belief in a slow, gradual evolution in attitudes and values.[1] This was to be expected since the first stages of any movement, before ideals are forced to confront hard realities, are always the most passionate and exciting time. In place of revolutionary zeal came a slow but steady growth in a whole range of progressive ideas, values and practices that can be generally described as holistic. They ranged from new approaches to health care and health maintenance to new ways of understanding personality and behavior; from novel techniques for improving sports performance to new spiritual ideas and practices. The common element was a sense that there is an essential wholeness or unity in things, whether it be mind and body, the individual and society or the individual and God. The holistic philosophy—the philosophy of the New Age—is that true health, happiness and wisdom lie in recognizing, and living, this simple but profound truth at every level of life.

The steady growth of holistic ideas and practices was accompanied by another, related phenomenon. Nagging questions in fields as diverse as medicine, psychology, evolutionary theory, physics and philosophy were continuing to bedevil the attempts of scientists and others to find satisfactory solutions. The overall pattern suggested that the purely analytical Western approach to solving problems, valuable though it might be, was inadequate to answer, or even address, certain basic questions.

The development of holistic ideas in the U.S. continued despite a major shift in the political and social landscape beginning in the early 1980's. The election of Ronald Reagan ushered in a new and far more conservative mood in American society and threw liberals and progressives of every stripe on the defensive. Although the pendulum swung back to some extent with the election of Bill Clinton in 1992, it returned even more forcefully to the right with the election of George W. Bush in 2000 and again in 2004. By that time liberalism was in full retreat, fueled by the fear of terrorism, the increased power of corporate interests and the rise of fundamentalist Christianity. As the 21st century was getting under way, an Age of Aquarius seemed very far away, and some even suggested that a new Age of Conservatism might be dawning instead.

Still, the narrow margins of victory for conservatives in 2000 and again in 2004 highlighted a sharp split in the American electorate and a deep reservoir of progressive sentiment among large numbers of Americans. That split is not new—it is a longstanding feature of the American psyche that dates back to the early days of the Republic. In Chapter 4 I argue that it represents the natural tension between two basic bodily energies. Seen in that way, the history of American society and politics illustrates the evolution of human consciousness as the struggle, and gradual integration, of two fundamental human instincts.

The Power of the Holistic Principle

The message of this book is that, as holistic understandings continue to evolve and move closer to the mainstream, we in the West are on the verge of discovering a new and deeper dimension to our existence: the life energy realm, which lies between, and connects, the everyday world and the domain of Spirit. Life energy and its profound influences on body and mind have been known and accepted in Asia for centuries. In the West they will eventually revolutionize how we see ourselves and virtually every aspect of our lives.

Because of life energy's unique ability to integrate seemingly separate and even contradictory ideas and processes, it can help fill in a number of important gaps in our understanding. Consider the following examples:

1. In medicine, a rising tide of dissatisfaction with conventional health care has led to a steady growth in the popularity of alternative therapies. Those therapies now account for more total patient visits than conventional medical treatment. Many alternative therapies are life energy-based and range from acupuncture to shiatsu, from Tai Chi to medicinal herbs, from polarity therapy to magnets. The most important reason for their popularity is that the Western

medical system, for all its sophisticated tools and many successes, leaves out a critical component of human health. Too many conditions go undiagnosed and untreated because the Western medical model lacks not only the techniques but the concepts to address the whole person or even identify the source of many complaints.

Chapter 2 shows that the missing component in the Western medical model is the life energy system. Like the human body itself, the energy system is a complex, highly organized structure that interacts constantly with both body and mind. Stresses of various kinds can cause energy imbalances, and when they become severe or last for long periods, disease can result. Chapter 2 uses hypothetical case studies to show that three major diseases of our time—heart disease, cancer and diabetes—may all be due, in some cases and to some extent, to chronic energy imbalances.

2. Since Freud began to unravel the mystery of the Unconscious a century ago, it has remained a vague and fuzzy concept because Western science lacks the conceptual framework and vocabulary to make it tangible and real. This has greatly slowed psychology's progress in developing into a true science and has denied psychotherapists valuable tools for treating emotional disorders. The overall message of Chapter 3 is that the Western psychological model, like the Western medical model, is incomplete because it leaves out the life energy system. Most basically, the Unconscious is a complex, highly organized structure made of life energies. It can be seen as a kind of invisible energy brain that works in concert with the physical brain, which mirrors it, and is the unseen link connecting mind and body. Because life energy is a bridge connecting the mental and physical parts of our experience, energy principles can give new meaning to terms like holistic health and the mind-body connection.

Chapter 3 explores Western psychology through the lens of life energies to shed new light on a number of familiar ideas. For example, Freud's three stages of infantile development closely track the growth of three distinct energies in the body. The unhealthy fixations that can take root during those periods correspond to imbalances in their respective energies.

Energy principles can give new insight, too, into emotional conflicts that are universal parts of human experience: the natural tension between anger and compassion, love and fear and other important pairs of emotions. Those tensions, which can interfere with relationships or lead to full-blown illness if they become severe enough, are "hard-wired" into the psyche through the structure of the energy system. The ancient diagrams of traditional Chinese medicine graphically illustrate those relationships and, when updated to reflect modern understandings, they can help give new answers to old questions, such as:

- What is depression? Is it a biochemical disorder, an emotional disorder, an energy disorder or all three?
- How is a person's sense of connection to other people represented in energy terms? How can that connection be weakened and what can be done to strengthen it?
- Can love truly conquer fear? Is there an energy relationship in the body that represents this truth?

In showing that our emotional lives are tangibly embodied as a network of organized and structured life energies, Chapter 3 introduces a main theme of this book. Just as the laws of physics, chemistry and other sciences govern the physical world and its energies, the laws of life energy govern the world of consciousness. The 20th century saw the discovery of radio and television waves, X-rays and many other invisible phenomena that were astonishing in part because they could not be seen. The 21st century is likely to witness the discovery of a similar unseen world of life energy forces that will change our understanding of consciousness in equally important ways.

3. Most popular systems for understanding personality—Jungian typing, Myers-Briggs, the Enneagram and others—approach the subject indirectly, using a variety of different models and terminologies. In Chapter 4 I explore personality more directly, in terms

of the five basic energies that make it up. To do so I use two complementary systems: the Chinese Five Elements and Western astrology. I show how Five Elements principles can help clarify the teachings of astrology by identifying the energy combinations that make up the twelve signs of the Zodiac. I illustrate the truth of astrology, and the value of merging it with the Five Elements, through the birth charts of several well-known historical figures including several U.S. presidents.

In Part 2 of Chapter 4 I show how the same energies that make up individual personality are basic to every relationship. Using the Enneagram, a popular behavior and personality typing system, together with the Five Elements, I show how the harmonies and tensions between differing personality types can be understood in terms of well-known energy relationships.

In Part 3 of Chapter 4 I expand the role of life energies further to include the forces that shape society itself. Using the United States as an example, I show how society's evolution is, in a fundamental sense, a story of the tension between Wood and Earth energies, their gradual development and movement toward integration. The current split in U.S. society can be seen as a consequence of those tensions, and energy principles may hold clues as to how they will ultimately resolve themselves.

4. Recent trends in science, healing, spirituality and other disciplines all highlight the importance of better understanding what we mean by knowing—in particular, the difference between ordinary thinking and intuition. In Chapter 5 I define intuition as a direct knowing made possible by the sensing of life energies—in the human body, in one's surroundings or in the mind of God. I describe three kinds of intuition, each of which represents the sensing of life energies in a different way or on a different level.

Movement and coordination, like intuition, depend on energies and information that flow out of the Unconscious. Since many of those energies originate in the body, I suggest that there may be a kind of body brain that works in cooperation with the head brain, facilitating both movement and certain kinds of intuition.

5. For all its great successes, the strong material bias of Western science places serious limitations on its ability to answer or even address certain important questions. A current example is the apparent conflict between science and faith over the question of evolution. In Chapter 6 I argue that the conflict is an illusion made possible when randomness and chance became unofficial parts of Darwin's theory. Using the teachings of both Eastern and Western philosophy along with the insights of medical intuitives and discoveries in quantum physics, I argue that evolution is not an automatic, mindless process but the result of a consciously executed design by God. Life energy, I argue, is the invisible connecting link through which God orchestrates the development of living things.

6. The integrating power of life energy extends finally to religion and spirituality. In Chapter 7 I discuss life energy's role since ancient times as a tool for spiritual growth. The yogis, saints and sages of India and other countries perfected techniques for redirecting the flow of energies in the body, leading to higher awareness. The trend toward direct spiritual experience in the West is a sign that we are gradually incorporating the lessons of Asia into a new and deeper kind of spirituality.

An important part of that process will be the eventual healing of the most fundamental split in Western religion—between Judaism and Christianity. Using energy principles and the teachings of Western astrology and Jewish mysticism, I argue that Judaism's own Tree of Life contains symbols of the two faiths and of their eventual reconciliation. The Jewish mystical tradition itself, I suggest, supported by evidence from both the Old and New Testaments, points toward Jesus as the Messiah promised to the Jewish people in the Book of Isaiah. His role in Judaism, however, is likely to be quite different than it is in Christianity, in part because of the trend toward direct inner experience.

Throughout this book I have drawn heavily on the wisdom and traditions of China and India where life energy has been a living force for many centuries. I use traditional ideas in outlining generally how energy principles apply to health, personality and spiritual practice. Most of the specific interpretations, however, are my own. For a non-physician, non-psychologist, non-philosopher and non-scientist, this has been an ambitious and even audacious undertaking. To the extent that some of my interpretations may be wrong, the responsibility is entirely mine. To the extent that they are right, they often illustrate how simple and straightforward energy understandings can be.

That many of the ideas in this book are being presented for the first time is evidence of how undeveloped our knowledge of life energy is—it truly is in a state of infancy. My hope is that this material will be taken in the spirit in which it is offered: as a sketch of the outlines of a large and complex picture, the details of which will be filled in by specialists in many fields.

CHAPTER ONE
THE LIFE ENERGY BLUEPRINT

Human life energy, also called *chi* ("chee"), *prana, ki* and *dahn* in various Asian countries[2] and by other names in other traditions, is, like gravity and electromagnetism, an elemental force of nature. Though derived from Indian and Chinese philosophy, it is no mere theory or abstraction but a living force that we can touch, feel and manipulate with our hands. It hovers in and around the tissues in a kind of hybrid intermediate space, neither physical nor spiritual but connected to both. It flows through every human body in carefully prescribed channels; it interacts at every moment with our cells, tissues and organs; and it profoundly affects the operation of our minds and bodies. Life energy is the fountainhead of human life and our tangible link to the realm of Spirit.

Because of its strategic location at the intersection of mind, body and Spirit, life energy virtually defines the term holistic and is perhaps the ultimate holistic tool for maintaining better physical and emotional health and promoting spiritual growth.

Like democracy, evolution and relativity, life energy is a fundamentally powerful idea, a key to a deeper and more complete understanding of what it means to be human. As a new era begins, the network of energy pathways in the body can serve as a guide, or blueprint, to physical and emotional wholeness and to the discovery of our true identity as spiritual beings.

The Symmetry of Chinese and Indian Teachings

In Asia, where knowledge of life energies has reached its fullest flowering, there is a certain symmetry in how that knowledge has evolved. India and China, Asia's two oldest and largest nations, each developed a unique tradition stressing a different aspect of life energy's role and a different part of the energy system. Taken together they trace the major outlines of the full life energy blueprint; used together, they can provide a complete framework for personal growth along with the practical tools needed to achieve it.

PART 1. CHINA AND THE MERIDIAN SYSTEM

China's understanding of life energies is best known in the West
for therapeutic techniques like acupuncture and Chinese herbal
medicines. China's traditional emphasis on health and healing led
it naturally to the meridian system, an elaborate network of pathways near the surface of the body.

    The meridians are ideal for medical diagnosis and treatment
because meridian energies are easy to reach and manipulate and
because only one kind of energy flows in each meridian. The meridians, too, come in pairs whose contrasting energies fit neatly
into China's *yin-yang* world view. Using the meridians as their primary tool, the ancient Chinese created a subtle and highly sophisticated system for diagnosing and treating illness and, to a lesser
extent, for understanding human personality and behavior.

Yin, Yang and the Shape of Our World

China did not discover life energy's important health influences
directly; that knowledge came indirectly as a byproduct of Chinese
philosophy and spirituality. Chinese sages saw the duality of life—
the play of opposites—as its most striking and important feature.
They imagined a reality, before the universe began, in which there
were no opposites, no separation and no conflict: no pleasure and
pain, no selfishness and kindness, no love and hate, only pure being. In modern scientific terms, their view corresponded to what
existed before the Big Bang gave birth to the universe, before there
was space, time or the inevitable tension and conflict of earthly
life. It would be impossible even to describe, or name, such a state
of things. Taoism, one of China's great philosophy-religions,
acknowledges that difficulty in the opening verse of its basic text,
the Tao Te Ching:

> The Tao that can be told is not the eternal Tao
> The name that can be named is not the eternal name,
> The nameless is the beginning of heaven and earth,
> The named is the mother of ten thousand things.[3]

Through simple but powerful poetry, the Tao evokes a deep mystery underlying human life and hints at a reality just beyond our understanding. On a more everyday level it sets out the principle of opposites that would become the cornerstone of traditional Chinese medicine:

> The ten thousand things carry yin and embrace yang
> They achieve harmony by combining these forces.[4]

The "ten thousand things"—all the things of the created world—are understood to be in a natural state of tension. That tension is symbolized by *yin* and *yang*, the complementary opposites that give shape to our world. When *yin* and *yang* are in balance, there is harmony and happiness; when they are out of balance, there is disharmony and conflict. This, in a nutshell, is the basic principle of traditional Chinese medicine.

The Chinese incorporated their understanding of *yin* and *yang* into their study of the human body. *Yin* and *yang,* they discovered, expressed themselves physically in the balance between heat and cold, dryness and moisture, tension and relaxation and other common pairs of opposites. By balancing the energies that underlay these physical phenomena, Chinese physicians learned to restore and maintain good health.

The Chinese discovered that the emotions, too, interacted in certain specific ways and that the mind, like the body, was subject to the laws of *yin* and *yang.* Although the emphasis in Chinese medicine has always been more on physical than emotional health, the early psychological insights of China provide an elegant and powerful framework for understanding personality and human behavior in new ways.

The Chinese discovered, too, that a tangible but mysterious force, or energy, in the body—one that they could feel and influence with their hands—could help harmonize *yin* and *yang.* They called it *chi*—we translate it as life energy—and through careful study and observation, they ultimately identified five distinct energies, the pathways through which they flowed and how they interacted. That knowledge developed into the Chinese meridian and Five Elements systems.

THE TWELVE PRIMARY MERIDIANS

The body has twelve primary energy pathways that nourish the internal organs and mind and body as a whole. They crisscross the body from head to toe, each carrying a specific type of life energy. The twelve primary meridians are shown is side view in Figure 1.

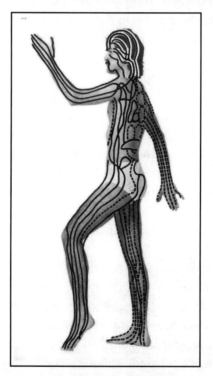

FIGURE 1.
THE TWELVE PRIMARY MERIDIANS

Along each meridian are a series of highly sensitive energy centers (acupuncture or acupressure points) which, when stimulated with fingers, needles, heat or magnets, affect mind and body in predictable ways. Chinese medical texts list 360 traditional points, along with hundreds of point combinations, for treating virtually every kind of physical or emotional complaint. Researchers continue to discover new meridians, sub-meridians and sub-sub-meridians, along with additional points.

The meridian network, like the body itself, represents a highly complex, subtle and finely calibrated network of activities. The body's energies can be seen as a kind of invisible template that embodies a person's total physical, mental, emotional and spiritual being. According to medical intuitives who can perceive energies directly, every bodily activity and every thought, feeling and impulse down to the tiniest movements inside individual cells has a counterpart in the energy realm.

Life's Duality and Meridian Pairs

To understand how *yin* and *yang* interact in the body, a good starting point are the six meridian pairs that make up the twelve primary pathways. One member of each pair carries *yang* energies that flow from the head down, while the other carries *yin* energies that flow from the feet up. There is a natural polarity or tension between each pair just as there is in the body as a whole. Some of the qualities of *yin* and *yang* energies, and of people with *yin*– and *yang*-dominant personalities, are as follows:

YANG	YIN
Warm	Cool
Intense	Relaxed
Physical\Material	Emotional\Ethereal
Active	Passive
Projective	Receptive
Hardy, Resilient	Sensitive, Vulnerable
Ambitious	Self Sufficient
Superficial	Deep
Self Interested	Giving
Masculine	Feminine

The differences between sister meridians illustrate the *yin-yang* structure of the system as a whole. The two Earth meridians, for example, are stomach and spleen. The *yang* energies of stomach embody the appetite for food and other material pleasures. Stomach energies are hardy and resilient; they resist control by other energies, tending to control or even dominate them instead.

By comparison with stomach, the energies of spleen are gentle, sensitive and vulnerable. They embody, among other things, a person's need for emotional nourishment, especially love. Unlike the energies of stomach and the other *yang* meridians, *yin* energies are easily weakened, blocked or even overwhelmed.

The chronic excess of aggressive *yang* energies in people today is a kind of internal mirror of life in the modern world. In Chapter 2 I show that the explosive growth of illnesses like heart disease and diabetes is, to a considerable degree, a reflection of the unhealthy dominance of *yang* energies.

THE FIVE ELEMENTS: BLENDING ART AND ENGINEERING

The ancient Chinese were keen observers, not just of the human body, but of the natural world around them. They discovered five distinct energies in the body along with a remarkable pattern of correspondences between those energies and forces of nature. The Five Elements system is one of those rare creations that blends art with engineering, poetry with utility. The beautiful parallels between body energies and natural forces is evidence of what I call Aesthetic Design in nature. On a more pragmatic level, Five Elements relationships are a valuable tool for understanding and improving both physical and emotional health.

As a system with only five major working parts, the Five Elements cannot hope to capture the full complexity of body processes or the nuances of human personality. Other systems can do those things more effectively. But what it lacks in precision and detail the Five Elements makes up for in depth and power. The five energies are primary natural forces and their interactions correspond to some of the most basic and important human experiences.

The Five Energies: a Mirror of Nature

The names of the five energies suggest just how fundamental they are to life. Earth, Fire, Metal, Wood and Water energies are as essential to the life and health of every person as their counterparts are to the life of the physical world. The qualities of the energies, their influences on body and mind and the interactions between them reflect the natural forces that gave them their names.

- **FIRE.** The most vital of the energies, Fire takes its inspiration from the sun. Fire nourishes the body's most critical organ, the heart, and the circulatory system as a whole. Its warmth and expressiveness enliven the joyful, outgoing Fire-type personality. Fire is the energy of summer, when warmth and vitality are at their peak. Fire is unique in having four meridians to itself, two *yin* and two *yang*.[5]

- **METAL**. Metal, the energy of structure, intellect and personal values, takes its name from the strongest of natural building materials. Just as iron and steel provide a durable inner core for physical structures, Metal energy is the foundation of the character and intellect. Metal is the energy of sadness and loss as well and Metal corresponds to autumn, when the joy and vitality of summer begin to fade. Metal types are organized, intelligent and morally upright. Metal energy flows in the lung and large intestine meridians.

- **WATER**. Water is an energy of depth, tenacity and spiritual vision. Water is the complementary opposite of Fire, *yin* to Fire's *yang*. Water is the energy of winter, when outer life becomes dormant and survival depends on the strength of one's inner resources. Like a deep pool, Water energy is mysterious and opaque, hinting at both profundity and danger. Water types are tough, resilient and often solitary. Water energy regulates fluids in the body and flows in the bladder and kidney meridians.

- **WOOD.** Wood is the energy of dynamism, growth and expansion. The image of a tree growing upward toward the sky captures something of the essence of Wood. Wood types are strong, adventurous and bold. At their best they are visionary pioneers. Wood energy nourishes the eyes, a symbol of Wood's role in promoting both inner and outer vision. Wood is the energy of springtime, the season of maximum growth and expansion. Wood energy flows in the gall bladder and liver meridians.

- **EARTH.** Earth is a transforming energy that nourishes the organs of digestion, helping convert raw materials into fuel for both mind and body. Earth types are sociable, caring and compassionate. Earth energy flows in the stomach and spleen meridians. Earth has no distinct season of its own.

The Five Elements Diagram

The five energies and their interactions are traditionally shown in one of two ways. The original Five Elements diagram places Earth at the center of the system, with the other four energies circulating around it (Figure 2).

Some modern authorities still use the Earth-centered arrangement to emphasize Earth's primary importance. One writer describes Earth as "the pivot of reference for all the other elements."[6] Another refers to Earth as "the fulcrum around which the other four transformations take place."[7] These views reflect the original teachings of Chinese medicine as found, for example, in *The Yellow Emperor's Classic of Medicine* or *Nei Jing Su Wen*: "The symbology of the earth is to nourish all things in nature. It is all-encompassing...This is why it does not correspond to any one particular time. It has a hand in every element."[8]

Earth, having no season of its own, came to be associated with the transitions between seasons, a natural place for an energy of transformation. But although Chinese medicine, at least initially, gave Earth a special place in the energy system, it never fully explained why Earth deserved such special status. In Chapter 3 I argue that Earth is the energy of love, the transforming human emotion and the centerpiece of one's emotional life.

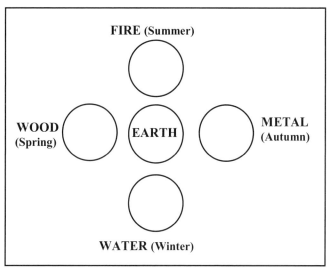

FIGURE 2.
THE ORIGINAL FIVE ELEMENTS DIAGRAM

The Mirror Expands:
the Nurturing and Controlling Cycles

Earth lost its central position when, still in ancient times, practitioners discovered a new set of relationships among the energies. In the Nurturing and Controlling Cycles, each energy naturally strengthens one of its neighbors and restrains, or controls, another. The Nurturing and Controlling Cycles are shown in Figure 3.

The solid lines represent nurturing influences between adjoining energies. Wood, for example, nourishes Fire and Fire in turn nourishes its neighbor Earth. The dotted lines, which connect energies across the circle, are controlling influences. Wood controls Earth and is controlled in turn by Metal. This system of checks and balances is a natural mechanism by which the organism maintains overall health. If one energy becomes excess or deficient, other energies tend to nudge it back into balance. In Chapter 2 I liken the

Nurturing and Controlling Cycles to the principle of homeostasis in Western medicine: a state of physiological balance that is essential

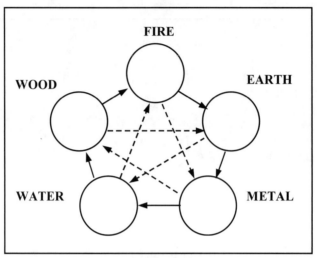

FIGURE 3.
THE NURTURING AND CONTROLLING CYCLES

to good health and that the body constantly strives to maintain. The case studies in Chapter 2 show how serious long-term disruptions in Nurturing and Controlling Cycle relationships can gradually undermine health.

The Nurturing and Controlling Cycles proved to be such valuable tools for diagnosis and treatment that the modified diagram eventually replaced the original Earth-centered arrangement. Earth's central position in the system was obscured and today is often forgotten.

The Poetry of the Five Elements

The body's energies and their activities reflect nature in elegantly simple and beautiful ways. The parallels are shown on the following page.

THE NURTURING CYCLE

IN THE BODY	AS IN NATURE
Fire energy nourishes Earth energy	The sun warms the earth
Earth energy nourishes Metal energy	The earth produces metal ores
Metal energy nourishes Water energy	Minerals enrich the blood and the sea
Water energy nourishes Wood energy	Water makes plants grow
Wood energy nourishes Fire energy	Wood makes fire burn

THE CONTROLLING CYCLE

Water energy controls Fire energy	Water quenches fire
Fire energy controls Metal energy	Fire melts metal
Metal energy controls Wood energy	A metal axe chops wood
Wood energy controls Earth energy	Vegetation controls erosion
Earth energy controls Water energy	A riverbank contains a river's flow

The Controlling Cycle and the Value of Conflict

The Controlling Cycle, like a good story, is based on tension and conflict. Therefore it is more interesting than the Nurturing Cycle and, not surprisingly, it contains more useful insights. If the complete energy blueprint is a portrait of life as a whole, the Controlling Cycle illustrates some of life's most important challenges. The struggle between freedom and fear, self interest and compassion, personal autonomy and the rules and values of society, and even love and hate are all embodied in the natural tensions of the Controlling Cycle. Reconciling those tensions is a primary part of the journey along what I call the Horizontal Pathway of Growth. Progress on that path—in the individual, in relationships and in society as a whole—is a major theme in the chapters that follow.

PART 2. INDIA AND THE CHAKRA SYSTEM

If China's knowledge of the meridian system is an expression of China's special genius for understanding life energies, India's comparable achievement has been in its understanding of the chakras. India's knowledge of life energies is deep and comprehensive. It includes the dualities of *yin* and *yang,* which are known in India as *ida* and *pingala.* India, too, has its own traditional healing system, Ayurvedic medicine, based on the balancing of life energies. But India's supreme contribution has been the spiritual attainments of its seers, sages and yogis and the knowledge they have passed down of chakra energies and their role in spiritual growth.

The chakras are a group of seven vertically aligned energy centers along the spine (Figure 4). Their physical arrangement symbolizes the ascent toward higher consciousness or what I call the Vertical Pathway of Growth. The chakras and meridians together trace the main outlines of the full life energy blueprint.

Writers, philosophers and poets have found countless ways to describe the duality of human nature—the blend of the divine and beastly—that lies within every human heart. The Protestant theologian Karl Barth described it as follows.

Heaven is the creation inconceivable to man,
earth the creation conceivable to him.
He himself is the creature on the boundary
Between heaven and earth.

The chakra system embodies the energies of both heaven and earth as well as the boundary between them. The chakras suggest, despite Barth's doubts, that human beings have an inborn capacity to cross over that boundary and experience the realm of Spirit.

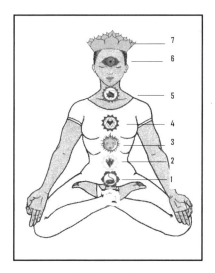

FIGURE 4.
THE CHAKRAS

The Lower Chakras

The energies of the three lower chakras are traditionally seen as the bearers of everyday instincts and emotions like hunger, sexual desire, fear, pleasure, egotism and anger.[9] Those same energies flow in the meridians and are represented in the relationships of the Nurturing and Controlling Cycles. The Horizontal and Vertical Pathways are thus not truly separate—they overlap in the chakras. The structure of the energy system confirms that everyday living and spiritual growth are not separate activities but are complementary parts of a single overall process.

The first and second chakras—the first located between the anus and genitals and the second below the navel—carry a heavy concentration of both Earth and Water energies. The first chakra, the traditional Earth chakra, receives grounding energies through the earth and is associated with the Earth qualities of human connection and group identity. The second chakra has its own strong Earth associations—with parenthood, healing and compassion.

Both the first and second chakras have strong Water associations as well. The first chakra embodies basic drives and feelings including the survival instinct and the Water emotion of fear. The second chakra, the traditional Water chakra, tends to close when repressed fears begin to constrict and limit the personality (see Chapter 3). Water, too, is a primary energy of rhythm and music, and in Chapter 5 I discuss the second chakra's important role in movement and body control.

The overlapping energies of the first and second chakras illustrate how complex the chakras are, particularly when compared to the meridians. It would be difficult or impossible to pinpoint treatments or address specific complaints using chakra therapies. The chakras, too, are too deeply embedded in the body to be easily reached by fingers, hands or needles. These are all reasons why the Chinese chose the meridians rather than the chakras as the foundation of their medical system.

The third chakra, in the solar plexus area, is known as the power chakra; an alternate name might be the Wood chakra. Third chakra energies are concerned with the needs of the individual ego and with the Wood values of personal ambition, power, achievement and control. Third chakra energies are in natural tension with the Earth energies of the first, second and fourth chakras.

The Heart Chakra: a Gateway to Spirit

The fourth chakra, or heart chakra, is the midpoint of the chakra system and the center of the life energy blueprint. Love is its defining emotion and its transforming energies are a gateway to the chakras that lie above and to the higher realms of Spirit.

In Chapter 3 I argue that Earth is the energy of love. Thus in both the original Five Elements diagram and the chakra system, Earth is at the center of the human organism.

In Chapter 7 I argue that the heart chakra has a special importance in today's world. It can be seen as a symbol of the age that is now dawning and which, like the heart chakra itself, will one day serve as a point of transition from everyday concerns to those of Spirit.

The Upper Chakras

The upper three chakras, like the chakra system as a whole, overlap to some extent with the meridians in processing the energies of everyday living. The fifth chakra, in the throat area, is responsible for self expression, especially speech, including the will to assert oneself. A talkative, expressive person is likely to have an open and well developed throat chakra, while someone who is shy or reticent is more likely to have weakness or even blockage in the throat chakra.

The sixth chakra, located between the eyebrows, is responsible for abstract thought and illustrates a basic difference between head and body energies. The lower chakras are closely tied to the body and to everyday needs and emotions, but the sixth chakra is free—it transcends the physical plane and embodies the energies of pure ideas and symbols. Many of those ideas, however, are used in everyday life. People who are logical, analytical and mentally well-organized have strong sixth chakra energies. If those energies are complemented by well-developed lower chakra energies, the person is likely to be energetically and emotionally whole. But when sixth chakra energies dominate too much, thinking crowds out feeling and the person is said to be "living in his head." I discuss the Head type personality and some of its strengths and weaknesses in Chapter 3.

The sixth chakra embodies the energies of other non-physical experiences, especially intuition and spiritual awareness. The sixth chakra is often referred to as the Third Eye or Spiritual Eye. Its full opening is synonymous with highly developed intuition and deep spiritual realization.

The seventh chakra, or crown chakra, is located at the top of the head. It carries the energies of the deepest and most transcendent spiritual awareness. Its opening is the ultimate goal of yoga and other forms of meditation.

PART 3. THE TREE OF LIFE:
MERIDIANS AND CHAKRAS COMBINED

In Jewish mystical tradition, the Tree of Life is a diagram of the various faces or aspects of God. The Tree is now believed to represent both divine and human energies. That correspondence is only one of many examples in this book of the truth of Genesis 1:27:

> So God created man in his own image, in the image
> of God created he him; male and female created he
> them.

The Tree is shown in Figure 5. A number of modern writers have equated its seven vertical levels with the seven chakras.[10] I agree with that view and take it a step further. The Tree of Life, I argue, is a depiction of both chakras and meridians and their interactions. The central column and the Tree's seven vertical levels represent the chakras, and the three pairs of energy centers on either side represent meridian energies in natural tension in the Controlling Cycle. The connections between the central column and the right and left sides represent, among other things, the transition from everyday awareness to spiritual intuition—the meeting of the Horizontal and Vertical Pathways. The Tree of Life is thus the most complete picture of the full life energy blueprint in any major spiritual tradition.

In Chapter 7 I discuss the energy centers of the Tree of Life in detail and suggest that the Tree, like the heart chakra, has a dual

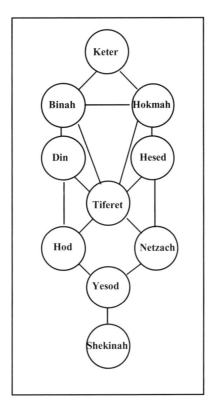

FIGURE 5.
THE KABBALISTIC TREE OF LIFE

importance in today's world—not only as a tool for personal growth but as a symbol of the evolution of Western society and religion. Two of the Tree's energy centers, I argue, represent Judaism and Christianity and the historical periods when they began to develop. A third center, and one that integrates the energies of the other two, represents the period we are now entering. The implication is that the two faiths will be reconciled sometime during the current age.

The Aura, Extraordinary Vessels, Strange Flows...

The chakras, the twelve primary meridians and the Tree of Life make up the main outlines of the life energy blueprint but it is not a complete picture. The aura—the energy envelope that surrounds every person and connects the individual with the environment—is a rich, multi-layered structure connected to the chakras. Like the chakra system, the aura embodies every aspect of human life: physical, mental, emotional and spiritual. The aura is a valuable source of information for medical intuitives who read health, illness and personal history in the aura's colors and forms. I discuss the aura and the work of two prominent medical intuitives in Chapter 5.

Within the meridian system, there are many other energy channels in addition to the twelve primary meridians. The Extraordinary Vessels, a group of superior pathways that consolidate the activities of individual meridians and influence whole segments of the system, are among the most important. Other, less well defined patterns of energy movement such as Strange Flows apparently influence mind and body in important ways.

In these pages I discuss the parts of the energy system that I understand best and that most clearly convey the ideas I wish to express. Others with a broader and deeper knowledge of other aspects of the system have made, and will continue to make, their own contributions. It will be decades, possibly centuries, before we have a complete understanding of the energy system and its full importance.

The Holistic Impulse

If the energy system is a blueprint for human growth, what is the guiding influence that encourages us to follow that blueprint, grow, change and evolve to higher levels? The chakas and the Tree of Life show, among other things, that the energy realm is a place where human and divine influences meet and merge. The energy system is a natural vehicle through which God can interact with, and invisibly guide, human life.

The holistic growth process, in both individuals and society, is, I argue, an expression of God's will acting through the unseen influences of life energy. I refer to that force as the Holistic Impulse.

Whatever the physical or emotional factors that contribute to growth—will power, new insights, the evolution of new values in society, genetic changes or other factors—all are ultimately grounded in life energies and all come, in the end, from God. In the chapters that follow I argue that God's connection to human life through the energy system can help clarify phenomena ranging from evolution to free will to spiritual awareness itself.

CHAPTER TWO
LIFE ENERGY AND PHYSICAL HEALTH

The Western prescription for good health maintenance is to eat a balanced diet, get plenty of exercise and keep stress under control. This is sound advice as far as it goes but it leaves out a fourth major component of a healthy mind and body: a well-balanced energy system. Chronic energy imbalance, like improper diet, lack of exercise and excessive stress, can gradually undermine health and increase the risk of both major and minor illnesses.

A person living with significant energy imbalance is like a plant growing in a deficient, unbalanced soil. Just as a plant can get along for a while without the right combination of nitrogen, phosphate and other nutrients, people don't get sick immediately when their energy system goes out of balance. There is usually a lag time, sometimes a long one, between energy imbalance and the onset of illness. In the meantime, chronic energy excesses and/or deficiencies gradually wear down the body's defenses. The person often has a vague sense that something is wrong but neither she nor her physician is usually aware of what the problem is or what can be done to fix it. Because energy imbalances don't show up in standard physical exams or in lab tests or X-rays, Western medicine is simply unequipped to diagnosis or treat these early warning signs of illness.

Energy Therapies East and West

Energy-based therapies and techniques have been widely used in Asia for centuries for medical treatment, health maintenance and general fitness. They are steadily gaining in popularity in the West because they are simple, effective and relatively inexpensive.

Acupuncture, which is now partially covered under some health insurance plans, has been proven experimentally to relieve pain and have a number of other health benefits. Shiatsu, a recognized form of medical treatment in Japan, is, like acupuncture, based on the balancing of meridian energies but uses fingers and hands rather than needles. Tai Chi is commonly used in the West to increase mobility and help relieve the pain and stiffness of arthritis. Herbal therapies can be effective in relieving specific complaints and for maintaining good overall health. Magnet therapies, which work by literally pushing and pulling energies through the system, are used for pain relief and general rebalancing. Reiki and therapeutic touch can reduce stress and are said to accelerate recovery from surgery.

The Incomplete Western Medical Model

The trend toward CAM, or complementary and alternative medicine, is increasingly evident in the U.S. in both education and government policy. It was reported in 1998 that 64% of U.S. medical schools offered at least one course in CAM.[11] Harvard Medical School has been a leader in the movement toward alternative medical education. In the abstract of an article in the Annals of Internal Medicine in 2003, four staff members from Harvard Medical School and two other teaching centers said that "Increased use of complementary and alternative medicine (CAM) has made it imperative that these topics be included in medical education from the preclinical years through residency and beyond."[12]

In 1998 Congress established the National Center for Complementary and Alternative Medicine with an annual budget of $68 million. Its purpose is to support research into the safety and effectiveness of alternative therapies. In 2000, the White House established a Commission on Alternative Medicine whose goal is to develop recommendations to guide the development of CAM in the U.S., including the education of practitioners and guidelines for insurance coverage.

The above trends confirm what a great many people already know instinctively: that something significant is missing in the Western understanding of human health. That gap expresses itself in a variety of ways, but the most basic reason for it is that the Western medical model is incomplete—it does not include the life energy system. It thus leaves out a basic component of the human organism and one that constantly interacts with and influences both mind and body. Western medicine therefore lacks both the concepts and the tools needed to understand the complete human being and fully address health and illness.

Energy Homeostasis

The notion of balance, which is central to Chinese philosophy and energy healing, is not unknown to Western medicine. Homeostasis, a state of biochemical and functional balance within the organism, is a central principle of Western physiology. The body has built-in mechanisms for maintaining homeostasis, and if it is upset for any reason the body tries to return to it as quickly as possible; in the meantime, there can be significant risks to health.

There are at least two patterns of overall balance in the energy system that can be seen, in a loose sense at least, as a kind of homeostasis. In the first, the body nourishes the energy system by creating life energies from food and oxygen and absorbing energy from sunlight and other sources in the environment. The energy system in turn nourishes the tissues, providing the raw material that keeps mind and body running smoothly. If any part of the cycle is interrupted or becomes inefficient, the energy system, body and mind all suffer. In Chapter 3 I show how an illness like depression may, in some cases, represent a disruption in the first kind of energy homeostasis.

Energy Types, Healthy and Unhealthy Equilibria

The Nurturing and Controlling Cycles illustrate a second kind of energy homeostasis. As we saw earlier, each energy is ideally strong enough to nurture one of its neighbors and control another, but not so strong that it overwhelms other energies or throws the whole system out of balance.

When the system of energy checks and balances is running smoothly, good health tends to follow. But unlike physical homeostasis, perfect energy balance is not only uncommon, it is downright rare if in fact it ever occurs at all. One major reason is that most people, simply by virtue of their natural temperament, live with a certain amount of built-in energy imbalance. Fire types, for example, are by definition strong or dominant in Fire energies. They tend to be warm, outgoing and expressive and to have the other natural strengths of their type. Inevitably, however, dominant Fire tends to distort other energies somewhat through the Nurturing and Controlling Cycles. Each of the types has its own characteristic imbalances and certain health risks associated with them.

From an energy perspective, disease most often occurs when energies stay too long in an unhealthy state of equilibrium—when energy homeostasis is upset for too long. In the examples that follow, the Wood or Wood-Fire type is vulnerable to diseases of intensity or excitement; the Metal or Metal-Water type is at risk for illnesses of constriction and stagnation; and the Earth type is subject to illnesses of indulgence and excess. In each case the person's dominant energies, which are ideally a major life asset, have become a potential liability because they have grown too strong.

CASE STUDY #1. GEORGE'S *YANG*-TYPE SYNDROME: WOOD, FIRE AND THE COMPULSION TO SUCCEED

George is an energetic and highly motivated person with a strong desire for career success and the prestige that goes with it. He is outgoing and has reasonably good social skills, although his assertive, intense and sometimes aggressive personal style sometimes puts other people on the defensive. George is vulnerable to frustration and anger and there is a chronic undercurrent of hostility in his manner. George is a leader by nature and has a successful business and a number of satisfied employees to prove it. He devotes long hours to his job and often finds that he leaves too little time for relaxation, family life or fun.

George is a classic Wood type with all the earmarks of dominant Wood energies: an intensely active, energetic nature, an instinct for leadership and control, a strong competitive drive with a heavy emphasis on work and financial success, and a tendency toward frustration, hostility and. anger. People like George are often referred to as workaholics; I call George's pattern Compulsive Work Syndrome.

George's vibrancy and enthusiasm are signs of strong Fire energy which, like Wood, is a *yang*-type energy: active, dynamic and projective. Wood strengthens Fire through the Nurturing Cycle and the qualities of the two energies tend to merge and reinforce one another. George might be described as a Wood-Fire type and, more generally, as a *yang*-type personality. His attitudes, values and behavior express the *yang* values of modern 21st century society—an emphasis on competition, material success and recognition.

Metal Imbalance and the Distorted Triangle

A striking thing about George is how driven he seems. Like many ambitious modern people, his frenetic desire to succeed and accomplish seems out of proportion to his actual needs. There appears to be another, hidden agenda, one that is unknown not only to the people around him but perhaps even to George himself. The strange sense of compulsion that drives him—the seeming need to keep proving his inner worth through outer achievement—points to another energy ingredient in George's behavior.

Metal, the energy of form and structure, is the foundation of moral and ethical values and of one's sense of duty and responsibility. When a person feels, consciously or unconsciously, that he has failed to do his duty or live up to his obligations, the sense of guilt and inadequacy is embodied in imbalanced Metal.

It is surely no coincidence that Metal is the energy in natural tension with both Wood and Fire, George's dominant energies. George's overall pattern suggests that three separate imbalances—in Wood, Fire and Metal—have combined to create the powerful, and remarkably stable, pattern of attitudes and behaviors that define his personality.

Figure 6 shows George's energy profile as an imbalance in three of the five basic energies, a pattern I call the Distorted Triangle. It comes into being, and is held in place, by the simple but powerful forces of the Nurturing and Controlling Cycles. Three steps are necessary to set the cycle in motion.

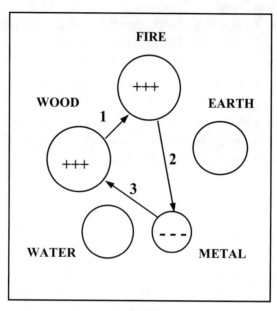

FIGURE 6.
COMPULSIVE WORK SYNDROME
AND THE DISTORTED TRANGLE

1. George's dominant Wood energies strengthen his naturally strong Fire through the Nurturing Cycle, making it a powerful force in its own right.
2. Fire exerts strong pressure on Metal through the Controlling Cycle, weakening Metal which is already depleted from a conscious or unconscious sense of guilt or inadequacy.
3. Because Metal is weak, it cannot properly control Wood, so George's dominant energy grows even stronger. Wood is now able to strengthen Fire even more; stronger Fire further weakens Metal; Metal is less able to control Wood; and the cycle continues.

At some point the three energies reach an equilibrium point and the cycle stops. George is left with significant imbalances in Wood,

Fire and Metal. The driven, compulsive pattern of his daily life reflects the distorted energy pattern within. George can easily continue to live this way for years, perhaps decades, because the forces that hold the pattern in place are in an extremely stable, if unhealthy, state of equilibrium.

George's energy syndrome is known in the West as Type A personality.

Type A Behavior and the Heart

Type A Personality became a popular term in the 1960's and gained special prominence when groups like the Framingham Heart Study made it part of their research. The Framingham study was a landmark investigation into the origins of heart disease. It began in the 1960's and followed the health progress of thousands of subjects over many years. Its findings were a major influence on our present-day understanding of heart disease and its origins. Among other things, the Framingham study was instrumental in identifying high blood pressure and high cholesterol as primary coronary risk factors.

Different groups have defined Type A Personality in somewhat different ways but the main features include 1) an unusual competitiveness and ambition, 2) a general sense of urgency, 3) open or concealed hostility and 4) a perceived need for control. All of these are typical signs of Wood energy dominance.

The Framingham study included several personality profiles, including the Type A cluster, to see whether attitudes and behaviors were linked with a greater risk of heart disease. In a 1978 article published in the American Journal of Epidemiology, a group of researchers reported on a part of the Framingham study involving 1822 subjects aged 45 to 77. The researchers reported as follows:

> Women (aged 45-64 years) with coronary
> disease scored significantly higher on the
> Framingham Type A behavior, emotional
> lability, aging worries, tension and anger

symptoms scales than women free of CHD (coronary heart disease). The prevalence of CHD was significantly higher among working women and housewives classified as Type A than as Type B behavior. Among men under 65 years, Framingham Type A behavior, aging worries, daily stress and tension were associated with the prevalence of myocardial infarction (MI). [Framingham II]

In a similar study reported on in 1980 by the same group, 1674 subjects were followed for eight years. The group reported that

Type A women developed twice as much CHD and three times as much angina as Type B women...Men exhibiting Framingham Type A behavior, work overload, suppressed hostility (not showing anger) and frequent job promotions were at increased risk of CHD especially in the age group 55-64 years. Type A behavior was associated with a twofold risk of angina, myocardial infarction, and CHD in general, as compared to Type B behavior (Framingham III).

In the years since the Framingham study, medical science has discovered a number of factors, including the release of stress hormones into the bloodstream, that may help account for the link between Type A behavior and heart disease. In Chinese medicine, Fire energy governs the health of the heart and blood vessels and a chronic excess of Fire is the energy equivalent of physical stress on the circulatory system. Wood energy is associated with emotional intensity and high blood pressure is a common complaint among Wood types. The Wood-Fire dominance of the Type A personality thus fits well with the findings of the Framingham study.

In recent years, many people have begun to follow their doctors' advice and address cardiac risk factors such as high cholesterol and high blood pressure. New drugs like statins and calcium channel blockers can lower cholesterol levels and blood pressure even when dietary and lifestyle changes fail. Heart disease rates have declined in proportion to those changes. But the Type A personality pattern remains and, since there are as yet no drugs to effectively rebalance distorted Wood-Fire-Metal energies or adjust the emotions and impulses they represent, energy therapies are a natural choice for modifying Type A behavior.

Breaking the Cycle of Tension

In an unhealthy pattern like George's, the body's instinct for self-healing is frustrated by the remarkable stability of the Distorted Triangle pattern. It often lasts for so long, and begins to feel so natural, that it may not even occur to someone like George that anything is wrong or that change is possible. George may eventually come to believe that "This is just the way I am."

Yang personalities, by definition, need a certain amount of intensity to feel fully alive. For that reason many Type A's choose such demanding jobs that they may feel, rightly or wrongly, that they could not perform effectively if their motivation were to lessen even a little. The material rewards of compulsive work can be very substantial, too, and are a major disincentive to change.

Even for Type A's who want to change, imbalances can be so well-entrenched that it can be almost impossible to break the cycle of tension without outside intervention. Muscle tension is usually the outer layer of imbalance and, even when a person goes on vacation, it can take a week or more for a very tense body to relax. By that time the vacation is over and the person has never had a chance to see what a more relaxed pattern of living would be like.

Peeling the Onion: Shiatsu and Other Energy-Based Therapies

Given even slight encouragement, the energy system begins to reorient itself into healthier patterns. Energy therapists know this and leave plenty of time between treatments to give the energy system time to absorb and consolidate the changes that a therapy session brings.

There are many effective therapies for rebalancing energies. Some of the most popular include acupuncture, shiatsu, magnet therapy and Chinese herbs. Traditional massage, although not an energy therapy *per se*, can be helpful since vigorously massaging the tissues inevitably reaches and stimulates energy pathways.

Of all the popular energy therapies, shiatsu is one of the most effective and enjoyable because it combines the precision of acupuncture with the gentle, nurturing quality of human touch. Shiatsu was developed in Japan and, for many Japanese, is a primary tool for both medical treatment and general health maintenance. Shiatsu, which means "figure pressure," is based on the same principles as acupuncture and works by stimulating and rebalancing meridian energies. In shiatsu, however, the practitioner treats, not just individual pressure points, but entire meridians from one end to the other. As they work, many shiatsu practitioners give special attention to important pressure points along the way. Some therapists place magnets or apply heat to selected points to make the treatments more effective and last longer.

Shiatsu is particularly effective for relieving muscle tension, the outer layer of imbalance and a key to breaking the energy logjam in overstressed workers. For someone like George, muscle tension is the physical expression of excess, stagnated life energies. Type A personalities and others who suffer from overwork tend to have tight, constricted muscles in the neck, shoulders, back and legs. These are the pathways of the bladder and gall bladder meridians, which carry the Water and Wood energies of drive, intensity and decision-making.

If George takes advantage of energy therapies to disperse some of his excess *yang* energies, he will begin feeling more relaxed almost immediately. The rebalancing of Wood and Fire will stimulate other positive changes through the Nurturing and Controlling Cycles. Deeper imbalances that had been masked by muscle tension may reveal themselves. Energy therapies are often compared to peeling an onion. As one layer of tension and imbalance peels away, another, deeper layer often appears. The process may ultimately uncover long-buried emotional conflicts. For a compulsive worker like George, these could include repressed feelings of guilt or inadequacy embodied in imbalanced Metal.

If he persists, George will reach a point where the irritable, compulsive edge to his personality begins to soften, signaling that his energy system is coming into better balance. As it does, he can reduce the frequency of treatments until, finally, he can maintain good energy balance with occasional maintenance treatments. Although he will always be a Wood type and a hard worker, George can, with the help of energy therapies, significantly improve his energy profile, reduce his level of stress and improve his chances for a long and healthy life.

....

George illustrates some of the health risks for the dynamic, intense *yang*-type personality. At the opposite end of the spectrum is the quieter, more introspective and retiring *yin*-type. A major risk for the *yang* type, as we have seen, is that energies will become too powerful and project too forcefully, in effect blowing the cork out of the bottle. The risk for the *yin* type is just the opposite: that energies will shrivel and turn in upon themselves, body processes will slow down and the bottle's contents will curdle and go rancid.

CASE STUDY #2. BETTY'S *YIN*-TYPE SYNDROME: REPRESSION AND ENERGY STAGNATION

Betty is a Metal or Metal-Water type and everything about her shows it. She is neat, well-groomed and highly organized. Her manner is polite but restrained, gracious but reserved and somewhat formal. Though not lacking in warmth, Betty does not express feelings openly but keeps a tight lid on her emotions. A bright and articulate person, she has trained herself to relate to others mainly through ideas. Though well-liked for her honesty, integrity and intelligence, Betty stimulates more respect than passion from her friends and associates.

Betty considers herself healthy and has no major physical complaints. She has noticed, however, that although she is still young, her vitality has declined and she feels less energetic and enthusiastic than before. She exercises less, stays home more and is less socially active than in the past. Sometimes she has trouble sleeping and often wakes up at 5 or 6 A.M. with vague feelings of unease or sadness and finds it hard to go back to sleep.

Although she doesn't think of herself as depressed, Betty has several common symptoms of depression: reduced energy level, less enthusiasm and enjoyment of life, fewer social contacts and sleep problems. Betty, who suffered some serious emotional losses when she was young, was not encouraged to talk openly about her feelings but instead bottled them up inside. She has continued the same pattern as an adult, rarely speaking about the pains and disappointments in her life. She likes to think of herself as a stoic and of her accepting, uncomplaining nature as a virtue.

Yin Stifling *Yang*: Betty's Distorted Triangle

Betty is a *yin*-type personality and her energy profile is shown in Figure 7. It is the exact mirror image of George's. George's dominant Wood and Fire energies grew until they overwhelmed the delicate *yin* energies of Metal, but Betty's dominant Metal is in full control. Because she failed to fully process a number of difficult emotions, their energies were trapped in her tissues. Many years later they are still there, inhibiting her full expression of feeling and, to some extent, stifling her personality.

Betty's Distorted Triangle has come into being through the same three-step process as George's, only in reverse:

1. Her swollen Metal energies have weakened Wood to the point where Wood's natural dynamism is hard to find in Betty's personality.
2. Because Wood is weak, it cannot properly nourish Fire, damp-

ening Betty's warmth and enthusiasm and reducing her pleasure in living.

3. Her deficient Fire, in turn, cannot properly control Metal, so Metal grows even stronger, and the cycle continues.

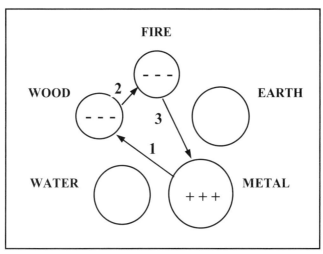

FIGURE 7.
BETTY'S DISTORTED TRIANGLE
A *YIN*-TYPE IMBALANCE

The three energies continue to distort one another until, as with George, an equilibrium point is finally reached and the cycle stops. Betty, like George, is left with three of her five energies significantly out of balance. The pattern is unhealthy but stable and Betty can easily go on this way for months or even years. Eventually, if the pattern is not corrected, her physical health may begin to suffer.

Health and the Metal-Type Personality

Most of the health risks in a pattern like Betty's are associated with excess Metal or its natural consequence, deficient Wood. The Metal organs, the lungs and large intestine, are responsible for processing and discharging respiratory wastes (carbon dioxide) and digestive wastes. Metal energy processes certain difficult emotions as well, especially grief and guilt. Metal imbalance can make it hard to discharge either physical or emotional wastes or both. In this chapter I focus on the physical health risks of Metal imbalance.

Metal types, because of their natural restraint and inhibition, are vulnerable to illnesses associated with tightness and constriction. This often expresses itself superficially as cold hands or feet. Internally, there can be a corresponding tension or constriction, especially in the Metal organs, the lungs and large intestine. Constipation can be a symptom of the Metal type's tendency to "hold things in." If the problem becomes chronic, colon cancer can be a risk. Since a high fiber diet is the simplest way to insure regularity, Metal types in particular are wise to include plenty of fiber in their diet.

In Chinese medicine, inflammation is seen as a symptom of "heat" in the body. Colitis, an inflammation of the colon, can be a consequence of trapping Metal energy, and the heat associated with it, in the colon. Asthma, a chronic constriction and inflammation of the respiratory passages, can be triggered by pollens or other impurities but its root cause is unknown to Western medicine. In some cases at least, asthma is almost certainly a result of trapped energy and heat in the Metal organs, the lungs and bronchial tubes. The constriction of the airways in asthma mirrors the emotional constriction of the Metal type personality.

Other organs and tissues can be affected by trapped Metal energy. Inflammations such as bronchitis, laryngitis and dermatitis all represent stagnated energy, and heat, in Metal or Metal-related organs. Sometimes a therapy as simple as a magnet placed on a nearby energy point can disperse stagnated energies and relieve bronchitis or other inflammations.

Wood Energy and the Liver

For someone with Betty's energy profile, liver deficiency is another potential source of health risks. The liver, a Wood organ, is one of the body's most complex and versatile working parts. It does literally dozens of important jobs including the manufacture of many essential enzymes and other substances. The liver's protective functions are a vital part of immune defense and include the following:

1. The liver removes toxins, other foreign materials and metabolic wastes from the blood.
2. The liver kills or neutralizes viruses, bacteria and other pathogens.
3. With the help of killer white blood cells and other immune components, the liver's special immune cells attack and destroy cancer cells.

In traditional Chinese medicine, the liver and its energies are essential to overall health. Liver energy nourishes the liver itself and regulates the flow of energies throughout the body. If liver energy is weakened or restricted, there can be a general slowing down and stagnation of body processes. If the stagnation is severe and continues long enough, it is believed to contribute to the formation of tumors.

Liver Energy Deficiency, Depression and Cancer Risk

The liver's role in immune function may be especially important for someone like Betty who lives with chronic depression. A number of studies have pointed to a possible correlation between chronic depression and the risk of cancer. Energy principles suggest that liver energy deficiency may be an underlying factor linking the two.

Researchers have long suspected a depression-cancer connection. In 1981, a study of 2,000 electrical workers in Chicago found that those who suffered from depression were twice as likely as others to develop cancer. Follow-up studies were inconclusive but a study at the National Institute of Aging supported the findings of the Chicago study. Researchers investigated the relationship between chronic depression and cancer in people over 65 years of age. The study was of 4825 people from Massachusetts, Iowa and Connecticut. The results, published in the Journal of the National Cancer Institute, found that depressed subjects had an 88% greater chance of developing cancer.

A growing body of evidence lends support to these findings. One study confirmed the observations of doctors that, when a person has suffered a major life loss such as the death of a spouse, the survivor is more likely to develop cancer during or soon after the grieving process.[13]

Western researchers, of course, see the cancer-depression connection as purely physiological with no role for life energy. One theory is based on evidence that natural killer (NK) immune cells are less active in depressed people. Another observation is that T lymphocytes, another type of immune cell, are less able to replicate themselves when a person is depressed. In both cases it appears that a slowing down of body processes may be a factor in the decreased immune response in depressed people.

Life energy principles may help explain these findings. In Chinese medicine, as we have seen, liver energy deficiency can be associated with both depression and a slowdown in body processes. The sluggishness of immune cells in depressed people could represent just such a bodily slowdown at the cellular level. If so, the link between depression and cancer may, in some cases at least, be an indirect one—a liver energy deficiency that contributes to both disorders. Betty's *yin*-type energy syndrome, if it is severe enough and lasts long enough, may have a depressive effect on both her emotions and on the operation of her immune system.

If studies one day confirm the liver energy-depression-cancer connection, energy therapies may become an important tool for cancer prevention.

Energy Quantity and Quality

For both Betty and George, the amount and intensity of their life energies are not only important health factors, they are forces that help define their personalities. Much of the difference between a dynamic *yang* type like George and a more retiring *yin* type like Betty is in the power and intensity of their energies. On the surface at least, life energy's importance depends mainly on its quantity. To some extent, life energy is a kind of simple fuel that powers mind and body.

On a deeper level, energy quality is, if anything, even more important than energy quantity. As we will see in Chapter 3, the quality of our daily experiences mirrors the quality of the energies that underlie them. Love, generosity, kindness and good will—and anger, fear, mistrust and hatred—are all embodied by energies of a particular positive or negative charge. It may be that, at the cellular level too, positive and negative energies are active in the ongoing struggle between health and illness.

Traditional Chinese medicine makes no distinction between benign and malignant tumors. It places all abnormal growths in a single category and attributes them all to what it calls "congealed blood." By modern standards this is a crude formulation, but it is understandable given the ancient origins of Chinese medicine and the fact that there were no instruments in ancient times to examine human cells or even know that cells exist.

Traditional Chinese medicine can therefore say that Betty may be at risk of a tumor because her body processes have slowed down, but not whether that tumor will be benign or malignant. As for Western medicine, studies like those cited above may ultimately confirm a link between a slowdown in body processes and the risk of cancer, but not why some people with sluggish body processes get cancer while others don't. There must be some additional factor at work, and the evidence from intuitive healers suggests that energy quality may be that factor.

Benign and Toxic Energies

Energy therapists can often sense what they call malicious or toxic energies in the bodies of their clients, particularly when cancer is present. Some energy healers can sense a struggle between the positive healing energies they transmit into their clients' bodies and the malevolent energies lurking in cancer cells. This kind of anecdotal evidence suggests that cancer cells, and possibly other disease-causing organisms, may not just be mindless collections of harmful molecules but may have a kind of conscious evil intent. That possibility gives new meaning to the term malignant as applied to cancer and suggests that restoring or maintaining health is more than just a mechanical process of keeping the body's machinery in good repair. It may depend as much on maintaining a positive balance of energies in the body.

For someone like Betty, who is mildly depressed and already lives in a somewhat negatively charged energy environment, paying attention to energy quality could have important health benefits. Spiritual masters teach that positive thoughts and feelings generate positive life energies while negative thoughts generate and attract negative energies. If Betty lets herself fall into a pattern of chronic worry or negative, pessimistic thinking, she may attract negative energies that could tip the balance toward illness. But if she works to maintain a positive mental and emotional outlook, the positive energies she generates may help her maintain long-term good health.

Are Life Energies Conscious?

The possibility that life energies may have beneficial or harmful intent raises the question of whether, in some meaningful sense, life energies are conscious. It is an important question for several reasons, including the following:

1. If life energies are conscious, it helps explain their remarkable responsiveness to human touch, attention and will. I discuss that topic in Chapters 3 and 7 and its importance in bodywork therapies, body-centered psychotherapies and energy-based meditation techniques.
2. If life energies are conscious, it raises the possibility that the body as a whole has its own independent awareness. If so, the body's overall "happiness" or "unhappiness" is presumably an

important factor in health. Healers and others who recommend that we cultivate a positive and supportive relationship with our bodies are therefore giving sound advice.

3. If life energies are conscious, it may help explain how, as I argue in Chapter 6, God guides the processes of evolution. God, I argue, orchestrates the development of living things by influencing the life energies that drive mutations. If life energies are conscious, God may "instruct" life energies to bring about mutations in accordance with His plan.

4. If life energies are conscious, the human mind can be seen as a collection of billions of bits of life energy, each of which is a tiny individual mind which, perhaps unknowingly, is part of a much larger mind. The image evokes another, similar image: of several billion human beings whose individual minds, whether they know it or not, are part of God's all-embracing mind. If the analogy is valid it is another example of the truth of Genesis 1:27—that human beings are made in the image of God.

....

George and Betty illustrate some of the health risks that can arise from the interplay of excesses and deficiencies among several energies. Peter's pattern is somewhat different: his health may be undermined by excess and deficiency within a single element.

CASE STUDY #3. PETER'S PATTERN:
THE PRICE OF CONSUMPTION AND COMPETITION

Peter is a product of the early 21st century society in which he lives. Although not as intensely driven as George, Peter's formidable Wood energies are evident in his competitive drive and in his strong desire for career success and the prestige and recognition that go with it.

Peter's Wood energies, although strong, are equaled or even surpassed by powerful Earth energies. Peter has the relatively round, fleshy body of the Earth type and his sociable, caring and compassionate temperament confirm that Earth, not Wood, is his dominant energy. Peter has the Earth type's special fondness for food, drink and the almost unlimited supply of material goods that modern life has to offer.

Peter feels generally satisfied with his life but, as he approaches middle age, he finds it harder to control his eating habits. At the same time he feels less energetic and motivated to exercise than in the past. He finds himself eating more sweet and salty foods and is gradually adding weight around his middle.

Peter's energy profile mirrors the twin engines of consumption and competition that drive him. Like the forces of modern society itself, his dominant *yang* energies have become swollen and distorted and are placing undue pressure on, and depressing, his more fragile *yin* energies. The strength of his *yang* energies makes Peter especially vulnerable to imbalances in the two Earth meridians, stomach and spleen. His energy profile is shown in Figure 8.

Much of Peter's Earth energy imbalance is due to the excessive strength of the energies of stomach and gall bladder. Like twin bullies on the schoolyard, the two toughs leave each other alone, instead attacking other, more vulnerable parts of the system. Gall bladder, the *yang* Wood meridian which governs work, competition and decision-making, overwhelms the delicate *yin* energies of the spleen meridian. Peter's craving for sweets is a typical sign of spleen energy deficiency.

Stomach, the *yang* Earth meridian, is too strong to be affected by gall bladder's power and is free to exert its own dominance over kidney. Kidney's weakness tends to sap Peter's vitality and discourage him from getting the exercise he needs. Peter's craving for salty foods is a natural consequence of his chronic kidney energy deficiency.

Peter's twin Earth energy imbalances may be a key to his particular health vulnerability. Both of the Earth meridians, stomach and spleen, have an important influence on the body's regulation of blood sugar. The two imbalances together may, over time, degrade the body's ability to produce enough insulin and/or use it effectively. Peter is therefore at special risk for diabetes.

Stomach Excess and Insulin Resistance

Stomach energy governs the physical appetite for food as well as the more general appetite for material pleasures of all kinds. In today's consumer society, stomach excess is virtually universal but

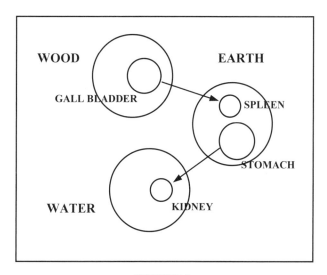

FIGURE 8.
PETER'S EARTH ENERGY IMBALANCE:
A PROFILE OF 21ST CENTURY STRESSES

can be a special problem for an Earth type like Peter. Because of how their bodies metabolize food, Earth types tend to gain weight easily, especially around the middle, and the result can be a condition called insulin resistance. When it appears, the body's cells are not able to absorb and use enough insulin to control blood sugar.

Insulin resistance is now well established as a major factor in the development of adult-onset diabetes.[14] The condition forces the body to produce abnormally large amounts of insulin until finally, for unknown reasons, the body's insulin-producing capacity begins to break down. Blood sugar becomes chronically elevated and the person has diabetes.

Because excess stomach energy is correlated with excessive appetite, and because obesity is the most common cause of insulin

resistance, there is a fairly clear correlation between stomach energy excess and the risk of diabetes. Earth energy's role becomes
even more important when we consider the other Earth meridian,
spleen, and the possible effects of long-term spleen energy deficiency on the body's ability to produce insulin.

Spleen Deficiency and the Pancreas

In Western medicine the spleen is considered an important part of
the immune system but nothing more. In Chinese medicine the
spleen and its energy system have a far broader influence. The
wide-ranging pathway of the spleen meridian is a clue to its importance. It begins at the tip of the big toe and flows through the feet,
legs, groin, abdomen, chest and arms before exiting at the finger-
tips. On its way through the body it passes directly through both
the pancreas and spleen. Among its many important jobs, the
spleen meridian provides the pancreas with the continuous supply
of life energy it needs to do its work.

In the pancreas special cells called beta cells manufacture insulin and release it into the bloodstream. If the supply of life energy
to the pancreas is reduced for any reason, the beta cells must still
keep producing insulin even though they have been deprived of
their normal amount of life energy.

If an overweight person like Peter has both insulin resistance
and spleen energy deficiency, his pancreas is forced to function under two significant stresses: 1) it must produce more than the usual
amount of insulin to overcome insulin resistance and 2) it must do
so with insufficient life energy. Because energy excesses and deficiencies can go undetected for long periods, Peter may have been
living with these combined stresses on his pancreas for years or
even decades.

To further aggravate the problem, people with spleen energy
deficiency, as I noted above, tend to have a craving for sweets. Because Peter responds to that craving by eating larger than normal
amounts of sugar, his body needs even more insulin to neutralize
the extra sugar in his bloodstream. Peter therefore lives with three

separate, significant, long-term stresses on his body's ability to produce enough insulin.

Although medical science does not yet know why the beta cells of diabetics stop producing insulin, the above pattern suggests that, in some cases at least, the pancreas may simply become exhausted. Under the constant demand to produce too much insulin with too little fuel over too long a period, it may be that the beta cells simply wear out. One authority[15] believes that other factors are responsible—either a genetic influence or some toxic effect on the cells—but he does not cite any studies to support that hypothesis.

Further research will show precisely why the beta cells of diabetics stop producing enough insulin. Whatever the reason, there is little doubt that obesity plays a major role in insulin resistance and diabetes. Therefore energy therapies to disperse excess stomach energies have real preventive value. If it turns out that spleen energy deficiency is a second important factor, correcting both stomach and spleen imbalances will be strongly indicated. In that case, special energy points called *luo* ("low") points will be extremely useful. *Luo* points are connecting points between sister meridians that have the unique ability to transfer energy out of an excess meridian and into its deficient sister, rebalancing both. If studies ultimately show that diabetes stems from an overall Earth energy imbalance, the Earth energy *luo* points may become a preventive treatment of choice.

....

Completing the Western Medical Model

The above examples illustrate the close interrelationship between life energies, attitudes, emotions and physical health. They show that body, mind and energy system are linked at the most basic level. For every major illness like heart disease, cancer or diabetes, there are dozens of less serious conditions in which energy imbalances play an important role. Energy therapies are a valuable preventive tool for major and minor illnesses alike.

The energy disturbances that underlie disease develop slowly and usually last a long time before illness strikes. In the meantime there is ample opportunity to identify and correct imbalances before they begin to affect the tissues and cause physical damage.

Anything as simple, effective and inexpensive as shiatsu, acupuncture, magnet or herbal therapies is bound for eventual broad acceptance. The tipping point will probably come when research conclusively shows their preventive value; insurance coverage will quickly follow. Within a relatively short time, the standard Western medical exam will probably include an annual energy assessment along with blood tests and other routine screening procedures. A well-balanced energy system will join exercise, good nutrition and stress management as one of the four basic requirements for long-term good health.

CHAPTER THREE
LIFE ENERGY AND EMOTIONAL HEALTH

In each of the examples in Chapter 2, the attitudes and emotions played a pivotal role in the development of physical disease. This is no coincidence. We have seen that individual energies embody both physical and mental aspects of experience, linking body and mind at the most basic level. Whatever the grouping of factors—ambition, Wood energy and the cardiovascular system; inhibition, Metal energy and the immune system; or appetites, Earth energy and blood sugar regulation—a disturbance in one part of the system inevitably affects the other two parts.

Because these relationships are so fundamental, it is fair to say that every human being is made up of three basic components: mind, body and energy system. A simple diagram illustrates this principle:

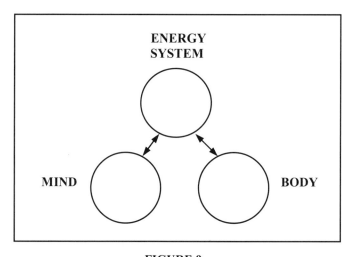

FIGURE 9.
THE THREE BASIC COMPONENTS
OF THE HUMAN ORGANISM

The two-pointed arrows represent direct, two-way relationships between the energy system and both mind and body. Direct body-energy interactions include the following: 1) life energy nourishes and fuels the cells, tissues and organs and 2) body processes such as breathing and digestion generate and release life energies. Direct mind-energy interactions include the following: 1) life energy is the raw material out of which our thoughts and emotions are made and 2) thoughts, emotions and attitudes generate positive and negative energies.

Figure 9 is as important for what it leaves out as for what it includes. There is no arrow connecting mind and body directly. The two interact with each other indirectly, via the life energy system. In each of the disease patterns In Chapter 2, for example, attitudes and emotions first caused imbalances in the energy system, and those imbalances in turn contributed to harmful physical changes. The process works in reverse as well. Later in this chapter I discuss body chemicals such as serotonin, which influence mood by binding to receptors in the cells. The binding of these "molecules of emotion" apparently releases the life energies that embody human feelings.

Two Basic Principles

Figure 9 illustrates two principles that can help clarify, or even redefine, what we mean by holistic health and mind-body relations:

1. Holistic health is a state of balanced interaction among the three components of the human organism—mind, body and energy system.
2. Life energy is the connecting link between mind and body and is the force or energy or process that makes mind-body interactions possible.

In this chapter I explore some of the energetic roots of the emotions and of certain emotional conflicts and disorders. As in Chapter 2, body, mind and energy system must all be considered for a full understanding. Just as the emotions are a crucial factor in physical health, biology is a fundamental influence on emotional health. Recent studies confirm that many emotional illnesses have their origins in body chemistry or even genetic inheritance. Even when this is the case, life energies are still important. We saw in Chapter 2 how patterns can develop in which attitudes, behaviors, life energies and body processes all mingle together and influence one another, blurring the distinction between cause and effect. In such cases correcting the overall pattern of imbalance may be more important, and more effective, than trying to uncover an ultimate cause. This is very much in the spirit of traditional Chinese medicine, which is less interested in pinpointing cause and effect than in identifying and correcting unhealthy patterns.

The link between life energy and the emotions is strikingly illustrated in the work of one of Western psychology's greatest pioneers. Ironically, he was a man who considered himself, above all, a scientist of the mind, but whose insights mirrored, to a remarkable degree, the intuitive understandings of ancient China and India.

PART 1. FREUD'S VISION: ANTICIPATING LIFE ENERGY

Sigmund Freud is generally regarded as the father of modern psychology. His conceptions of the Unconscious, repressed emotion, infantile stages of development and other phenomena revolutionized our understanding of the mind.

Freud's star has dimmed somewhat in recent years for several reasons. Modern psychology now places far greater emphasis on the biological basis of emotion than in the past. Freud, too, almost certainly exaggerated the importance of the sex drive in human behavior. But even if Freud's work was imperfect and his analytical approach is currently out of fashion, his insights were profound and their influences will be long-lasting. Nothing illustrates that better than placing some of Freud's ideas alongside life energy principles. Though he apparently never studied Eastern healing methods or other energy-based teachings, several of Freud's seminal ideas closely track the structure of the life energy system. They reflect his intuitive understanding that mind and body, though seemingly separate, are united at a deeper level of organization.

WHAT IS THE UNCONSCIOUS MADE OF?

Freud believed that certain ideas from the physical sciences could be applied to psychology. His first principle was that consciousness is driven by a force he called psychic energy. Freud visualized the mind's energy, not as a vague abstraction, but as a tangible force that organizes itself into concrete structures such as the Id, Ego and Superego. Freud thus understood that the realm of consciousness, like the physical world, is a place of structure and organization and that psychic energies follow definite laws. One of those laws, Freud believed, was that the mind's energies may disappear from view but are not destroyed.

Freud borrowed his idea from the European physicists Mayer and von Helmholtz, who had recently developed the Law of the Conservation of Energy. It states that physical energies can be converted into various forms but cannot be destroyed.[16] Freud reasoned that psychic energies, like physical energies, were permanent and that, if a person lost touch with a certain memory or emotion, the energy embodying it had simply gone out of awareness; in principle, it could be reawakened and experienced again. That insight formed the basis of Freud's concept of repressed emotion and, more generally, of the Unconscious.

The work of energy therapists confirms that Freud was right and that repressed emotions do indeed have a concrete existence: as life energies trapped in the tissues. Fear tends to settle in the lower two chakras or the kidney meridian; anger is trapped in the third chakra or the liver meridian; grief migrates to the fourth chakra or the lung meridian; and so on. Energy therapists can identify, locate and treat these blockages and imbalances, encouraging the energies to free themselves and improving emotional health.

Because repressed emotion and life energies are so closely related, it can be useful to define repressed emotion in terms of life energies. A repressed emotion is an emotion that one has not fully processed and that has become trapped in the tissues in the form of stagnated life energies that are unavailable to consciousness.

The Unconscious as an Energy Brain

Freud's theory of the Unconscious was a natural extension of his notion of repressed emotion and of the idea that psychic energies are structured, organized and permanent. Because both our bodies and minds are constantly doing remarkable and complex things without any conscious help from us, the psychological community and the public at large long ago accepted the Unconscious as a fact. But today, a century after Freud began to explain it, the Unconscious remains almost as vague a concept as it was in Freud's day. For the most part it is little more than a handy label for processes and phenomena that Western science is simply unequipped to understand or explain.

The reason for the lack of progress is simple. The Western model of the human organism does not include the life energy system. Therefore it cannot answer the most basic question about the Unconscious: what is it made of? Presumably it is made of *something*. The amazingly complex and efficient activities of body and mind must be held together by some concrete, organized structure.

The Unconscious, as medical intuitives perceive it, is an intricate network of life energies that embody everything we know, feel, think and are. It includes a great deal of information including, among other things, every piece of knowledge we have acquired and every experience we have had in our lives. Remarkably, information from any part of that vast storehouse of knowledge is available at a moment's notice. All we have to do is place our attention on what we want to think about or remember and it instantly appears. The process is so effortless and automatic that we take it for granted. But the mind can do these remarkable things only because the Unconscious is so extraordinarily well-organized, and because its contents are concretely recorded in a meaningful language—the language of life energies.

Seen in this way, the Unconscious is a kind of invisible energy brain that works in concert with the physical brain, which mirrors it. The energy brain is an unseen bridge connecting mind and body.

The Energy Body

The insights of medical intuitives suggest that the Unconscious, or energy brain, underlies not just the physical brain but the body as a whole. The aura, or human energy field, is an extension of the seven chakras and duplicates the body in seven increasingly subtle layers.[17] The energies within those layers represent every human activity—physical, mental, emotional and spiritual. Thus, at the energy level, mind and body are ultimately one. They seem separate to us because we experience them, not in their true energy form, but as reflections in the physical and mental realms. I discuss the aura and the interplay of mind and body energies in more detail in Chapter 5.

The Coherence of Freudian Theory

A longstanding objection to Freud's theory of repressed emotion, and more generally of the Unconscious, is that it lacks coherence. This is a technical term that simply means the theory is too vague and speculative to qualify as science. One writer states the problem as follows:

> The difficulty with Freud's theory is that it offers us entities (repressed unconscious conflicts, for example) which are said to be the unobservable causes of certain forms of behaviour, but there are no correspondence rules for these alleged causes - they cannot be identified except by reference to the behaviour which they are said to cause...And this does raise serious doubts as to whether Freud's theory offers us genuine causal explanations at all.[18]

In fact, energy therapists routinely locate the sources of repressed unconscious conflicts in the body, and they do so by using the "correspondence rules" of Chinese medicine. For example, repressed fear settles in the kidney meridian and repressed anger in the liver meridian. Freud's theory of repressed emotion is thus not vague or speculative at all but is validated and confirmed by well-established energy principles. To the extent that Western psychology fails to recognize this, it is because Western psychology is an incomplete system.

LIFE ENERGY AND FREUD'S THREE STAGES

Freud's insights into the Unconscious were grounded on the principle that energy is the building block of the mind. His theory of early childhood development says, in effect, that those building blocks come in several varieties. Although Freud was not aware of Five Elements energies, his theory identified three of those energies—Earth, Metal and Wood—and the periods in a young child's life when each begins to develop. The adult conflicts that can result from stresses during those periods, and which Freud called fixations, represent imbalances in the respective energies. Freud's three stages may be a time, too, when the Earth, Metal and Wood type personalities begin to develop.

The Oral Stage and Earth Energy

Freud's first stage is the Oral Stage, from birth to two years, when a baby is nursing and receiving more or less constant attention from its mother. The baby learns to love and to trust that it will be loved in return. For Freud, conflicts during the Oral Stage could lead to Oral Stage Fixation: adult feelings of insecurity, a need for constant reassurance and chronic difficulty finding the right balance between giving and receiving.

The Oral Stage represents the development of Earth energies in the infant and young child. In Chinese medicine Earth is associated with physical and emotional nourishment—food and love—and the mother-child relationship embodies the satisfaction of both needs.[19] Healthy, free-flowing Earth energies give a person the balanced ability to love and trust and to inspire love and trust in return. An Earth imbalance leads to the same symptoms as Oral Stage

Fixation—insecurity, lack of trust and a need for continual reassurance. People with Earth imbalance/Oral Stage Fixation often resort to clinging or manipulative behaviors to satisfy their needs and wants. A parent with the fixation may be smothering and overprotective, refusing to let the child grow up and develop a healthy sense of independence.

The major stresses during the Oral Stage are shown graphically in the Controlling Cycle (Figure 10). The tension between Earth and Water represents the struggle between the need for love (Earth) and the fear and mistrust that can lead to insecurity if those needs

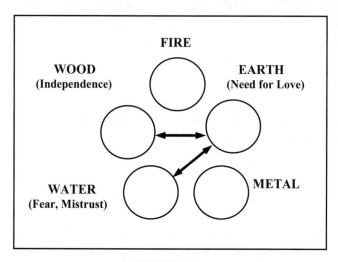

FIGURE 10.
MAJOR TENSIONS DURING THE ORAL STAGE

are not met (Water). The tension between Earth and Wood represents the balance between the baby's (and sometimes the parent's) need for love and security (Earth) and the independence that the child ideally develops as it grows up (Wood).

The Anal Stage and Metal Energy

Freud's second stage is the Anal Stage, ages 2-3, when the child learns to use the toilet. The child's attention is focused on body functions, cleanliness, and learning when it is appropriate to "hold things in" and "let things out." Conflicts during this stage can lead to Anal Stage Fixation. Anal retentive types tend to be compulsively neat and orderly, careful, anxious and emotionally withholding. They are vulnerable to feelings of guilt and emphasize control and restraint over freedom and spontaneity. These are all symptoms of Metal or Metal-Water imbalance which was illustrated by Betty in Chapter 2. Because the Metal organs, the lungs and large intestine, are the organs of elimination, the connection between the Anal Stage and Metal energies is beyond doubt.

The primary tensions during the Anal Stage are between Metal and its Controlling Cycle neighbors Wood and Fire (Figure 11). In

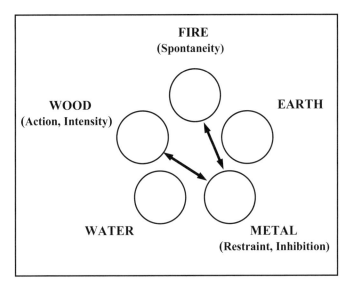

FIGURE 11.
MAJOR TENSIONS DURING THE ANAL STAGE

the anal retentive type, the inward-turning *yin* qualities of Metal dominate and stifle the spontaneity of Fire and the dynamism and intensity of Wood. In Part 2 I describe some of the specific emotional risks of that pattern.

The Phallic Stage and Wood Energy

In Freud's Phallic Stage, ages 3-5, the child competes with one
parent for the attention of the other. Freud portrayed the Phallic
Stage mainly as a struggle over sex. His famous Oedipus Complex,
in which the child has fantasies of killing one parent and marrying
the other, has a sexual aspect but is clearly a struggle for power as
well. The same is true of Castration Anxiety, the young boy's fear
that his jealous father will mutilate him.

Whether the primary factor is sex or power or both, the Phallic
Stage is clearly a time when Wood energies take center stage in the
young child's life. Wood is the energy of both sexuality and power
as well as competition, egotism, anger and aggression—all parts of
the child's experiences, or at least his fantasies, during the Phallic
Stage.

Phallic Fixation is associated with qualities that point to Wood
or Wood-Fire dominance: recklessness, excessive self-assurance,
narcissism, vanity and pride. The Phallic Stage is the first major
struggle between the child's Wood energies and the two energies in
natural tension with Wood—Earth and Metal (Figure 12). The desire to be strong, dominant and even violent (Wood) clashes with

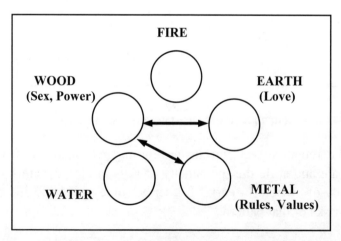

FIGURE 12.
MAJOR TENSIONS DURING THE PHALLIC STAGE

the child's love for his parent (Earth). The desire to impose his will (Wood) collides with his developing sense of rules and appropriate behavior (Metal). In Part 2 I discuss some of the unhealthy outcomes of those tensions when they occur in adults.

....

Freud was able to identify the three stages of early childhood development because he was sensitive to what might be called the poetry of the body—the symbolic relationships between physical needs and desires and their emotional counterparts. As a physician who believed that psychology was, or at least could be, a true science, Freud would have been gratified to know that the poetry of the body is made possible by concrete energies that link the child's feelings with the physical aspects of its experience.

Five Energies, Three Stages of Development

Freud's theory leaves an important question unanswered. If the Oral, Anal and Phallic Stages correspond to the development of Earth, Metal and Wood energies, when do the other two energies, Fire and Water, begin to develop? Are there separate stages for them and if not, why not?

Freud described two more developmental phases—the Latency Stage and the Genital Stage—but the first is a relatively dormant period and the second is a kind of second Wood phase when sexual feelings continue to develop. Fire and Water apparently do not have their own separate stages. One reason may be that, although there are five energies and five general personality types, the five types can be distilled into three even more basic categories. I alluded to that earlier in describing George as a Wood-Fire or *yang*-type personality, and Betty as a Metal-Water or *yin*-type personality. Because the two pairs of adjoining energies—Wood-Fire and Metal-Water—share certain qualities and tend to blend into one another, and because they strengthen each other through the Nurturing Cycle, it may be that they develop together during the same childhood phase. If so, Earth energy begins to develop during the Oral Stage, Metal and Water during the Anal Stage and Wood and Fire during the Phallic Stage.

The Enneagram: Head, Heart and Gut Types

Seeing personality in terms of three categories—*yin, yang* and something in between—is an approach used in the Enneagram, a system that has become increasingly popular in recent years. The Enneagram is one of the strangest yet one of the richest and most intriguing of the many systems for understanding behavior. Its insights can shed light on personality as an expression of five basic energies but only three general types.

The Enneagram (Greek for "Picture of Nine") originally developed as a tool for spiritual growth.[20] It was handed down through ancient sources in Asia, finally finding its way to the Russian philosopher Gurdjieff in the twentieth century. In recent years teachers in Latin America and the U.S. have further developed and popularized it. The Enneagram is now used by psychologists, social workers and other professionals in the U.S. and elsewhere. Informal Enneagram groups have sprung up in many places, and members are enthusiastic about the insights it brings to their relationships and self-understanding.

The Enneagram diagram is shown in Figure 13. It classifies each person as one of nine types, each of which is referred to by a number. The lines connecting each type with two other types show the paths of growth and regression for each type.

One of the Enneagram's important insights is that we can divide the nine individual types into three groups: Thinking (Head) types, Feeling (Heart) types and Instinctual (Gut) types. With some qualifications, these categories correspond to the *yin*-type, Earth-type and *yang*-type personalities. The similarities are most evident in the three types that most clearly represent thinking, feeling and instinct.

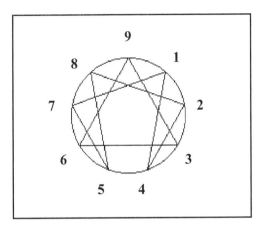

FIGURE 13.
THE ENNEAGRAM

"The Boss, " "The Observer" and "The Lover"

Each of the nine types has a name that captures something of its essence. Of the three Gut or Instinctual types, the Eight—known as "the Boss"—is the purest expression of instinctual energies. The Eight is forceful, aggressive and has a natural talent and desire for leadership and control. When resisted he can respond with anger and, if necessary, with force. Those qualities are the hallmarks of the Wood-dominant personality and perhaps of someone for whom the Phallic Stage was an especially important time.

Among the Feeling or Heart types, the Two—known as "the Lover"—best expresses the emotional nature of the type. Two's are caring and compassionate but can become manipulative, clinging or controlling if they feel their needs and wants are not being met. The Two is an Earth type and, under stress, shows signs of Freud's Oral Stage Fixation.

The Five, known as "the Observer," is the clearest example of the Thinking or Head type. The Five is intelligent, organized and, of the nine types, the least connected to his feelings. The name Observer captures the Five's tendency to experience life from a distance, through ideas rather than emotion. Head types are some-times referred to as fear-based types, and the Five's combination of intellect and repressed fear identifies him as a Metal-Water type. The Five may have learned to practice restraint and avoid feelings in part from conflicts during the Anal Stage.

The Enneagram and Five Elements Aligned

The parallels between Five Elements and Enneagram types leave little doubt that the Enneagram is based on life energy principles. The two diagrams confirm it. If we place the Enneagram inside the Five Elements circle (Figure 14), the purest examples of Head, Heart and Gut types line up closely with the energies that make them up. The Eight, the most Wood-dominant of the types, is next to Wood energy; the Two, the most Earth-dominant type, adjoins Earth energy; and the Five, the best example of the Metal-Water type, is between Metal and Water energies.

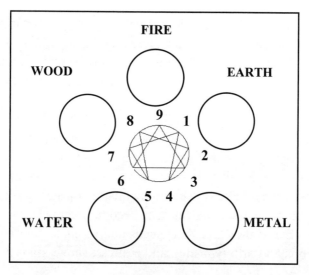

FIGURE 14.
THE ENNEAGRAM AND FIVE ELEMENTS ALIGNED

There are parallels, too, between the growth paths of Enneagram types and tensions within the Controlling Cycle. The growth path for the Eight, for example, is the line connecting the Eight with the Two. One writer on the Enneagram describes the Eight's growth process as follows:

> When healthy Eights move to Two, they identify with others rather than against them...Integrating Eights have empathy and compassion...They learn the power of love rather than being obsessed with power.[21]

These words describe one of the most fundamental of all human conflicts and one discussed at length in the chapters that follow: the natural tension between Wood, the energy of independence and self-interest, and Earth, the energy of sharing, compassion and love. Figure 14 confirms that the line connecting the Eight and Two is the same line that connects Wood and Earth in the Controlling Cycle.

The paths of growth and regression for several of the Enneagram types correspond more or less to Controlling Cycle tensions. The parallels are not perfect because both diagrams are simplified models of the complex phenomenon that is human personality. The parallels illustrate, in a general way, that the Enneagram, like virtually every system for understanding personality, is based ultimately on life energies.

The Enneagram framework is important here for another reason. It highlights the unique role of Earth in the energy system and in human life. The Head, Heart and Gut types are expressions of *yin, yang* and a third quality, embodied by Earth, that is neither *yin* nor *yang*. Head and Gut Types—*yin* and *yang* types—represent the tension and imbalance that make up the everyday world of opposites. The Heart type, or Earth type, is the only type that does not have a natural opposite. The reason is that Earth is neither an energy of dynamism and projection (*yang*) nor one of withdrawal and reflection (*yin*). It is instead a primary energy of connection. At its best, Earth transcends *yin* and *yang* and harmonizes life's opposing forces through the power of love and compassion.

PART 2. THE FIVE ELEMENTS AND EMOTIONAL HEALTH

Whether one believes that personality is mainly a product of genetics, life experience or both, most people express the influences of one or two dominant energies. They give each person certain emotional strengths as well as vulnerabilities. Just as in physical health, when a person's dominant energies become so strong that they disrupt the overall balance within the system, the seeds can be planted for illness. Energy imbalances can underlie disorders ranging from mania to depression, from anxiety to paranoia.

Since each of the energies carries at least one primary emotion, energy balance directly affects how joyful, fearful, loving, sad or angry a person is likely to be. The following sections describe the role of each of the five energies, and its relationships with its Controlling Cycle neighbors, in emotional health and illness.

FIRE ENERGY: THE "NORTH POLE" OF PERSONALITY

A healthy personality can be defined in many ways. If we think of it as the ability to interact freely with, and enjoy, other people and daily activities, Fire is a kind of leading edge, or North Pole, of the personality. Fire embodies joy, enthusiasm, excitement, sociability, extroversion and romantic love. Fire, along with Earth, is a basic connecting force that promotes physical intimacy and the ability to enjoy, and draw energy from, other people. Because Fire is associated with qualities we think of as *yang*—warmth, activity, dynamism and extroversion—Fire is, generally speaking, a *yang* energy and an important component of the *yang*-type personality.

In Chinese medicine Fire is the abode of *shen*, or spirit, a basic animating and enlivening force. Whether, as the Chinese believe, *shen* is a real, distinct entity—a kind of circulating spirit in the body—or merely a metaphor for personal vitality, a healthy s*hen* reveals itself as the sparkle in a person's eyes and a vibrancy in the personality.

Fire has important associations with the Unconscious and with deep unconscious processes such as creativity and spiritual awareness. Personal charisma, too, is a mysterious quality associated with strong or dominant Fire energy.

Fire embodies the instinct for freedom, a key reason for its importance to emotional health. In the Controlling Cycle, Fire exists in a natural state of tension with Metal and Water, each of which tries to limit personal freedom in a different way.

Fire and Water: the Struggle between Happiness and Fear

If Fire is the energetic North Pole of personality, Water is a kind of South Pole, *yin* to Fire's *yang*. Water balances and restrains Fire's exuberance and excitement with seriousness, thoughtfulness, depth and caution. Water, too, is the domain of fear and its more contemporary cousin, anxiety. When Fire and Water are well developed and well balanced, a person is both joyful and realistic, optimistic but not naïve. The person is aware both of life's opportunities and dangers and is able to navigate the two with a combination of enthusiasm and prudence.

Water is home to *jing,* which translates as essence and is associated with genetic inheritance and stages of personal development, including maturity and aging. If *shen* is a lamp fully illuminated, *jing* is a kind of electrical potential waiting to be connected. The presence of *shen* and *jing* in the Fire-Water axis demonstrates the fundamental importance of the two energies in personality.

When Fire Defeats Water: *Jing*, Risk-Taking and the Fantasy of Invulnerability

Water's natural role is to control Fire but Fire can, if it is strong enough, reverse the usual relationship and, in the Chinese phrase, insult Water. An insult to Water obscures fear and, among other things, disrupts the normal balance between enthusiasm and caution. The result can be dangerous, sometimes deliberately risky behaviors including substance abuse, unsafe sex or driving at high speeds. In substance abuse there is often an element of escapism suggesting that the person is not only out of touch with fear but is actively running away from it. This is a further clue that the excess in Fire is due, at least in part, to a significant imbalance in Water.

It is no coincidence that young people in particular tend to

indulge in risky behaviors. The young have both naturally high enthusiasm—strong Fire—and a false but powerful sense of their
own invulnerability—weak or undeveloped Water. Although normal up to a point, youthful risk-taking suggests that *jing,* the energy of maturity and personal development, is slow to awaken. It
may be that therapies to strengthen Water energies and disperse excess Fire can help stimulate the development of *jing,* restore the
normal Fire-Water balance and promote greater emotional maturity.

Fire and Metal: the Price of Civilization

If Fire and Water represent the conflict between happiness and
fear, Fire and Metal embody the equally basic conflict between
freedom and restraint. Metal, the energy of rules, values and structures, wants to "civilize" the personality and make people conform
to society's norms. Metal thus corresponds closely to Freud's Superego. Fire's natural response is to resist Metal and maintain as
much spontaneity and freedom as possible.

When Fire and Metal are relatively well balanced, a person can
be spontaneous but not impulsive, fun-loving but not irresponsible.
When Fire dominates Metal too much, discipline and the awareness of rules and norms can begin to break down. The results can
range from impulsive or eccentric behavior to a hedonistic obsession with pleasure and disregard of duties and responsibilities. The
expression "burning the candle at both ends" aptly describes the
person with unrestrained Fire energies whose intense passion for
life overwhelms boundaries, structures and the daily routine.

Fire Unbounded: an "Excess of Joy"

The more extreme, pathological effects of unrestrained Fire come
about when Fire becomes so strong that it overwhelms both of its
Controlling Cycle neighbors. Any of the five energies, if it becomes strong enough, can do the same. When Fire is all-powerful,
the Chinese refer to the condition as "an excess of joy." Excitement

runs rampant and Fire becomes a kind of law unto itself, acting without restraint from either side, literally destroying the system of checks and balances the Controlling Cycle represents. This is the energetic picture in mania, when excitement is unrestrained by fear, inhibition, rules or structures (Figure 15).

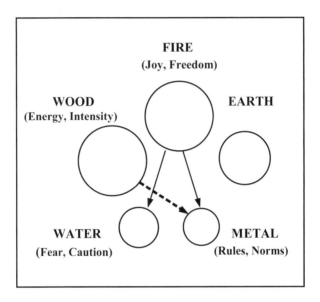

FIGURE 15.
THE ENERGETIC PATTERN IN MANIA

For some people, manic episodes can have a spiritual component, and a person in the midst of such an experience may feel a close connection to God even while behaving in a way that seems bizarre or even crazy to an outside observer. Although mental illness and spiritual awareness may seem unlikely partners, they can have certain things in common. Both mania and ecstasy are intense experiences associated with highly concentrated Fire energies. Each represents, in its own way, a cutting of the usual connections with everyday life. The crucial difference is that, in spiritual awareness, the broken connections are replaced by new, healthy and meaningful connections at a deeper level.

Because manic behavior usually includes both excitement and

intense activity, it is not simply an expression of unrestrained Fire but of Fire and Wood working together. This is natural since, as we have seen, Wood and Fire are the two most *yang* of the five energies and mania is perhaps the ultimate *yang* behavior.

In energy terms, mania may be a more extreme example of an imbalance we saw in Chapter 2. George was a Wood-Fire type whose powerful instinct for activity and accomplishment made him a hyperactive Type A personality. Since the same Wood-Fire energies, operating at a much higher level of intensity, are the force behind mania, Type A behavior and mania may be seen as related syndromes that occupy different places on the same energy continuum.

The Earthly Limits of Fire: a Metaphor for Daily Life

The restrictions that Metal and Water impose on Fire are a symbol of life's basic limitations. Fire, which represents the pure joy and freedom of being, is hemmed in on one side by fear—a restraint from within—and on the other side by rules and structures—a restraint from without. Life after about the age of two is a matter of adjusting to, and working within, these twin constraints on happiness and freedom.

Although we rightly think of mania as an abnormal, pathological condition, unrestrained Fire in its pure form may represent a natural and healthy state of being. How difficult is it, after all, to imagine a place where joy is not limited by fear and where freedom is not constrained by rules? Such a place sounds like Heaven, and the mysterious associations of Fire with creativity, romantic love and, above all, spiritual ecstasy suggest that Fire contains the seeds of a joy that transcends earthly life.

Fire Blending into Metal: When Joy is Tinged with Sadness

Metal, the energy of rules, structures and values, is the energy of sadness as well. Fire and Metal represent the polar opposites of joy and sorrow, celebration and loss. In their natural connections to the seasons, Fire and Metal are the energies of summer and autumn respectively. When the joy and freedom of summer come to an end, the Metal energies of autumn begin to awaken. In cold northern climates like New England, the turning of the leaves to red, yellow and gold and the clear, soft October sunlight create a sense of beauty mingled with impending loss that is pure, distilled *yin* and *yang*. Joy and sadness merge into a single, powerful emotion, a sweet melancholy that has inspired some of the world's great Romantic poets:

> Where are the songs of Spring? Ay, where are they?
> Think not of them, thou hast thy music too...
> While barred clouds bloom the soft-dying day,
> And touch the stubble-plains with rosy hue...
> Hedge-crickets sing; and now with treble soft
> The red-breast whistles from a garden-croft;
> And gathering swallows twitter in the skies.
> ——from "To Autumn" by John Keats

The romantic temperament captures the essence of life as a beautiful but fleeting experience, the bittersweet merging of Fire with Metal. The romantic's passionate appreciation for life reveals the strength of his Fire energies. But Metal is never far away either— in the tinge of sadness even in the happiest of times, and in the romantic's love of nostalgia, the celebration of times past and things lost.

The mingled joy and sadness of the romantic temperament hint at the dark side of Metal energy, which emerges fully when Metal's *yin* tendencies are not balanced by the *yang* influences of Fire and Wood. The consequences of imbalanced Metal are the topic of the next section.

STRUCTURE, STRENGTH AND RIGIDITY: METAL'S DOUBLE-EDGED SWORD

Metal is a fundamental force in modern society. In a sense, it is the energy of civilization itself. Metal embodies the laws, moral and ethical principles and social norms that make society work. When a person accepts and internalizes those structures, Metal becomes the foundation of character. Metal is closely associated with Freud's concept of the Superego.

Metal is the energy of both moral and mental structure, of both character and thinking, and is a primary force in the intellect. As society becomes more complex and the demands on people's mental abilities grow, Metal energy is increasingly prized. Because modern society handsomely rewards intellectual achievement, there is a strong incentive for people today to develop their Metal qualities to the fullest.

The benefits of strong Metal are obvious but they come with certain unavoidable risks. As with each of the energies, Metal's greatest strengths can be among its most serious potential liabilities. The structure and stability that give the Metal type his strength of character can make him rigid, dogmatic or self-righteous. Under stress, the Metal type's gift for organization and detail can degenerate into obsessive or compulsive behaviors—a way of dissipating anxiety through structure, repetition and ritual. Most serious of all, the Metal type's emphasis on thinking over feeling, and his tendency to push away and repress difficult emotions, can plant the seeds of depression and other serious disorders.

The Two Prongs of Depression

Wood is the energy of activity and Fire of happiness. When Wood and Fire are strong and well-balanced, a person leads a satisfying, active and engaged life. But when Fire declines and enjoyment begins to fade, there is a natural tendency to pull back and curtail social and other activities. As inactivity increases, mood slips further and the person feels even less motivated to stay active and involved. A negative Wood-Fire cycle can be set in motion that may end in depression. In energy terms, Wood and Fire are the two prongs of depression.

We saw in Chapter 2 how Wood and Fire, the two energies in natural tension with Metal, can become part of a Distorted Triangle pattern in which Metal weakens Wood directly and Fire indirectly through the Nurturing and Controlling Cycles. If Metal is even more dominant, it can weaken both energies directly by over-whelming Wood and insulting Fire. Meanwhile, the other *yin* energy, Water, which is compatible with Metal and is nourished by it, may aggravate the problem by further weakening Fire. The pattern is shown in Figure 16.

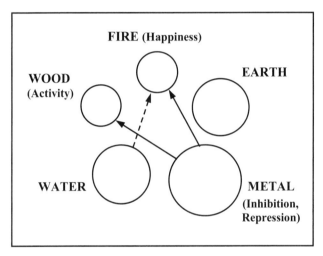

FIGURE 16.
THE TWO PRONGS OF DEPRESSION

Because depression is a *yin*-type disorder often associated with introversion and the repression of emotion, the *yin* or Head type personality may be especially at risk for depression. The Head type, as we saw earlier, is a Metal or Metal-Water type who pushes away feelings and relates to life mainly through ideas. The Head type's special vulnerability to depression is immortalized by one of the best-known figures in English literature.

The Prince of Denmark

Hamlet, probably the most famous Head type in history, wanted to

92 A PROMISE OF EDEN

avenge his father's death but could never summon the will to act. Instead, he thought about, and talked about, the problem until it was too late. His soliloquy beautifully captures the Head type's dilemma:

> Thus conscience doth make cowards of us all,
> And thus the native hue of resolution
> Is sicklied o'er with the pale cast of thought,
> And enterprises of great pith and moment,
> With this regard their currents turn awry,
> And lose the name of action.

Hamlet's idealism and desire for justice are evidence of his strong Metal energies but his behavior shows that those energies are seriously out of balance. Hamlet's maddening preoccupation with thinking rather than doing is a virtual caricature of the Metal type's restraint and inwardness. The obsessive quality of his thinking, too, is characteristic of Metal imbalance.

Hamlet's own words confirm that, like many Head types, he is not pure Metal but rather a blend of Metal and Water. Fear and lack of will are typical signs of Water imbalance and, when Hamlet acknowledges that "conscience doth make cowards of us all," he reveals the role of fear, and imbalanced Water, in his failure to act. Fear only reinforces the Metal type's natural restraint, transforming caution into passivity and, in Hamlet's case, a kind of paralysis. Hamlet is a classic example of the imbalanced Metal-Water Head type: brooding and introspective, idealistic yet afraid, desiring justice yet lacking the will to act. Although clearly angry, Hamlet's anger is strangely muffled, so is not strong enough to overcome inertia and propel him into action.

Repressed Anger and Depression

A good case can be made that Hamlet is clinically depressed. His father was recently murdered; his uncle, the murderer, married his mother; and Hamlet himself openly considers suicide. In energy terms depression, passivity and repressed anger are natural partners since all are associated with distorted Wood energies. Liver energy, a form of Wood, is the bearer of anger which in Chinese medicine is known as "liver fire rising." When Wood is depressed, both activity and anger tend to be stifled.

Whether repressed anger causes depression, depression causes anger to be repressed or—which is more likely—anger, depression and energy form a complex pattern in which an ultimate cause is hard to find, there is a clear energetic link between depression and anger. Freud was apparently at least partly right when he declared that depression is anger turned inward.

Depression and Biology

There is growing evidence that biochemical imbalances lie behind many emotional disorders including depression. Whether body chemistry is the root cause of these illnesses is a complex question that involves genetics, biochemistry, temperament, life experience, energy dynamics and possibly other factors. It is hard to isolate a root cause from so many factors, and in fact there may not be a root cause in any practical sense. The Asian approach—to identify and correct patterns of imbalance—may be more in keeping with the holistic quality of human experience.

The interaction of mind, body and energy system takes on new meaning when viewed from the perspective of individual cells. Just as Einstein showed that matter and physical energy are interchangeable, energy principles, with the help of modern science, suggest that matter, life energy and the emotions are constantly creating and transforming themselves into one another.

Matter, Energy and Two Kinds of Nourishment

Chinese medicine teaches that *chi*, or life energy, can exist in a number of forms depending on its origin and function. Two major categories are prenatal and postnatal *chi*. Prenatal *chi* is an energy one is born with, is limited in supply and is gradually used up over the course of a lifetime. Prenatal *chi* is closely related to *jing* and reflects a person's genetic inheritance and affects processes like maturity and aging.

Post-natal *chi*, or *gu chi* ("goo chee"), is an energy that is created continuously to provide mind and body with the fuel they need to live. *Gu chi* is acquired through food, oxygen and probably sunlight. When a person eats, drinks and breathes, the body gets two kinds of nourishment—physical nourishment for the cells and energy nourishment for the life energy system.

Gu Chi and the Cells: Updating Chinese Medicine

The ancient Chinese, who did not have the luxury of modern science to help them understand how life energies behave, described *gu chi* in a general sort of way: as an energy spontaneously created out of food, drink and air, which then circulated throughout the body, nourishing and energizing body and mind.

We can use our modern understandings to update the principles of Chinese medicine and perhaps begin to explain how *gu chi* arises at the level of individual cells. Since the cells are where the body receives its most basic nourishment, applying the concept of *gu chi* at the cellular level is consistent with the principles of traditional Chinese medicine.

The body's cells create a wide range of important chemicals and energy principles suggest that these substances, and their varying activities, represent the storage and release of different kinds of life energy. Mitochondria, for example, are tiny power plants within the cell that produce ATP, a basic body fuel. Since Wood is the energy most closely associated with physical and mental activity, the ATP mechanism could be a way for the body to create, and make use of, some form of Wood energy.

Another kind of biology-energy connection is less speculative and is supported by recent medical research. The documented link between certain cell activities and the emotions suggests that life energy plays a central role in connecting body and mind at the cellular level.

Life Energy and Emotion: A Western Scientist's View

Candace Pert is a neuroscientist and author of *Molecules of Emotion: Why You Feel the Way You Feel.* She is a pioneer in the study of the biochemical basis of emotion. Her work has shown that proteins called neuropeptides, by attaching themselves to receptors in cells throughout the body, bring about changes in mood and feeling. She refers to these proteins as the "molecules of emotion" and presents them as powerful evidence that body and mind are connected at the most basic level.

In her book, Pert ponders an explanation for the ability of mind and body to communicate with one another. She concludes that life energy is a likely candidate:

> For me the key concept is that emotions exist in the body as informational chemicals, the neuropeptides and receptors, and they also exist in another realm, the one we experience as feeling, inspiration, love—beyond the physical. The emotions move back and forth, flowing freely between both places, and in that sense, they connect the physical and nonphysical. Perhaps this is the same thing that Eastern healers call the subtle energy, or prana— the circulation of emotional and spiritual information throughout the bodymind.[22]

Camdace Pert's work may help explain how body chemicals, life energy and the emotions are woven together in a disorder like depression.

Serotonin, Wood Deficiency and Depression

The brain chemical serotonin plays a major role in emotional health. As a neurotransmitter its job is to transmit nerve impulses in the brain by traveling from one nerve cell to another and binding to a receptor in the receiving cell. When serotonin is functioning normally, a person's mood tends to be positive. But when serotonin is unable to do its job efficiently, studies have shown that depression and certain other emotional disorders are more likely.

Many popular antidepressant drugs work by preventing the removal of serotonin from the spaces between brain cells after they have done their work. By essentially flooding the brain with serotonin, SSRI's (selective serotonin reuptake inhibitors) can prevent or relieve the symptoms of depression and certain other disorders.

Serotonin's important role in maintaining mood suggests that it may be, not just a molecule of emotion, but a molecule of happiness itself. Since Fire is the energy of happiness, the binding of the serotonin molecule to its receptor could be one of the body's ways of creating and releasing a form of Fire energy.

Research has shown that serotonin dysfunction is not due to an isolated weakness or defect in one part of the system but to a more general slowdown in the whole serotonin mechanism. The transport of the chemical into, out of and between cells becomes less efficient, and receptors have a reduced ability to bind with the serotonin molecule.[23]

These findings suggest that depression could, in some cases at least, be the result of a general sluggishness or inactivity in the serotonin system. It recalls Betty's syndrome in Chapter 2. Betty suffered from depression that had its roots in a Wood energy deficiency and a consequent slowdown in body processes. I noted the research findings there suggesting a possible connection between a bodily slowdown and reduced immune cell activity. The serotonin studies suggest something similar—that a Wood energy deficiency, and the inevitable slowdown in body processes that accompanies it, may cause serotonin molecules, receptors and the whole serotonin system to become relatively inactive. The result could be that the body is unable to produce enough Fire energy, contributing to depression.

The Biochemistry of the Five Elements: a First Step

Research will one day show whether there is a link between Wood energy deficiency, serotonin function and depression. If so, it could be a first step in identifying the biochemistry of the Five Elements. If serotonin releases Fire energies when it binds to its receptor, and if it does so more efficiently when Wood energy is strong, it confirms one leg of the Nurturing Cycle: that Wood energy nourishes Fire energy (Figure 17).

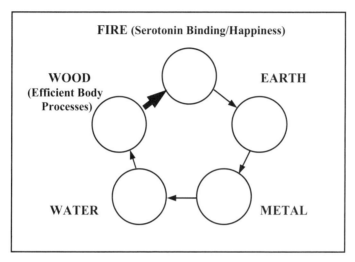

FIGURE 17.
SEEKING THE BIOCHEMISTRY OF THE FIVE ELEMENTS

As research continues and more molecules of emotion are discovered, we may find that grief, fear, anger, sadness and even love are embodied in biochemical processes. In each case, life energy will be the connecting link between body and mind. Those discoveries may encourage new therapies, perhaps combining drugs, energy techniques and talking therapies, to address the important role of all three human components—mind, body and energy system—in emotional health.

SAD, Heaven and Earth

Seasonal Affective Disorder, or SAD, is a mild to moderate depression associated with a lack of sunlight during the winter months. Although SAD's cause is unknown, daily light therapy has been shown to be effective in relieving, or at least reducing, its symptoms. The link between life energy and the emotions suggests that sunlight, like food and oxygen, may contain both physical energies and life energies that are important in maintaining mood.

C.W. Leadbeater, an early 20th century writer in the Theosophical tradition, identified an energy in sunlight which, he believed, helped explain its ability to fight depression. In his book *The Chakras*, Leadbeater writes:

> We all know the feeling of cheerfulness and well-being which sunlight brings to us, but only students of occultism are fully aware of the reasons for that sensation. Just as the sun floods his system with light and heat, so does he perpetually pour out into it another force as yet unsuspected by modern science—a force to which has been given the name "vitality."[24]

Leadbeater's reference to "vitality" recalls the Western philosophical tradition known as Vitalism—the belief that there is an *elan vital,* or vital force, that animates living things. *Elan vital*, in fact, is life energy and, if Leadbeater is right and sunlight contains mood-enhancing life energies, they are presumably a form of Fire energy.

Traditional Asian teachings support Leadeater's view. *Chi* enters the body from both the heavens above and the earth below. *Yin* energy enters through the feet and *yang* energy, including the enlivening energy of Fire, enters through the head.

Leadbeater believes that people who suffer from seasonal depression do so because they are unable to absorb enough vitality from sunlight:

> In the wintry and melancholy climes miscalled the temperate, it too often happens that for days together the sky is covered by a funeral pall of heavy cloud, and this affects vitality just as it does light... When vitalized atoms are thus more sparsely scattered, the man in rude health increases his power of

absorption, depletes a larger area, and so keeps his strength at a normal level; but invalids and men of small nerve-force, who cannot do this, often suffer severely, and find themselves growing weaker and more irritable without knowing why.[25]

Absorbing Energy through the Feet

Light therapy may be the simplest and most effective way to relieve the symptoms of SAD. Another method is to obtain the *yang* energies of Fire, not from the heavens above, but from the earth below.

Although the body absorbs *yin* energies through the feet, it has the power to transform *yin* into *yang* and vice versa and in fact does so continuously. The structure of the energy system is such that, as energies travel through the body, they flow alternately through *yin* and *yang* meridians, transforming themselves as they go.

The 20th century Japanese healer Shizuto Masunaga, who was instrumental in developing modern shiatsu, discovered a series of extensions to the twelve primary meridians. They include a branch of the heart meridian, a Fire meridian, that begins on the bottoms of the feet. It is a natural pathway through which the *yin* energies of the earth can be absorbed through the feet, converted into *yang,* then sent upward into the body.

Tai Chi, which stresses lower body awareness and improves energetic contact with the earth, can be helpful in relieving the symptoms of SAD. With practice, one can feel energies collecting on the bottoms of the feet, then flowing upward through the legs and into the body. In Chapter 5 I discuss Tai Chi and how it can improve energy flow in some of the body's important energy centers in the lower body.

Obsessive-Compulsive Disorder

When a person's natural instinct for structure and organization becomes distorted, feelings and behavior can take on a compulsive edge. For extroverted, action-oriented, *yang*-type personalities— George in Chapter 2 for example—Metal imbalance can manifest itself as Compulsive Work Syndrome. For introverted *yin*-type personalities who are more vulnerable to anxiety, the result may be obsessive-compulsive disorder instead.

In OCD there are usually two symptoms—highly ritualized behavior and anxiety—that point to a twin imbalance in Metal and Water. The two energies, as we have seen, adjoin each other on the Five Elements circle and may begin to develop together during the same early childhood stage.

Ritual is the purest and most distilled form of organization and is therefore a natural form of expression for the Metal or Metal-Water type. Metal types take comfort, security and even meaning from a sense of order and structure—from knowing, as the familiar saying goes, that "there is a place for everything and everything is in its place." Because ritual is so soothing and satisfying for Metal types, they use it instinctively as a way of relieving anxiety. One writer describes the range of compulsive behaviors as follows:

> Compulsions may be comparatively simple, such as uttering or thinking a word or phrase of protection against an obsessive thought. But some are almost unbelievably complex—as in the elaborate dressing, washing or bedtime rituals that can take up hours every day.[26]

OCD, which may occur in as many as 2% of the population, is apparently more common in people of high intelligence.[27] Since Metal is the energy of the intellect, this further supports the conclusion that OCD is essentially a Metal, or Metal-Water, disorder.

WOOD ENERGY AND ITS TENSIONS: A PORTRAIT OF CIVILIZATION

Wood energy and its natural tensions with Earth and Metal represent some of life's most basic challenges. Wood is the energy of egotism, self interest and anger and, in its more extreme forms, violence and cruelty. Wood naturally opposes both Metal, the energy of rules and values, and Earth, the energy of caring, compassion and love. The quality and strength of the three energies are major influences on life at every level—on the individual's emotional balance and maturity, the harmony or discord in relationships, and whether society adheres to the Social Contract or the Law of the Jungle. Figure 18 shows Wood's Controlling Cycle relationships with its neighbors; it is, in effect, a portrait of civilization itself.

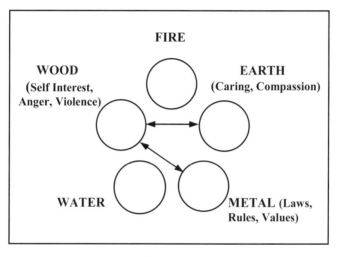

FIGURE 18.
WOOD ENERGY AND ITS TENSIONS:
A PORTRAIT OF CIVILIZATION

Wood Dominance and Antisocial Behavior

The DSM-IV is a standard diagnostic manual for mental health professionals. It describes a common syndrome, Antisocial Personality Disorder, or APD, which, according to the author, occurs in up to 75% of the U.S. prison population:

> Patients with Antisocial Personality Disorder chronically disregard the rights of other people;

they cannot or will not conform to the norms of society...Some are engaging con artists; others may
be graceless thugs...Although these people are
often superficially charming, many are aggressive
and irritable. Besides substance abuse, there may
be fighting, lying and criminal behavior of every
conceivable sort. These people may claim to have
guilt feelings, but they do not seem to feel genuine
remorse for their behavior.[28]

These words could have been written to describe Wood's dominance over Earth and Metal through the Controlling Cycle. A person with APD "cannot or will not conform to the norms of society"
because his aggressive Wood energies have overwhelmed the
structure and restraint of Metal. He is able to "chronically disregard the rights of other people" and "not seem to feel genuine remorse" because the Earth energies of caring and compassion are
either undeveloped or have been weakened or blocked by Wood's
dominance. Wood is therefore in complete control and its more extreme qualities are fully in evidence—the person may be
"aggressive and irritable" and may engage in "fighting, lying and
criminal behavior of every conceivable sort."

Tracing the energy outlines of a disorder is one thing; finding
practical uses for that knowledge is another. As with depression
and many other emotional illnesses, the root cause of APD is unknown. According to James Morrison, author of the DSM-IV, it is
probably due to a combination of genetics and life experience. If
genetics or early emotional traumas are a major factor, the energy
imbalances of APD may be symptoms as much as causes of the destructive behavior. On the other hand, as we saw with George,
Betty and Peter in Chapter 2, when a person's life pattern becomes
imbalanced in some significant way, biology, energy and the emotions can become intertwined to the point where root causes are
hard to find. The best course may be to find practical ways to
change the overall pattern.

Energy therapies will probably not cure APD or other serious
behavioral disorders, but they might be helpful in relieving symp-

toms. In some cases they may uncover buried emotional conflicts that can be addressed in other ways. At the very least, energy therapies can help disperse excess Wood energies in APD and perhaps reduce anger and the chance of violence.

Crime as a Disease

Energy therapies for criminal offenders may sound like an unrealistic fantasy, and they are not likely even to be considered until society makes some far more basic choices, such as spending more resources on rehabilitation and less on punishment. Although current trends are moving in the opposite direction, the pattern is likely to reverse itself for several reasons. One is that meeting cruelty with cruelty is self-defeating and only makes society's problems worse.

Even more basic, our understanding of what crime is, and how it is related to disease, is slowly evolving. For many years alcoholism was thought of as a character flaw and alcoholics were considered, if not criminals, at least deserving of society's contempt. But when a gene was discovered that predisposes people to alcoholism, a moral weakness was instantly transformed into an illness worthy of sympathy and compassion. The difference was that we had found something tangible in the body that helps account for behavior. The unspoken assumption is that we are either free agents, and therefore fully responsible for our actions, or we do things because we are made that way and therefore deserve understanding and support.

The uncomfortable fact is that we do most things because we are made that way, and having two separate categories—one for good people who are innocent victims of illness and another for bad people who choose to be criminals—is an artificial distinction. That fact will be driven home forcefully if, one day, researchers discover a gene for Antisocial Personality Disorder or some other major cause of criminal behavior. We will then have to face the fact that crime, like alcoholism and other destructive behaviors, is an illness.

Even if no ATP gene is found, we know from life energy principles that people who disregard the rules of society and ignore the interests of others are living with a seriously imbalanced energy system. Whatever the source of those imbalances—childhood neglect or abuse, lack of education, inadequate role models or other negative life experiences—the APD sufferer, like the alcoholic, behaves as he does because of how he is made. He responds to the feelings and impulses embodied in his life energies which, like his genes, are part of his internal structure and cannot be controlled directly. If we accept the idea that the life energy system is part of the human organism, energy-based disorders are diseases in the same sense that gene-based disorders—and the common cold—are. Society needs to protect itself against criminal offenders, but it will start solving the problem of crime only when it starts treating criminals like the sick people they are.

Hyperactivity—APD's Mild Cousin

A less serious, but still troublesome, form of Wood dominance is Attention Deficit Hyperactivity Disorder or ADHD. ADHD affects mostly children and young people and its signs are constant, often inappropriate physical activity along with distractibility and trouble focusing on schoolwork or other tasks. The syndrome often fades away as the child grows older but sometimes lasts into adulthood. The signs and symptoms of ADHD and APD suggest that the two disorders are rooted in the same pattern of energy imbalance and that ADHD is a kind of child-sized, relatively innocent version of APD. That may help explain why, according to the DSM-IV, ADHD is sometimes a precursor to Antisocial Personality Disorder in adults.

Wood, the energy of activity, is a primary force in ADHD. As in the APD adult, the child's dominant Wood energies apparently depress or block out the influences of Earth and Metal. While the APD adult may show that he "cannot or will not conform to the norms of society" by robbing a bank or stealing a car, the ADHD child may leave his seat in school or start running or climbing inappropriately. The APD adult "chronically disregards the rights of others" by lying, cheating, assaulting or even killing. The ADHD child, who often lacks the social skills to know what other children want or need, can seem selfish, uncaring or out of touch.

According to the DSM-IV, ADHD tends to run in families, an indication that it may be genetically based. Morrison believes the same may be true of APD, raising the hope that a gene or genes may be found for both disorders. As with APD, energy therapies may be helpful in ADHD by dispersing excess Wood and reducing the child's need to be constantly in motion.

Compulsive Work Syndrome and the Weather

George in chapter 2 represented the intense, achievement-driven Type A personality whose Wood-dominant pattern of living I referred to as Compulsive Work Syndrome. The pattern is becoming increasingly common throughout the U.S. but probably originated with the Puritans in 17th century New England. The Puritan work ethic left such an indelible impression that the term has become a permanent part of our language.

In Chapter 2 I argued that Compulsive Work Syndrome stems, not just from Wood dominance, but from the effects of imbalanced Metal. The Puritans are a case in point. They were motivated by a constant awareness of Original Sin—a basic sense of inadequacy as human beings—that drove them to work unceasingly and to be suspicious of pleasure of any kind. Those attitudes, together with their rigidly moralistic beliefs and their eagerness to judge others whom they deemed unworthy, were all signs of seriously imbalanced Metal. The Salem witch trials were a tragic distortion of the desire to do good by rooting out evil.

Like their Puritan forebears, modern-day New Englanders tend to work long hours, take life and work very seriously and don't object to sacrificing pleasure or free time for the sake of duty and responsibility. Those habits are probably residues, in part, of Puritan influences but there may be another, more mundane explanation as well. Unlikely as it seems, Compulsive Work Syndrome, not only in New England but in other places where it is most common, could be due in part to the weather.

People who live in cold northern climates tend to be relatively serious, sober and hard-working. Many of the groups best known for their strong work ethic and no-nonsense approach—the Japanese, the Germans, New Englanders and New Yorkers—all live in places with severe winter weather.

People from warm, sunny regions—Spain, Italy and other Mediterranean countries, the American South and Southwest and the tropics—are generally more carefree and lighthearted with far less tendency to overwork. Even within single countries such as Spain, France or Italy, the heavy industrial and economic centers tend to be in the north, while people in the south have a more relaxed, carefree attitude.

One reason for these differences is probably that warm, sunny climates produce a greater abundance of Fire energies. Fire, the energy of joy and high spirits, encourages people to enjoy life fully and balance work with plenty of free time and relaxation. Better weather, too, provides more opportunities to be outdoors.

Severe winter weather, however, does more than just deprive people of adequate Fire—it places severe stress on the body's Metal energies and organs. Metal flows in the lung meridian, which nourishes the lungs, upper respiratory tract and skin. All of those parts of the body are exposed to winter cold and are the targets of winter illnesses like colds, sore throats, flu, bronchitis and pneumonia.

When Metal is chronically weak, as we have seen, it cannot properly control Wood. If, in addition, a person is naturally Wood-dominant, Wood energies may become excessive, setting the stage for a naturally hard worker to become a compulsive worker. If a whole population happens to be Wood-dominant—the Japanese, the Germans or New Englanders for example[29]—and if they happen to live in a cold northern climate, the resulting Metal-Wood imbalance may help create an entire population of workaholics. The pattern is shown in Figure 19.

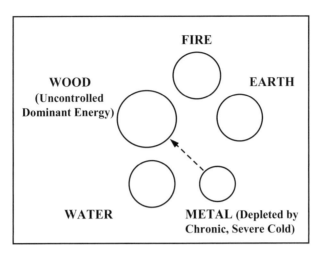

FIGURE 19.
COMPULSIVE WORK SYNDROME AND THE WEATHER

If climate combined with temperament can affect the behavior of whole populations, a more general question is: To what extent are attitudes and behaviors in general a function of energy balance? Can people be made more loving, more generous, more thoughtful or more compassionate by nurturing their life energies? What are the limits, if any, of energy techniques to promote, not just better emotional health, but stronger values and healthier and happier societies? These questions may be answered one day when the energy system is accepted as a full partner in the human organism.

EARTH ENERGY: THE CENTER OF OUR BEING

Earth energy, as I have suggested several times, belongs in a somewhat different category from the other energies. The pathways of the Earth meridians in the body are an indication of Earth's special importance. Of the six *yang* meridians, stomach, the *yang* Earth meridian, is the only one that runs along the inner, protected surface of the body—the abdomen and chest—rather than along the exposed outer surface on the back and sides. This suggests that stomach energy, like the energies of the *yin* meridians, is deeper and more fundamental to life than the other yang energies and is in need of more protection. Stomach energies are viewed as particularly important in the Japanese tradition, and a chronic deficiency is considered to be a significant risk to health.

No Excess of Love

The three previous sections dealt with the health risks of excess Fire, Metal and Wood energies. They included serious problems ranging from mania to depression to violence and criminal behavior. There is no comparable syndrome for Earth energy. Although certain eating disorders, dependencies and general self-indulgence may result from an excess in Earth, the most serious Earth disorders stem from deficiency, not excess. A major reason is that Earth, despite Chinese medicine's failure to acknowledge it, is the primary energy of love and human connection. That there can be an excess of anger, fear or sadness there is no doubt. There can even be, in the Chinese phrase, an excess of joy. But there is no such thing as an excess of love.

Nor is it easy to imagine emotional illness arising from too many connections with other people or with too strong a connection to one's surroundings. Lack of connection, on the other hand, is one of the most fundamental factors in emotional illness. Some of the most serious and profound disorders are due to a loss of contact with other people, with one's own body or with reality itself. I discuss the important role of Earth energy deficiency in some of those conditions below.

The Elephant in the Room

If, as the ancient Chinese believed, Earth is the central human energy—and if, as modern authorities agree, Earth is the energy of bonding between mother and child—there can be little doubt that Earth is the energy of love. Perhaps out of respect for the traditions of Chinese medicine, modern practitioners and writers have been reluctant to acknowledge that fact. A recent comprehensive text on Chinese medicine, and one cited in this book,[30] runs to nearly 500 pages. In the index, under "emotions," there are 23 entries. They range from anger, anxiety and bitterness to sympathy, timidity and worry. They include the basic emotions fear, grief, joy and sadness as well as more exotic entries such as cynicism and disdain. There is no entry for love. The text itself, a profound study of the physical, emotional and spiritual dimensions of Chinese medicine, omits almost any mention of love.

Another, even better-known text,[31] also cited in this book, runs to nearly 400 pages and it, too, has no entry for love in the index and makes only passing reference to love in the text itself.

These are by no means unusual examples. They accurately reflect the teachings of traditional Chinese medicine as it developed in ancient times and is still practiced today. Perhaps for cultural reasons, the ancient Chinese were reluctant to talk about, or even acknowledge, what is arguably the most central and important human emotion. That omission did not, and does not today, prevent Chinese medicine from being a highly effective therapeutic system, but it does limit it ability to fully address human emotion and its effects on both mind and body. Identifying the energy of love is a long overdue step which, I believe, can only make Chinese medicine a more complete and useful system.

Bonding and Love

The simplest reason for believing Earth is the energy of love is that love has no other place to go. The other four major emotions—joy, sorrow, fear and anger—belong to Fire, Metal, Water and Wood respectively. The symmetry of the Five Elements seems to require that Earth and love go together, but there are more substantial reasons. The most persuasive is that Earth is universally acknowledged to be the energy of bonding between mother and child. Although the authorities tiptoe carefully around the word love, the overall message is clear. Three writers refer to Earth's role as follows:

The Earth element dominates the oral-bonding and

first-separating stages of psychosocial development
for both parent and child. As the source of all material substances the Earth element is the nourishing
mother.[32]

The earth element helps establish an appropriate
boundary regarding the nourishment of self and
others...the quality of this balance is predicated in
part on the nature of our relationship to our mother
as it guides the course of our development from
conception to adulthood.[33]

The power of Earth comes from the capacity to
link, nurture and sustain.[34]

The author of the first excerpt, Dr. Leon Hammer, goes so far as to
say that mother's love is part of the bonding process, but he stops
short of referring to the child's feelings:

The capacity of the Earth mother for unconditional,
minimally egocentric love during the in-utero and
early oral developmental eras...will determine the
quality or quantity of the "bonding" between the
earth mother and offspring, as well as the latter's
bonding with itself and with the entire human
race.[35]

If we can assume that love is the emotion of bonding for both
mother and child, then the child's "bonding with itself and with the
entire human race" means that the child learns to love both itself
and others. Giving and receiving love is thus the primary and most
important function of Earth energy.

Freud had no doubt that a child learns to love in infancy.
Whether he exaggerated the importance of sexual feelings in in-
fants is another question:

According to [Freud], love as well as sexuality is
rooted in infancy (Freud, 1905). A person's first

love object is the mother. The mother's breast provides the infant not only with nourishment but also
a source of sexual pleasure which he will later on
seek from his adult lover.. Freud views love and
sexuality as an extension (or rediscovery) of their
infantile forms.[36]

Spleen, the Loving Mother

The two Earth meridians, as we have seen, mirror each other in
their functions. Stomach, the *yang* Earth meridian, governs the appetite for food and other material pleasures. Spleen, the *yin* Earth
meridian, embodies the need for emotional nourishment or love.
Donna Eden, in her book *Energy Medicine,* writes that Earth energy, and specifically spleen energy, embodies love but she points
out a certain paradox. Both the spleen organ and the spleen meridian are important parts of the body's immune system, and spleen
energy is used to manufacture white blood cells and antibodies that
attack and kill dangerous invaders. Eden likens spleen's role in immune defense to "women working in a munitions plant or Red
Cross nurses in a war zone."[37] When an actual invasion occurs,
"Spleen, the inner mom, can only love the enemy. Nothing else is
within its repertoire."[38]

   Spleen's dual role as both nurturer and defender fits everyday
life and is a striking symbol of motherhood itself. Every loving
mother plays exactly the same two roles for her children. Spleen
truly is the loving mother of the meridian system.

The Heart and Two Kinds of Love

The heart, as everyone knows, is the traditional abode of human
love. Few singers or poets have been heard to lament that "I lost
my love and my spleen is broken." The heart chakra, as we saw in
Chapter 1, is a central reservoir for the energies of love. The heart
meridian, which nourishes the heart, is another likely candidate.
But since the heart meridian carries, not Earth but Fire energies,

one might argue that Fire, not Earth, is the energy of love. One authority, Dr. Leon Hammer, believes just that. Hammer, one of the few writers on Chinese medicine who discusses love directly, gives the following description of a person suffering from what he calls heart *yin* deficiency:

> Love relationships lack the overflowing warmth, effusive ardor, and emotional effervescence usually associated with love. The subject will lack 'abandonment' and will never be rapturously carried away by inner drives.[39]

The above is a description of someone who is not fully experiencing romantic love, not the love of a parent, child, family or friends. Hammer does not claim that heart *yin* deficiency impairs family love; in fact, he acknowledges, in the earlier excerpt on mother-child bonding, that Earth, not Fire, embodies a mother's love for her child:

> The capacity of the earth mother for unconditional, minimally egocentric love...will determine the quality or quantity of the 'bonding' between the earth mother and offspring.

These things suggest that, just as there are two kinds of love, there are two kinds of energy that embody love: Fire, the energy of passionate, romantic love and Earth, the energy of the calmer, more centered and sometimes more unselfish love of family and friends. The two often appear together, as they should, since Fire and Earth adjoin each other on the Five Elements circle. Adjoining energies, as we have seen, tend to overlap, reinforce and blend into one another. This may help explain why some love affairs, based mostly on Fire, die out after the initial excitement and infatuation fade while others, built on a solid foundation of Earth, can last a lifetime. What marriage, after all, could survive if it had to depend forever on rapture and excitement? Deep affection, implicit trust, a comforting sense of closeness and support may be the contributions that Earth makes to relationships that last.

Earth Energy and Body Awareness

As the energy of love, Earth connects us to one another in the most powerful way. Earth's connecting power has another, equally important function—to ground us in the physical world by providing a strong sense of connection to our own bodies. The first and second chakras, as we saw in Chapter 1, are grounding chakras that carry a heavy concentration of Earth energies. When those energies are strong and free-flowing, a person has solid contact with her body and, through it, with her emotions, her surroundings and other people. If Earth is significantly weakened or blocked, all of those connections may suffer. The stage may be set for psychological disturbances both large and small.

Superficial Loss of Body Awareness:
the Type A/Plate Armor Type

If the loss of energies and feeling is not profound, a person may continue to seem outwardly happy and successful even though his internal life is unrewarding. Barbara Brennan, in her book *Hands of Light: a Guide to Healing Through the Human Energy Field,* describes a type of energy block that can undermine an apparently healthy person's ability to feel. She calls the pattern "plate armor" and describes it as follows:

> The plate armor...holds all types of feelings by freezing them. They are held in place around the body by a generalized field of high tension. It effectively helps the person build a well-structured life on the outer level....on the personal level, life will not be so fulfilling, because the plate armor effectively nullifies all feelings.[40]

The areas of high tension in the Plate Armor pattern include the shoulders and sides of the legs. These are highly sensitive areas along the gall bladder meridian, one of the Wood meridians. We have seen this pattern before. George in Chapter 2 was a Wood or Wood-Fire type whose excess Wood energies drove him to work excessively, leaving little time for personal satisfactions. George, a Type A personality, was vulnerable to diseases of the heart and circulatory system. According to Barbara Brennan, the plate armor type may suffer from "ulcers from overwork or heart problems from 'pushing' in life without personal nourishment."[41]

It is no coincidence that Wood energy in general, and gall bladder in particular, have the power to restrain or even depress Earth energy through the Controlling Cycle. A whole range of Earth qualities and concerns—love, caring, companionship, home, family, friends, community—are compromised when the Type A personality, or plate armor type, places an undue premium on the Wood values of work, achievement and personal recognition. The pattern is shown in Figure 20.

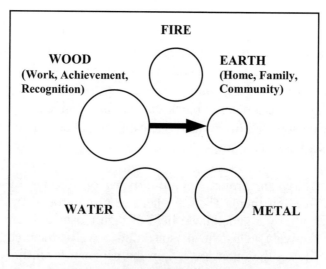

FIGURE 20.
DISTORTED WOOD AND EARTH ENERGIES
IN THE TYPE A/PLATE ARMOR PATTERN

Profound Loss of Body Awareness:
Tension, Fear and the Splitting of Consciousness

When Earth's other Controlling Cycle neighbor, Water, enters the picture, a person's loss of feeling and body awareness can become far more serious. Earth normally controls Water but, as we have seen, the usual roles are sometimes reversed. When that happens, the health consequences can be very significant.

If something happens to seriously disrupt the normal Earth-Water balance—a biochemical or genetic abnormality, a head injury, an overwhelming emotional trauma or other stress—Earth energies may be weakened to the point where the person begins to lose a basic sense of connection. That loss may reveal itself in various ways. It may become progressively harder for the person to feel love, compassion or other emotions, to socialize comfortably or even to have a normal awareness of his body and surroundings. At the far end of the spectrum are major illnesses like schizophrenia in which a person loses contact with reality itself.

The Schizoid Pattern and the Lower Chakras

The schizoid or "splitting" pattern, whose most serious form is schizophrenia, refers not to split personality—Dr. Jekyll and Mr. Hyde— but to a splitting of consciousness itself. When a person begins to lose touch with his own body, the world can lose depth and begin to seem flat and two-dimensional, like a TV screen or a picture drawn on a piece of paper. When energies become disrupted to that extent, there is unquestionably a major disturbance in both chakra and meridian energies.

The first and second chakras, as we saw in Chapter 1, are the traditional Earth and Water chakras and each has a heavy concentration of both energies. Together they are the grounding chakras that provide s solid connection to the earth, to one's own body and the surroundings. The disconnection that is the hallmark of the schizoid pattern is almost certainly a product of a disturbance in first and second chakra energies.

Loss of Body Energies—One Stereo Speaker Disconnected

Anyone who has ever shot a basketball with one eye closed knows that depth perception requires two eyes. For the brain and the mind to perceive things in three dimensions, a person must have two points of reference. The same is true of hearing. With one ear stopped up it can be hard to know where a sound is coming from. Stereophonic sound is based on the same principle: two speakers placed a few feet apart can create the illusion of an orchestra playing in a concert hall. If one speaker is disconnected, the sound becomes flat, two-dimensional and relatively lifeless.

A person living with a schizoid disorder is like a stereo system with one speaker disconnected. Like a basketball player with one eye closed, one of the organs that lets him experience the world in three dimensions is not working. His head chakras are open and he can perceive well enough to get around and function. But without a second point of reference—the energies of the body chakras—the perception of depth vanishes and the world appears flat and two-dimensional.

The Schizoid Pattern and the Controlling Cycle

A person living with a schizoid condition may experience the world in two dimensions but is still required to live and interact with other people as if things had depth and distance. The person is literally split into two parts—his mind, which lives in its own self-contained world, and his body, which he watches, in effect, from a distance as it goes about its daily business.

This strange way of living, not surprisingly, creates tension both physical and emotional. The Controlling Cycle may help explain how that tension keeps the schizoid pattern in place. Physical tension can be due to excess gall bladder (Wood) energies and is similar to that in the plate armor pattern in overstressed workers. Emotional tension, in the form of anger and frustration (Wood), can come from a sense of being chronically out of touch. The combined Wood energies of physical tension, anger and frustration put added pressure on the already fragile and weakened Earth energies of spleen (Figure 21).

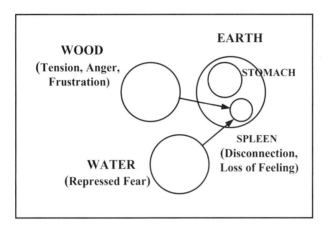

FIGURE 21.
FEAR, TENSION AND WEAKENED EARTH ENERGIES
IN THE SCHIZOID PATTERN

As Earth is weakened from one direction by Wood, Earth's other Controlling Cycle neighbor, Water, representing repressed fear, applies pressure from the other direction. Until something is done to free Earth from the combined stresses of fear, anger, frustration and physical tension, the schizoid pattern is not likely to improve very much.

Earth Energy, Schizophrenia and Diabetes

In the meridian system, as we have seen, the Earth energies of human connection are represented by spleen, the *yin* Earth meridian. The *yang* earth meridian, stomach, carries the hardier, more basic energies of physical appetites and pleasures. *Yin* energies, which are more subtle and delicate than *yang* energies, can be depressed through the Controlling Cycle even as the hardier *yang* energies stay strong or even excess. In the schizoid pattern, stomach excess can exist alongside spleen deficiency, especially if a person who feels disconnected and alone compensates by overeating.

If the pattern sounds familiar, it is because it is similar to Peter's pattern in Chapter 2. Peter's Earth energy deficiency was far less profound than it is here (in Peter's case, chakra energies may not have been heavily involved). But in both cases there is a combined stomach excess and spleen deficiency. For Peter the twin Earth imbalances were associated with an increased risk of diabetes. We might expect to see a similar risk in the schizoid pattern, and in fact there is such a risk.

Diabetes occurs at a much higher rate among schizophrenics than in the general population. According to a presentation sponsored by the Joslin Diabetes Center in Boston, the rate for schizophrenics is 2.7 times higher than for the population as a whole. This dramatic difference, according to one researcher, is probably due to a combination of factors:

> It has been suggested that the increased incidence of diabetes and the metabolic syndrome is a result of a genetic link. Others suggest that it results from a schizophrenic lifestyle which might include variations in nutrition and activity. Still others argue that the increased risk is brought on by some of the medications that are used to treat these conditions. While all of these factors may well play a role, it is difficult to determine to what degree each has an impact.[42]

The "variations in nutrition" that may increase diabetes risk could include both overeating and indulging in sweets, both of which, as we saw in Chapter 2, are responses to Earth energy imbalance. All of the factors cited in the Joslin study may be important, but an imbalance in Earth energies—which are essential to both emotional health and blood sugar regulation—could be a primary link between schizophrenia and diabetes.

WATER ENERGY: DEPTH, HUMILITY AND FEAR

To appreciate the importance of Water energy to health and happiness, one need only look at the two energies in natural tension with Water: Fire, the energy of joy and freedom, and Earth, the energy of love and connection. Water, the energetic South Pole of personality, balances and deepens life's experiences by encouraging an honest acceptance of life as it really is—a blend of love, happiness and freedom with disappointment, fear, loneliness and disconnection. Water is an energy of both infinite human potential and significant emotional risk. When healthy, well-developed and well-balanced, Water can be a source of deep understanding and the most profound spiritual awareness. When distorted or overly dominant, it can be the energy of neurotic fears and anxieties and, if imbalances become too severe, of isolation, suspicion and paranoia.

Neurosis: Fear, Anxiety and Disconnection

Many phobias and other anxiety disorders, whether biologically based or not, may be symptoms of an imbalance between Water and both of its Controlling Cycle neighbors.[43] The dominance of Water over Fire is clear—fear and anxiety crowd out joy and emotional freedom. But the Water-Earth relationship may be important as well since there may an element of disconnection that feeds anxiety. In agoraphobia, for example, a person feels anxious over the thought of leaving home and venturing into unfamiliar surroundings. Earth, as we have seen, is a fundamental grounding and connecting force, the energy of parental and family love, home and hearth and the pleasures of domestic life. If those energies are blocked or undeveloped, a person may find it harder to internalize a sense of being at home and to carry that sense into unfamiliar settings. Even the thought of leaving home may create a sense of disconnection serious enough to trigger anxiety.

Claustrophobia is the virtual polar opposite of agoraphobia—anxiety over not being able to go out, of being confined in small, enclosed spaces. The Earth-Water relationship is less clear in claustrophobia and, as in any neurosis, it can probably be traced in some cases to past traumas or other factors not directly related to life energies. But the feeling in claustrophobia of being trapped, whether in an elevator, a locked room or elsewhere, does represent a sense of disconnection—from the outside world as a whole. It may be that people whose Earth-Water relationship is out of balance are more prone to claustrophobia because their generally weak sense of connection makes it easier for confinement to trigger anxiety.

For many people the anxiety of anticipating a stressful experience—a dental appointment, a speaking engagement, a school exam—lessens or even goes away when the moment arrives. The expectation is often worse than the reality. This may illustrate yet another aspect of Earth's connecting power: its ability to link the present with the future, to connect how a person imagines something will be with how it really is. People who are able to take life's stresses in stride and avoid worrying excessively may benefit from Earth's power to place the future in a more realistic perspective.

Many fears and anxieties are made worse by keeping them secret and can be relieved to some extent by talking about and sharing them with other people. Psychotherapy is based in part on that principle—the power of Earth energy to lessen anxiety through sharing.

In the end the natural tension between Earth and Water may represent, more than anything else, the existential dilemma itself: the fact of having been born into the world as a separate being in need of love and support, and of having to struggle to find happiness and fulfillment in a world of loneliness and disconnection.

Profound Water Imbalance: Isolation and Paranoia

Many people with strong, well-developed Water energies live a healthy life of solitude and deep fulfillment. Monks, nuns, yogis and solitary adventurers among others all make good use of the depth and inwardness of Water. By severing some of the more superficial outer connections with everyday life, they are able to find deeper and more meaningful connections within.

Problems arise when a person sheds outer ties but fails to

replace them with equally good or better internal ones. The Water or Metal-Water Head type personality tends to seek solitude but, as we saw in Chapter 3, may be at risk for disorders such as depression. If both Earth and Water are seriously out of balance, more profound disorders are possible. Paranoid schizophrenia features the same Water-Earth imbalance as in neurosis but at a far deeper level. Fear, lack of trust and disconnection combine and are twisted into a disabling fantasy of persecution.

Energy Therapies to Relieve Fear

There is no fear in love, but perfect love casts out fear.
—1 John 4:18

The perennial struggle between love and fear, though documented since Bible times, is often dismissed as little more than a comforting sentiment. The structure of the energy system suggests otherwise. As we have seen, the healing power of love is not only real, it is built into the structure of every human body through the relationships of the Controlling Cycle.

Everyone has experienced the power of love and compassion to control fear. The support of family and friends can ease the way through an illness or other difficult life experience. Support groups of all kinds mobilize the healing power of shared struggle. Camaraderie in the military is a time-honored method for building morale and strengthening will. In these and many other ways, external connection and support generate and release Earth energies that overcome fear. Certain energy therapies appear to work in a similar way by transmitting a particular kind of healing energy.

Reiki and the Laying On of Hands

Reiki ("RAY-kee") is one of the simplest of all bodywork therapies—so simple, in fact, that it is not technically bodywork at all. Reiki is not a technique—the practitioner simply places his or her hands on, or near, the client's body and holds them there for a few minutes. A special type of healing energy is believed to flow from giver to receiver. There is no manipulation of the client's body, no pressure applied to meridians or pressure points, only simple contact between one person and another. Some practitioners make their treatments more effective by visualizing energy flow or by encouraging their clients to visualize energy or do affirmations. But a basic Reiki treatment requires only simple touch and nothing more.

Some Reiki practitioners say that Reiki illustrates the healing power of simple compassion; others describe it as the transmission of unconditional love. Reiki has been likened to the ancient healing practice of the laying on of hands. The energies of Reiki are passed on to practitioners through a special initiation, using healing symbols taken from ancient Asian religious texts. Reiki is thus closer to a pure spiritual healing technique than any other popular energy therapy.

Reiki is becoming increasingly popular as a support therapy for surgical patients, either before surgery or during recovery. It reduces anxiety and is said to help patients tolerate surgery better and heal faster. Reiki is available both at Reiki clinics and in a growing number of U.S. hospitals.

"Inner Reiki:" Cultivating a Supportive Relationship with the Body

The effectiveness of therapies like Reiki suggests that developing a consciously positive relationship with one's own body may have real health benefits. If another person's love and compassion have healing power, one's own caring, concern and appreciation for one's body should have a similar power.

I raised the question earlier as to whether life energies are conscious. Their responsiveness, and the positive and negative intent that some healers sense in their client's energies, could be evidence of that consciousness. Even if life energies have only the tiniest flicker of real awareness, sending love to trapped or imbalanced energies may, in principle, have the same healing effect as expressing love for another human being. This "inner Reiki"—self-healing through compassion and caring for one's own body—may be an another example of love's power to cast out fear.

PART 3. LIFE ENERGY AND BODY-CENTERED THERAPIES

Freud's belief that our mental and emotional lives are rooted in tangible energies did not end with him. His ideas helped inspire innovative theories and techniques that began to bring together mind, body and energy in new ways. Some of those teachings are based explicitly on the presence of unseen energies; others tap into the energy system by paying close attention to the body's role in emotion. Because all stress the importance of mind-body interactions, these techniques are referred to generally as body-centered therapies. The practices described below have all been important in the evolution of energy understandings in the West.

Reichian Therapy and Bioenergetics

Wilhelm Reich was a brilliant but eccentric Austrian psychiatrist who trained in Vienna in the early 20th century under Sigmund Freud. In the 1930's Reich began to speak and write about an energy he called "orgone" which he believed existed in every living being. He coined the term "body armoring" to refer to the muscular tensions that coincide with emotional defense mechanisms. He developed various techniques, including breathing exercises, bodywork and scream therapy, as ways of relieving tension and ridding the body of unhealthy influences.

After coming to the United States, Reich encountered serious legal troubles when he tried to manufacture and sell machines he called "orgone accumulators." He ultimately died in tragic circumstances, but only after contributing much to the Western understanding of mind and body and the energies that connect them.

The physician Alexander Lowen was both a patient and student of Reich and his own deep healing experiences with Reich convinced him of the value of body-centered therapies. After working for several years as a Reichian therapist, Lowen went on to develop his own system, which he called Bioenergetics.

Lowen believed there were five basic character types, each of which developed out of certain life experiences and each identifiable by the pattern of muscular tensions held in the body. Lowen developed techniques and exercises for resolving those tensions, sometimes combining them with psychotherapy.

Although Lowen did not use the meridian or chakra systems as a model for his system, he was aware of Asian teachings and acknowledged their value. In his book *Bioenergetics*, Lowen reproduced a drawing of an ancient Tai Chi posture known as the Taoist Arch, noting that it is virtually identical to one of his own grounding exercises, the Fundamental Stress Position.

Like Tai Chi masters and the originators of the Chinese Five Elements system, Lowen sensed the central importance of Earth energy in human life. He placed heavy emphasis on grounding—a solid sense of connection to the Earth—as a requirement for good physical and emotional health. Lowen regarded love, the Earth emotion, as the central point around which the rest of the psyche revolves.

Gestalt Therapy

Gestalt therapy was developed in the 1940's by Fritz Perls, a German-born, Freudian-trained psychoanalyst. Perls' ideas grew out of the teachings of Gestalt psychology in Germany and were heavily influenced by Wilhelm Reich, who was both mentor and analyst to Perls. Perls began his work in wartime Germany but ultimately came to the United States where he lived and worked until his death.

Gestalt therapy is based on the principle that every life situation represents a pattern of interacting factors—a Gestalt—and that the pattern as a whole is more important than any individual part. Identifying cause and effect is less important than understanding how a person functions within the overall Gestalt. The holistic view of experience that Gestalt represents closely parallels the teachings of traditional Chinese medicine.

Gestalt therapists encourage role-playing, physical movement, singing and other spontaneous activities that promote personal expression. They encourage their clients to concentrate on immediate feelings and perceptions, including body sensations, rather than trying to analyze their thoughts and behavior.

Because of its emphasis on patterns and immediate experience, Gestalt pays as much attention to the therapy process itself as to its subject matter. One writer says the following:

> Gestalt therapy focuses more on process (what is happening) than content (what is being discussed). The emphasis is on what is being done, thought and felt at the moment rather than on what was, might be, could be, or should be.[44]

Gestalt therapy is effective in part because it encourages people to contact and experience the emotional energies in their bodies rather than retreating into their heads. This is especially important for Head types, whose natural instinct is to avoid feelings.

The central importance of awareness in Gestalt therapy hints at the important role of life energies. Some Gestalt therapists see the relationship between energies and awareness as a basic part of the healing process. One writer describes his work as follows:

> Gestalt therapy alerts us to the interrelationship between awareness and energy. When awareness is scattered and bound up in unknown feelings and thoughts, energy flow is diminished throughout one's personality. A Gestalt counselor, by suggesting the practice of certain 'experiments' in awareness focusing, aids and amplifies a client's effort to free him– or herself from energy blocks mentally, emotionally and physically.[45]

Focusing

Focusing, like Gestalt therapy, promotes personal growth through the power of concentrated awareness. In Focusing the goal is to bring mind and body together in the most direct way possible: by locating the place in the body where emotional conflicts are felt, and by staying with that feeling—called a "felt sense"—until there is a change in awareness. The change signifies a step forward in personal growth.

Focusing was developed in the 1970's by Eugene Gendlin, a professor of psychology at the University of Chicago. Gendlin, a practicing psychotherapist, was disappointed in the high failure rate among people who went through psychotherapy. He devised a technique based on his observations of successful therapy clients and what they did during a therapy session.

The essence of Focusing is to make contact with a deep bodily knowing that straddles the boundary between the conscious mind and the Unconscious. One of the signs of the felt sense is that it feels unclear or even murky. The lack of clarity indicates that it lies on the fringes of consciousness—it is strong enough to be felt but not clear enough to be understood. When the shift occurs, the fuzziness often clarifies into a feeling of emotional release and, sometimes, a new insight. The conflict, even if not resolved completely, appears in a new perspective.

The Focusing technique gives a clue to what Focusing really is. After locating the felt sense in the body, the next step is to find a "handle"—a word, phrase, color or other idea or image that perfectly fits the felt sense. After finding a handle, the focuser goes back and forth mentally between the felt sense and the handle, feeling the connection and testing to see if the handle fits. After a little while, the shift may occur.

One writer, Marilyn Ferguson, believes Focusing may be a way of integrating the functions of the left and right sides of the brain. The handle may represent the left, or analytical side, and the felt sense the right, or "holistic" side. When the two meet the person may experience what Ferguson calls "whole brain knowing."[46]

Gendlin, too, believes that Focusing represents a more complete kind of knowing. He describes it as the awareness of "body and mind before they are split apart."[47]

Focusing can be a useful tool, not only for therapy, but to foster creativity. According to Marilyn Ferguson, "The felt shift is essentially identical to the freeing insight of the creative process."[48] She believes creative people have an instinctive gift for paying attention to vague impressions and that doing so helps those impressions flower into new ideas and meanings.

Focusing and Life Energy

Several aspects of Focusing highlight the important role of life energy:

1. The first step, identifying where emotions are felt in the body, is a way of locating the energies that hold repressed feelings.

2. Because the felt sense is often detected in the abdominal area or chest, it corresponds to the lower chakras or heart chakra, where many of the energies of repressed fear, sadness, anger and other emotions are held.

3. Concentrating on a sensitive place in the body makes use of life energy's unique responsiveness to attention and will. In Focusing as in shiatsu and other energy therapies, paying attention to energies encourages them to move and change—particularly if, as Gendlin recommends, one relates to the body in a positive, supportive spirit.

4. Finding a handle is perhaps the most ingenious part of Focusing. It appears to be a way of repairing the broken connections between the energies that embody memories and experiences and the ideas those energies represent. Focusing, in other words, is a way of reversing the process of repressing feelings and, as Gendlin suggests, of reuniting mind and body.

EMOTION WAVES AND THE LAWS OF PHYSICS

In the Introduction I compared our knowledge of the human mind today to our knowledge of the physical world a hundred years ago. A century from now we are likely to know things about consciousness and the energy realm that will be as astonishing to us as the scientific discoveries of the 20th century were.

Because nature tends to operate according to a limited number of basic principles, we may discover some striking parallels between the laws of physics and the laws of consciousness. We have already seen some of those parallels. Life energy behaves in certain ways like a kind of human electricity. It flows in "wires" called meridians, is collected in "substations" called chakras and provides the fuel that "lights up" the human mind and body. Life energies, like magnets, respond differently to positive and negative charges, and the north and south poles of magnets can influence health by pushing or pulling energies through the meridians.

Life energies may be similar to physical energies in another way. Light, sound, heat and other forms of physical energy exist in the form of waves or particles or both. Even gravity is now understood to travel in the form of waves. Inside the atom, electrons and other components have a strange wave/particle duality. Waves and particles are a basic feature of physical matter and energy at every level.

Though only speculation, it could be that life energies, like physical energies, exist and travel in the form of waves or particles or both. The flow of energies through the meridian system suggests that life energies may exist as tiny particles similar to electrons flowing through a wire. Life energy's wave nature, if it has one, is even more intriguing. It raises the possibility that our emotions may be embodied in waves of varying types and intensities. Just as the qualities of light, sound and heat depend on the properties of electromagnetic waves traveling through space, the qualities of our emotions could depend on the properties of emotion waves traveling through the energy system.

Wave Length, Frequency and the Quality of Feelings

For all kinds of waves, the length of a wave is the distance from the peak of one wave to the peak of the next. The frequency is the number of waves that reach a certain point—your eye or your ear for example—every second. High frequency, short wavelength energies are intense—X-rays, radioactive emissions, high-pitched squeals, whistles, power saws, sirens—while low frequency, long wavelength energies are more soothing and relaxing—foghorns, cellos, the roar of the ocean, the rumble of a train rolling through the countryside.

Why do high frequency energies make us tense and jittery while low frequency energies make us feel calm and relaxed? Certainly conditioning plays a role. If we hear a piercing, high-pitched whining sound, we may remember our last visit to the dentist. Or if we hear the deep blast of a foghorn, we may recall our last vacation at the seashore. But past experience aside, there may be something inherent in certain sounds and perhaps colors that evokes certain emotions in us. Presumably there is some kind of internal mechanism that links the two. Could our emotions exist as waves that somehow resonate with certain sights or sounds? Is an emotion a kind of inner tuning fork whose energies begin to vibrate when a matching tuning fork—a dentist's drill, a foghorn, a cello— begins vibrating nearby? If so, feelings like excitement, joy, panic and anger might exist as high-frequency, short wavelength waves, while calmness, peace, love and sadness may take the form of low frequency, long wavelength waves.

Wave Amplitude and the Passage of Time

The amplitude of a wave is the wave's height and it corresponds to the strength of the energy. Loud sounds and bright lights have high amplitude while faint sounds and dim lights have low amplitude.

If emotions exist as waves, furious anger and intense joy probably have high amplitude, while mild contentment or a vague sense of sadness have low amplitude. In physics, when light or sound waves travel through space, they gradually lose amplitude, becoming fainter and dimmer as they go. This may correspond to the journey of emotion waves, not through space but through time. Anger gradually diminishes, love sometimes fades, grief heals after a period of mourning. In each case, the amplitude of an emotion wave may gradually decline with the passage of time.

Wave Addition and Interference: the Nurturing and Controlling Cycles

Many kinds of physical waves—light waves, sound waves, ocean waves and others—tend to strengthen, weaken or even cancel each other out when they meet. The phenomenon is known as wave addition and interference and is a basic property of physical waves. In Chinese medicine, as we have seen, life energies naturally strengthen and weaken each other through the Nurturing and Controlling Cycles. Exactly how they do so is unknown, but the two cycles are a basic mechanism for keeping the energy system in balance. Energy therapists are well aware of their value and they use the principles of "life energy addition and interference" every day to improve energy balance, health and well being for their clients.

If emotions exist as waves, does Fire energy nourish Earth—is joy compatible with love—because joy waves strengthen love waves? Does Wood control Earth—and does anger destroy the sense of human connection—because anger waves are able to cancel out the waves of love and compassion? Does love triumph over fear because love waves can make the waves of fear shrink and disappear? When instruments are invented that can detect, measure and perhaps see the detailed structure of life energies, we may have answers to those questions.

When Freud discovered and named the Unconscious a century ago, he founded modern psychology and began the process of converting it into a science. Where that process will end is not known—but if students of consciousness one day discover that the structure and behavior of emotional energies is similar to that of physical energies, Freud's dream will have been realized beyond his wildest imaginings.

CHAPTER FOUR
PERSONALITY, RELATIONSHIPS AND SOCIETY

The same rich mix of energies that underlies physical and emotional health is at the core of every personality. A person's temperament, talents, interests, goals and capacity for rich and meaningful relationships are all expressions of Earth, Fire, Metal, Wood and Water energies. Most people are dominant in one or two, giving them certain natural strengths and weaknesses. Identifying one's Five Element type is an interesting and enjoyable exercise and can be a valuable tool for self-awareness and for maintaining better physical and emotional health.

Of course, trying to describe personality as the interplay of a few basic energies has obvious limitations. The simplicity of the Five Elements gives it a certain elegance and power but, as I noted in Chapter 1, no model with so few working parts can hope to capture the nuance and detail of something as complex as human behavior. Still, the Five Elements are an exceptionally rich source of insights because their energies are linked to elemental natural forces. Those connections in turn have inspired a varied collection of myths and symbols that can help bring personality to life.

In Part 1 I describe each of the five basic energy types, then illustrate them through the lives and careers of a number of well-known historical figures including several U.S. presidents. To do so I combine Five Elements principles with the teachings of a system not generally understood to be energy-based: Western astrology. Astrology, which is accepted by some and seen by others as naïve or even ignorant superstition, has its roots in several ancient philosophies. I use it here for several reasons:

1. To show that it works. The astrological birth chart truly does indicate a person's inborn tendencies, talents, strengths and weaknesses. The inspiration of Lincoln, the paranoia of Nixon, the cool brilliance of Jefferson—and our own individual strengths and weaknesses—are all reflected in the positions of the stars and planets at the moment of birth. This does not mean that heavenly

bodies hold absolute power over us or that we are helpless victims of irresistible forces. The arrangement of the planets is an outer symbol of the inner world of emotions and impulses that drives each of us. We are free to shape the course of our lives as we choose through our responses to those influences.

2. A second reason for combining the Five Elements and astrology is that the two systems make natural partners in exploring personality. Together they yield richer, more accurate and more useful insights than either system used by itself. One important reason is that the traditional Earth, Air, Fire and Water signs of astrology are really blends or hybrids of several energies. I identify the main energies that make up each sign and show how that knowledge can sharpen and refine astrology's insights.

3. Because astrology works, it is persuasive evidence that life energy's influences extend far beyond the individual and even beyond planet Earth itself. The links between the stars and ourselves, like those between nature and the Five Elements, point to an underlying beauty and unity in the universe that are at the heart of the holistic philosophy.

In Part 2 I move from individual personality to relationships and show how the same energy interactions that make for tension or harmony within the individual are at work in every relationship. Some of the same techniques that can improve individual health and well being may be a useful tool for improving interpersonal relations.

In Part 3 I expand the boundaries of life energy further to include the forces that shape society itself. Using the United States as an example, I argue that the evolution of society is, to a significant degree, a struggle between the competing influences of Wood and Earth. Just as the tension between those energies poses a fundamental challenge to every individual and every relationship, a truly healthy society can only come about when Wood and Earth have been balanced and integrated at a higher level.

PART 1. ASTROLOGY, THE FIVE ELEMENTS AND PERSONALITY

> Zeus had loved his old friend, and lifted him up, and set him among the stars as the constellation Sagittarius. Here, in the Zodiac, now above, now below the horizon, he assists in the regulation of our destinies, though in this latter time few living mortals cast their eyes respectfully toward Heaven, and fewer still sit as students to the stars.
>
> —from *The Centaur* by John Updike

Western Astrology—an Innocent Victim of the Enlightenment

In ancient times astronomy and astrology were part of a single discipline and those who practiced it were among the most respected members of society. Astrology as we know it probably began with the Chaldeans, a Semitic people who lived in Babylonia (now Iraq) around the 7th century B.C. The Chaldeans were gifted mathematicians and keen observers, and they prepared the first known ephemerides or charts of planetary movements.[49]

The Chaldeans' scheme of the heavens included the twelve major constellations, which developed into the twelve astrological signs we know today, beginning with Aries and ending with Pisces. The Chaldeans also developed the notion of houses, each of which occupies one-twelfth of the sky above or below the horizon. If a planet fell within the 6th house, for example, its influences were felt in the realm of health and illness; if it fell within the 2nd house, it affected wealth and prosperity; and so on. The houses have come down to us from the Chaldeans with some modifications.

Babylonian astrology was less concerned with personal affairs than with predicting floods, famines, wars and other major events. The Greeks adopted the Chaldean system, refined and improved on it, and created a system for understanding the individual based on the moment of birth. The great Greek astronomer and mathemati-

cian Ptolemy, who worked in the 2nd century A.D., is given much
of the credit for creating the astrological system we know today.[50]

Western astrology fell into disrepute in the 18th century during
the period of the Enlightenment in Europe. The Enlightenment,
which was in part a reaction to the superstition and ignorance of
the Middle Ages, separated purely rational disciplines from those
that contained any element of subjectivity, intuition or faith. Although the Enlightenment paved the way for modern science and
did the world a great service, it rejected some valid and important
ideas along the way. Astrology was one of them.

Planetary Energies and the Law of Karma

The basic principle of astrology is that the stars and planets emit
energies that interact with and influence human life energies in the
body. Astrology in its true form is a spiritual teaching and is
intimately linked with personal evolution and the Law of Karma.
The Indian spiritual master Swami Sri Yukteswar Giri described
astrology as follows:

> Astrology is the study of man's response to plane-
> tary stimuli. The stars have no conscious benevo-
> lence or animosity; they merely send forth positive
> and negative radiations….A child is born on that
> day and at that hour when the celestial rays are in
> mathematical harmony with his individual karma.[51]

Signs, Planets and the Four Elements

In Western astrology each of the twelve signs, or star groups, is
associated with one of four energy types: Earth, Air, Fire or
Water.[52] Leo, for example, is a Fire sign while Taurus is an Earth
sign. Each of the planets rules at least one sign and the sign and its
ruling planet have many qualities in common. The Sun, for example, rules Leo and both are strongly associated with Fire energy.
Venus rules Taurus and both carry the influences of Earth energy,

and so on. When a sign as seen from earth—Gemini for example—is behind a planet, the planet is said to be "in" that sign. The location of the planets and signs at the moment of birth determines, or at least corresponds to,[53] the personal qualities of a child born at that moment.

Hybrid Signs, Air and Metal, and Astrology's "Missing" Element

The richness of astrology lies in the myths and symbols associated with the signs and planets and in the distinctive human qualities each represents. The three traditional Fire signs, for example—Aries, Leo and Sagittarius—all carry Fire energies but each influences personality in a different way. The reason is that none of the three is a pure Fire sign; all are blends of Fire with other energies. The egotism and control of Leo come not from Fire but from Wood; the noble instincts of Sagittarius are rooted, not in Fire, but in Metal; Aries, which is ruled by the planet Mars, is, I argue, not a Fire sign at all but is mostly Wood, an element not even found in Western astrology.

If the Five Elements' only contribution were to show the important influences of Wood energy—astrology's "missing element"—it would quality as a major addition. But the Five Elements can clarify Western astrology as a whole, and make it a more accurate and complete system, by showing the unique combination of energies that make up each planet and sign.

Apart from Wood, the names of the elements in Western astrology are the same as in the Five Elements with one exception. The Air signs in astrology correspond to Metal in the Chinese system.[54] I therefore refer to the three traditional Air signs—Gemini, Libra and Aquarius—as Metal signs.

Why Western Astrology?

The Chinese long ago developed their own complex and sophisticated system of astrology to complement their Five Elements system. The two teachings together form a rich stew of insights representing the best of Chinese thought and intuition. One might ask: If the aim is to enrich astrology using the Five Elements, why use Western astrology? The reason is simple. Astrology is valuable and meaningful, in part, because it connects everyday life with the symbols and traditions of earlier times. Chinese astrology draws on Asian folklore and legends familiar to people raised in the Asian tradition. For Westerners, stories from our own heritage, especially Greek and Roman mythology, resonate with our experience: Venus, the goddess of love and the arts; Mars, the god of war; Leo the Lion, the King of Beasts; and so on. For Americans in particular, who are often accused of lacking a folk soul and of living in a society without cultural richness, the legends and myths of astrology can add a much needed layer of meaning to everyday life.

....

THE FIRE TYPE PERSONALITY

Fire types are warm, expressive, outgoing people with a fun-loving nature and good social skills. There is a lightness and brightness about Fire types and they enjoy and draw energy from other people. Fire types often have light hair and eyes, and blondes and redheads tend to have prominent Fire energies. Because of their charm and verbal skills, Fire types often choose occupations that bring them into contact with other people. Entertainers, politicians and salesmen are heavily represented among Fire types.

Fire types are comfortable with physical intimacy but not necessarily with unselfish love. Fire and Earth adjoin each other on the Five Elements circle and the loving and caring qualities of Earth tend to merge with the passionate, romantic, fun-loving qualities of Fire. A person's particular blend of Earth and Fire energies helps determine the balance of the two kinds of love in that individual.

Fire's natural tensions are with Water and Metal. A risk for Fire types is that dominant Fire can weaken Water, limiting

emotional depth. If a Fire type has unresolved fears—a Water imbalance—he may practice denial or avoidance, displaying a forced
optimism or even bravado that conceals the fear within. If Fire seriously weakens Metal, the Fire type can lose his usual sense of
boundaries and become undisciplined or irresponsible or take reck-
less and unnecessary risks.

THE FIRE SIGNS: LEO AND SAGITTARIUS[55]

LEO THE LION: STRENGTH, LEADERSHIP AND AMBITION

Leo, the sign ruled by the Sun, competes with Aries for the title of
firstborn among the signs. Its qualities and traditional symbol, the
lion, reflect Leo's exalted status. Leo is a sign of strength, confidence, optimism, personal charisma and natural leadership. People
with prominent Leonine energies combine charm with egotism and
generosity with ambition. Leos genuinely like other people but often feel a strong need to control them. Leo thus represents a blend
of Fire and Wood energies and is probably the sign in which the
two primary *yang* energies are most evenly balanced. The sign of
Leo tends to be prominent in the charts of political and military
leaders.

Leo Tempered by Libra: the Birth Chart of Bill Clinton

Former president Bill Clinton is an excellent example of the Fire or
Fire-Wood type personality, and of how those energies express
themselves through the sign of Leo. Clinton's chart, too, illustrates
a common pattern in which the rising sign, which represents the
outer public persona, can conceal other, sometimes less pleasant
traits associated with the birth sign. The same pattern is repeated,
as we will see, in the charts of George W. Bush, John F. Kennedy,
Winston Churchill and Thomas Jefferson.

Clinton's chart is shown in Figure 22. He has no less than four
planets in Leo—the Sun, Mercury, Saturn and Pluto (oval A). This
helps account for his remarkable vitality, charm, verbal skills and
gift for leadership. It helps explain his legendary ability to interact

tirelessly with other people, to enjoy the interaction and draw energy from it—all signs of powerful Fire energies.

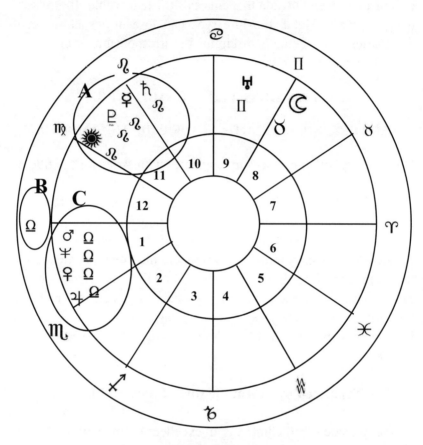

FIGURE 22.
THE BIRTH CHART OF BILL CLINTON[56]

In another, less well-balanced personality, the heavy emphasis on Leo might have led to a brusque, overly aggressive or even combative personal style (for comparison, see the birth chart of George W. Bush below). But in Clinton there were powerful moderating influences that softened his harsher Wood qualities, at least in public, and gave him a mild, even gentle, personal style.

The source of Clinton's gentleness is his rising sign, Libra (oval B). The rising sign is the sign dawning on the eastern horizon at the moment of birth. Along with the birth sign and the Moon sign, the rising sign is one of the three most important indicators in the birth chart. Libra, like Leo, has unusual prominence in Clinton's chart. It is not only his rising sign, he has four planets in Libra and all are in the First House (oval "C"). The First House is the area of sky just below the eastern horizon and any planet in that house has special importance.

Libra, a hybrid of Metal, Earth and Fire, is a sign above all of harmony and balance. Its symbol, the scales of justice, represents the Libran's instinct for conciliation and compromise along with an aversion to open conflict. Leo tempered by Libra captures the essence of Clinton's political style—forceful but never angry or bullying, seeking solutions through negotiation and compromise rather than confrontation. Libra, too, helps explain Clinton's tendency, criticized at times, to avoid conflict and to try to be all things to all people.

Clinton's sexual misconduct can be explained, in energy terms, in part by the conjunction of Mercury and Pluto (the two middle planets in oval A). A conjunction occurs when two planets, viewed from earth, are side by side at the moment of birth. The qualities of the two energies merge, sometimes with dramatic results. One writer says of the Mercury-Pluto conjunction: "Something of a power complex may be present, especially if the conjunction falls in Leo."[57] In Clinton's case the conjunction falls in Leo.

It is not surprising that Clinton's power complex played itself out, not in his public behavior, but in his private sexual life. Pluto, the ruler of Scorpio, has strong associations with both sex and power, but Libra's prominence virtually ruled out any public display of aggression. One of the secrets of Clinton's success, after all, was a gracious and caring personal manner that was particularly attractive to women, who saw him as a strong but sensitive champion of progressive causes. So, instead of expressing his need for power openly, Clinton did it in secret through a series of often daring extramarital sexual affairs. His choice of partners, situations and techniques all suggest that power, dominance and risk-taking were as important to him as sexual pleasure. Recalling the discussion of Fire energies in Chapter 3, the thrill of danger, even if it means courting disaster, can be a powerful motivation for Fire types. Clinton clearly let his dominant Fire energies overwhelm both Metal, the energy of rules and values, and Water, the energy of prudence and caution.

Clinton and Kennedy

Bill Clinton patterned his ambitions after one of his heroes, John F. Kennedy. Though the two men were different in many ways, there is an important similarity in their birth charts that reflected itself in the two men's lives. Both men had Libra as their rising sign, conferring a natural courtesy, charm and grace. For both, the courtly Libran façade concealed a secret, promiscuous sex life. The source for Kennedy was not a Mercury-Pluto conjunction but a heavy concentration of four planets in the Eighth House—the house of Scorpio which is ruled by Pluto and is strongly associated with sexuality. They included Venus, the planet of love and appetites, as well as the Sun. Both were in the sign of Gemini, associated with duality and sometimes permissiveness. Kennedy had three planets in sensual Taurus as well, giving him particularly strong appetites.

Besides sexuality, the Eighth House has associations with great wealth and with death. Tragically for Kennedy, his life, and untimely death, reflected all of those associations. Kennedy's chart is shown in Figure 29 and I discuss it in the section on Metal energy.

JUPITER'S NOBLE INFLUENCES: THE SIGN OF SAGITTARIUS

In Greek mythology Sagittarius was the centaur Chiron, half-horse and half-human, who was famous as a scholar, physician and prophet. Sagittarians often reflect the versatility of Chiron. They tend to be physically strong and active with a love of freedom and the outdoors, and they often take an intense interest in ideas and the life of the mind. Sagittarians, like their mythical counterpart, tend to carry themselves with a certain nobility and grace.

Sagittarius and its ruling planet, Jupiter, represent an unusually rich and complex blending of energies. This helps explain why some of history's most versatile and accomplished figures have been Sagittarians or have had Jupiter or Sagittarius prominent in their charts. One of England's most illustrious sons was an example of the many sides of the Sagittarian—a soldier-statesman-orator-politician with a broad historical vision, and who was both a gifted writer and a talented artist.

The Eloquent Warrior: the Birth Chart of Sir Winston Churchill

Churchill, who led Great Britain through the darkest days of World War II, had an extraordinary career that spanned most of the 20th century. His life illustrates both the brilliance and the unconventionality of the Sagittarian mind. Churchill was the son of an English lord and an American beauty, Jennie Jerome. A mediocre student, he was held back in school but eventually graduated from the Military War College at Sandhurst. He was captured during the Boer War in South Africa only to escape, rejoin the British forces and be hailed as a national hero.

Elected to Parliament, Churchill became First Lord of the Admiralty during World War I but was forced to resign after orchestrating the disastrous Gallipoli campaign. After a period of political exile, he returned to government and eventually became Prime Minister at the outbreak of World War II. His stirring speeches and indomitable will became a symbol of British strength in adversity. After the war, he wrote a multi-volume history of the conflict and another work, *The History of the English-Speaking Peoples*. He received the Nobel Prize in Literature in 1953. Recounting his difficult boyhood days when he was forced to repeat English classes while other boys were studying Greek and Latin, Churchill said, with characteristic simplicity, "I got into my bones the structure of the ordinary English sentence which is a noble thing."

In his later years Churchill took up oil painting and produced some remarkably good works. He died in 1974 at the age of 90.

His plaque in the floor of Westminster Abbey in London reads simply, "Remember Winston Churchill."

Churchill's birth chart is shown in Figure 23. The strong influences of Sagittarius are its most striking feature. Both the Sun and Venus are in that sign (oval A) while Jupiter, Sagittarius' ruler, is in the First House (oval B). Many of Churchill's best qualities—optimism, enthusiasm, breadth of vision, a sense of life as a noble adventure and a gift for writing—owe much to the positive energies of Sagittarius. Those qualities were enhanced by Churchill's Moon in Leo, another Fire sign that shares many of Sagittarius' energies.

Although in many ways a cultivated and highly civilized man, Churchill had a dark side that was most evident in his love of war. He admitted his fascination with it and is reported to have said about that quality, "It is a horrible way to be made." The seeds of aggression can be found in Churchill's birth chart. Both Sagittarius and Leo, although nominally Fire signs, have generous helpings of Wood energy. If encouraged by other influences, they can form the foundation of a warrior temperament. In Churchill's case Mercury is in Scorpio, suggesting an interest in the darker and more violent side of human affairs (oval C). Churchill's Mars in the First House is an indication of prominent Wood energies including a formidable temper.

As with Bill Clinton, John F. Kennedy and other leaders, Churchill's aggressive tendencies were moderated by the harmonious rising sign of Libra. Like the two presidents, Churchill's outer courtesy and grace concealed powerful unsatisfied Wood impulses within.

A wartime anecdote illustrates some of Churchill's more colorful Sagittarian qualities. While British, French and German troops were engaged in terrible trench warfare during World War I, Churchill, a high-ranking government official, made a visit to the front. He reportedly ordered a full-sized tin bathtub to be delivered to his headquarters. After the tub was filled with hot water, Churchill took off his clothes, climbed into the tub and, with shells and bullets whizzing around nearby, took a leisurely hot bath while puffing on a cigar. Whether true or not, the story illustrates the confidence and often outsized ego of the Fire or Fire-Wood type. It captures, too, the quirkiness of the Sagittarian mind along with the Sagittarian's unquestioning faith in his own good luck.

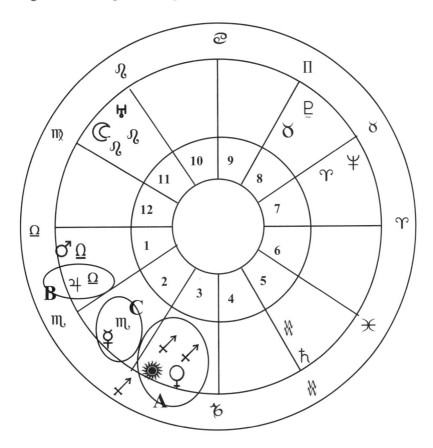

FIGURE 23.
THE BIRTH CHART OF SIR WINSTON CHURCHILL[58]

THE WOOD TYPE PERSONALITY

Wood types are intense, competitive, hard-driving people who tend to focus their energies on work and accomplishment. Wood types are bold and assertive and often have a pioneering, adventurous spirit. The Wood type's ego is strong and he has an instinct for leadership, control or even dominance. Physically, Wood types are often mesomorphs with strong, muscular, well-developed bodies.

Powerful Wood energies, balanced by other positive influences, have contributed to the character and achievements of some of history's greatest leaders. On the dark side of the Wood spectrum are cruel, self-absorbed, power-hungry people lacking any sense of empathy or compassion, including some of the greatest tyrants of both past and present.

THE WOOD SIGNS: ARIES AND SCORPIO

Wood is an important ingredient in several signs but in most cases is not the dominant influence. The two exceptions are Aries and Scorpio, each of which expresses the influences of Wood to the point that each can be most accurately described as a Wood sign.

THE SIGN OF ARIES: COURAGE,
BOLDNESS AND INDEPENDENCE

Aries, whose symbol is the ram, is the closest thing to a pure Wood sign in astrology. The best qualities of Aries are courage, boldness, directness and a highly energetic, independent spirit. The weaknesses of the sign include egotism, lack of empathy and a tendency toward aggression. Aries' link to anger and aggression is evident from its name. The constellation Aries was named after the Greek god of war, and Aries' ruling planet, Mars, was named after the Roman god of war.

When the dynamic, aggressive energies of Aries are balanced by other complementary influences, they can provide the drive and power for exceptional achievement. Examples include Dr. Martin Luther King, Thomas Jefferson and Johann Sebastian Bach. Dr. King's chart is shown below and Jefferson's chart appears in the section on Metal energy.

America's greatest civil rights leader since Lincoln was single-mindedly dedicated to the pursuit of racial equality in American life. He set a standard of vision, bravery, humility and sacrifice that have been equaled only rarely in U.S. history.

The Keystone of Character:
The Birth Chart of Dr. Martin Luther King

Martin Luther King was born on January 15, 1929, in Atlanta, Georgia. Thirty-nine years later he died there, the victim of an assassin's bullet. During his short life he led the struggle for civil rights in the U.S. that ended in landmark federal legislation and an end to many forms of racial discrimination.

Dr. King's birth chart is shown in Figure 24. If courage is the keystone of character, the rising sign of Aries was central to his personality and achievements (oval A). Aries' prominence explains Dr. King's fearlessness and direct, straightforward leadership style. Those energies gave him the fortitude to organize and march in demonstrations in hostile Southern cities; to go to prison willingly for his beliefs; and to continue making public appearances in spite of continued death threats. In his last public statement on April 3, 1968, the day before he died, he hinted at a premonition that his life might soon end:

> Well, I don't know what will happen now. We've got some difficult days ahead. But it doesn't matter with me now. Because I've been to the mountain-top....And I've looked over. And I've seen the promised land. I may not get there with you. But I want you to know tonight, that we, as a people, will get to the promised land. And I'm happy, tonight. I'm not worried about anything. I'm not fearing any man. Mine eyes have seen the glory of the coming of the Lord.

Dr. King's birth sign, Capricorn (oval B), balanced his boldness and courage with depth and spiritual vision. Capricorn, though nominally an Earth sign, carries the Water energies of humility, sacrifice and, at its best, deep spiritual awareness. The Water sign of Pisces has strong spiritual associations as well, and both Dr. King's Moon and Venus are in the sign of Pisces (oval C).

Dr. King's devotion to his life's work is symbolized by the

Sun's placement at the top of his chart. The Midheaven—the point directly overhead at the time of birth—is associated with a person's

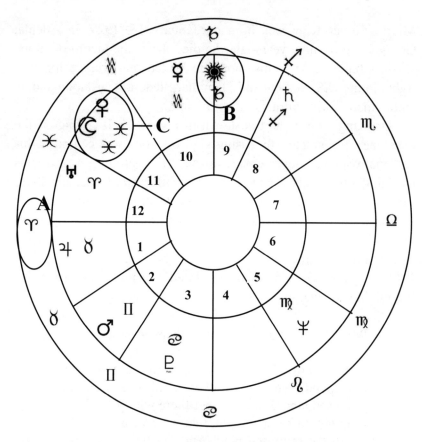

FIGURE 24.
THE BIRTH CHART OF DR. MARTIN LUTHER KING[59]

career and life aspirations. Martin Luther King was born shortly before noon and the Sun, in the powerful and complex sign of Capricorn, was at the highest point in the sky.

THE SIGN OF SCORPIO:
AN ELEMENTAL FORCE OF NATURE

If Aries is the purest expression of Wood energy among the twelve signs, Scorpio represents a more complex blending of Wood with other influences. Although traditionally classified as a Water sign, Scorpio is a powerful combination of Wood, Water and probably other energies. Wood and Water adjoin each other on the Five Elements circle and Water nourishes Wood through the Nurturing Cycle. The result is a kind of double dynamo that helps explain the peculiar intensity of the Scorpian personality.

Before Pluto was discovered, Mars was believed to be Scorpio's ruling planet. Both Mars and Pluto have much of the intensity, power and driving energy that are the hallmark of Scorpio. Scorpio's symbol, the (water) scorpion, evokes mostly the negative associations of the sign, especially danger and aggression. But Scorpio has many positive associations as well. People born under the sign of Scorpio often have a penetrating intelligence and intuition and the sign appears frequently in the charts of psychologists and psychiatrists. Scorpio's energies are purposeful and focused and Scorpios often achieve much in life.

Scorpio is associated, not only with the unconscious mind, but with depths of other kinds—the Underworld, crime, death and the afterlife, and natural disasters like earthquakes and volcanoes. Scorpio is closely associated with sex and, oddly, with high finance and great wealth. Plutocrats, whose name derives from Scorpio's ruling planet, believe in government by the rich.

The smoldering intensity of Scorpio's energies is illustrated by the charts of two prominent historical figures. The first was a famous warrior-dictator; the second found a more constructive outlet for his furious Wood energies.

The Warrior Mystique: the Birth Chart of Napoleon

Napoleon Bonaparte, Emperor of the French and Commander of the Army of France at the height of its imperial power, was a virtual force of nature in Europe during the early 19th century. In his relatively brief career, he made war on, and occupied, most of Europe as well as parts of Africa and Asia. His most grandiose, and disastrous, campaign was the attempted conquest of Russia. His army advanced thousands of miles, reaching the gates of Moscow only to find the city burned and deserted. The retreat of Napoleon's army through the frozen Russian countryside was an epic defeat and catastrophe. Napoleon was eventually dethroned and exiled to the island of St. Helena, where he spent the last years of his life, dying at the age of 51.

Napoleon's birth chart (Figure 25) shows the tremendous combination of aggressive energies that lay behind his drive, ruthless-

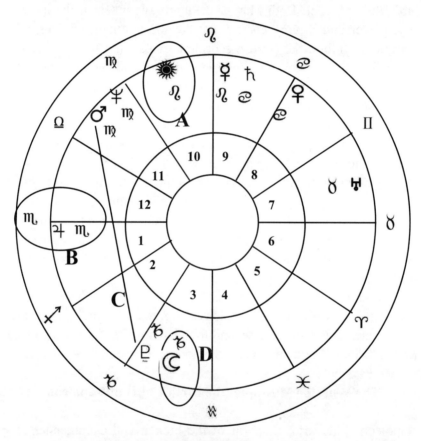

FIGURE 25.
THE BIRTH CHART OF NAPOLEON BONAPARTE[60]

ness and ambition. Born on August 15, 1769, on the island of Corsica, his birth sign is Leo (oval A). His Sun is in the 10th House, suggesting a dedication to career advancement at the expense of other interests. But a key to Napoleon's temperament is the sign of Scorpio, which is both his rising sign and the sign in which the important planet of Jupiter is placed (oval B). Fusing its Wood energies with those of his birth sign, Scorpio helped saturate Napoleon's inner and outer being with an instinct for control and domination.

The placement of Mars and Pluto further strengthened Napoleon's aggressive tendencies. The two planets are in a harmonious Trine relationship—120^0 separation—magnifying the effects of both (line C). Mars is in a complementary Sextile relationship with the Scorpio rising sign. Finally, Napoleon's Moon is in the chilly sign of Capricorn (oval D), a common placement for military leaders. It suggests a tendency toward depression, which occasionally afflicted Napoleon, as well as a certain emotional coolness or detachment. The latter quality probably made it easier for Napoleon to send men into battle, and often to their deaths, without feeling much remorse about it.

A more recent warrior-dictator, Benito Mussolini, had the same combination of Scorpio rising and Leo birth sign as Napoleon. Mussolini, who ruled Italy during World War II and joined forces with Hitler to make war on the Allies, is often shown in photos with an intensity and hint of menace reminiscent of paintings of Napoleon.

When Scorpio's energies are balanced by softer, more complementary forces, they can drive creative achievement of the highest order. A man who changed the face of classical music is an example.

Passion Erupting from the Depths:
The Volcano that was Beethoven

Ludwig van Beethoven has been described as the most disruptive force in the history of classical music. His explosive energy, the range of contrasting emotions he expressed and the forms he used to express them revolutionized the world of 18th century music.

Beethoven's unique blend of intensity, joy, loneliness, fury and spiritual ecstasy is more understandable given the extraordinary arrangement of planets in his birth chart (Figure 26). The two most important planets, the Sun and Moon, as well as Mercury are all in

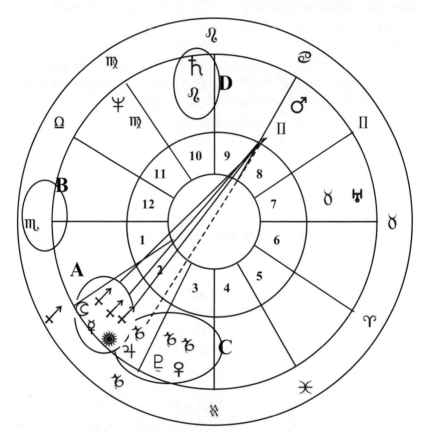

FIGURE 26.
THE BIRTH CHART OF LUDWIG VAN BEETHOVEN[61]

the dynamic Fire sign of Sagittarius (oval A). That alone might have accounted for many of Beethoven's creative gifts but he had, in addition, two important pairs of planets—the Sun and Jupiter and the Moon and Mercury (the four planets in the Second House)—in conjunction. Either pairing can indicate unusual personal qualities, exceptionally high intelligence or special talents.

To have both conjunctions in a single chart is rare and is probably a reliable indicator of genius.

Scorpio Rising: the Engine that Drove the Music

Beethoven's rising sign, like that of Napoleon and Mussolini, is Scorpio (oval B). His creative engine was thus energized by a powerful dynamo of Wood energies. Like the two warrior-dictators, Beethoven is shown in busts and drawings as a dark, brooding figure with an air of simmering intensity.

The placement of Mars added even more force to Beethoven's already formidable temperament. Mars is directly opposite the Sun, Moon and Mercury in the sky, in a stressful aspect called an Opposition (three solid lines). But Beethoven, thanks in part to Sagittarius' positive influences, directed his volcanic energies, not toward war and conquest, but into the highest artistic expression. His Third Symphony, Fifth Symphony and many other works are among the best examples in music of the constructive channeling of dynamic, intense Wood energies.

Human Limitation and the Rings of Saturn

Unfortunately for Beethoven, the extraordinary positive forces that moved him were opposed by almost equally powerful constricting and depressive influences. In astrology Jupiter is known as the Great Benefactor—a planet of joy, freedom, versatility, expansiveness and good luck. Saturn is Jupiter's opposite number, *yin* to Jupiter's *yang*. Saturn, and sometimes the sign of Capricorn which Saturn rules, can represent physical or emotional limitation or just plain bad luck. For those who believe that life is God's art, the rings of Saturn represent the limiting, constricting influences a person must contend with, including the karmic consequences of past lives.

Both Saturn and Capricorn are particularly prominent in Beethoven's chart. He has three planets in Capricorn—Venus, Jupiter and Pluto (oval C)—and Saturn itself is in its own house, the Tenth, giving it special force (oval D). Saturn is in the sign of Leo, an especially burdensome influence that makes it hard for a person to derive much pleasure from life. Finally, Saturn is near the Midheaven, the point directly overhead at the time of birth. The Midheaven, as we saw with Dr. King, represents a person's career and life goals. Saturn near the Midheaven suggests an isolated and lonely life, dedicated to work and little else. Saturn's placement at the top of Beethoven's chart evokes the image of a lonely king reigning in solitude, bringing joy to his subjects below but unable to experience much of it for himself.

Mars, the Fifth Symphony and Symbols of Greatness

Mars, as I noted, is in an extremely tense position in Beethoven's chart. Aries' ruler is in the Eighth House, the House of Scorpio, almost directly opposite the Sun, Moon, Mercury and Jupiter. Mars forms a stressful Opposition aspect, or 180° angle, with three of the four planets; the fourth planet, Jupiter, is slightly too far off-center to be technically in opposition (dotted line).

Beethoven's mighty Fifth Symphony is universally known and is often referred to as the Classic of classical music. Many people, even if they haven't heard the symphony in some time, can hum the first four dramatic bass notes—BUM-BUM-BUM-BUM!—the first three notes the same and the fourth note two steps lower and stressed. The short phrase, with its sense of tension and foreboding, repeats several times during the first movement, and those four notes have become a symbol of the Fifth Symphony and of classical music itself.

If the Sun, Moon, Mercury and Jupiter were musical notes in Beethoven's birth chart, they would be filled with tension because they oppose Mars, the Red Planet of intensity and anger. Three of the notes, which are in direct opposition to Mars, would be the same note; the fourth would be a different note, perhaps a slightly lower note.

Did the arrangement of the Sun, Moon, Mercury and Jupiter on December 16, 1770 over Bonn, Germany represent the first four notes of Beethoven's Fifth Symphony? Were those planets a cosmic symbol of the great man born on that day and of the immortal music to come? Or was it just a coincidence, an accident of geometry and timing and something with no meaning or importance? I discuss apparent coincidences and some of their possible meanings in Chapter 6.

THE WATER TYPE PERSONALITY

Water, the South Pole of personality, is the mirror image of Fire. Where Fire types are warm, joyful and expressive, Water types tend to be serious, introverted and thoughtful. Fire types are good talkers and Water types are good listeners. The brightness of the Fire type contrasts with the often dark and sometimes brooding quality of the Water type, who often has dark hair and eyes and sometimes a darkish cast to the complexion. Unlike Fire types, who seek out and are energized by other people, Water types seek solitude and are emotionally recharged by being alone.

Fire types tend to spread their attention among many interests while Water types can focus with great concentration on a single topic, exploring subjects in great depth. Fire types are energetic and tend to move quickly, while Water types are usually more deliberate but have greater stamina and endurance. At their best, Water types have a profound humility and great depth of understanding. When distorted and imbalanced, Water can warp the personality in the direction of fear, isolation, depression or even paranoia.

THE WATER SIGNS: CANCER AND PISCES

The three traditional Water signs all represent a complex blending of Water with other energies. Scorpio, which I have classified as a Wood sign, is a dynamic combination of mainly Wood and Water. Cancer and Pisces, too, reflect the qualities of Water intermingled with other powerful influences.

THE SIGN OF CANCER:
AFFECTION, LOYALTY AND DEFENSE

Cancer's symbol is the crab, one of the more descriptive images among the twelve signs. The crab, like the turtle, is a hard-shelled creature that carries its home around with it. Cancerians greatly value home and family life and their strong domestic values, loyalty and patriotism are among their greatest strengths. These are all Earth qualities and Cancer, the sign ruled by the moon, has a strong or even primary component of Earth energies.

The hard shell of the crab symbolizes, too, a rigid wall of protection that defends against perceived threats to a softness, or weakness, within. Cancerians sometimes suffer from inner fears and insecurities that make them defensive and reactive, responding even to minor slights with irritation or annoyance. They cling tenaciously to their beliefs, like a crab holding fast with its powerful claws, and their stubbornness is legendary. Kind and generous to those they love, Cancerians can be harsh and unforgiving to those who have threatened or offended them.

The Cancerian's strengths and weaknesses are rooted in the Earth and Water energies of the sign. At their best, Cancerians combine the loving and caring nature of the Earth type with the deeply developed feelings and creativity of the Water type. Outstanding examples have included Ernest Hemingway and Henry David Thoreau, both of whom were born under the sign of Cancer.

Water, the energy of listening, is the energy of music as well. Although Taurus and Capricorn are the primary musical signs, Cancer is often prominent in the charts of musicians and composers. The songwriter Richard Rodgers, his partner Oscar Hammerstein and Louis Armstrong were all born under the sign of Cancer.

Fear and insecurity—imbalanced Water and Earth—are the Cancerian's Achilles heel and they are most likely to express themselves openly when Cancer is the rising sign. People born with Cancer rising often have a difficult time when they are young, but with time and effort they build confidence and self-esteem and, in the end, make good use of their inborn talents.

When Cancer is the birth sign, a person's weaknesses are more likely to be disguised by other influences, especially when the rising sign is powerful. If Leo rises, there may be a dramatic disconnect between the person's outer behavior and inner feelings. The 43rd U.S. president is a good example.

When Aggression Masks Fear: the Birth Chart of George W. Bush

If not for the attacks of September 11, 2001, George W. Bush's entire presidency might have looked much like its first eight months: an emphasis on modest domestic goals, little interest in foreign affairs and an overall belief that, whenever possible, government should be a kind of passive caretaker rather than an active participant in the lives of its citizens.

September 11 shocked and galvanized both the nation and the president. Most agreed that the country's aggressive response in Afghanistan was justified; many disagreed with the president's decision to invade Iraq. Bush's warlike policies reflected the combined power of Leo and Cancer—the impulse to attack and defend—aggravated by other unresolved power conflicts.

Bush's birth chart is shown in Figure 27. Cancer is his birth sign (oval A) but Leo is the dominant force in his personality. Leo is not only Bush's rising sign, he has three planets in Leo—Mercury, Pluto and Venus—and all are in the First House, giving them great potency (oval B). Bush was thus born with a powerful blend of Fire and Wood energies in the forefront of his personality. Fire took the lead during the hard living and hard drinking days of his youth. Later, as president, the Wood energies of combativeness and aggression would take center stage.

As with Bill Clinton, Bush's rising sign represents a kind of outer façade that conceals the inner core of personality. Unlike Clinton, whose inner aggressiveness was masked by gracious Libran energies, Bush's aggressive Wood energies were on the outside, concealing fear and insecurity within. If Clinton revealed his secret aggressions only in private, Bush may have revealed his secret fears to no one, including himself.

Bush's predilection for power is further explained by the same Mercury-Pluto conjunction found in Clinton's chart (top two planets in First House). As with Clinton, the conjunction falls in Leo,

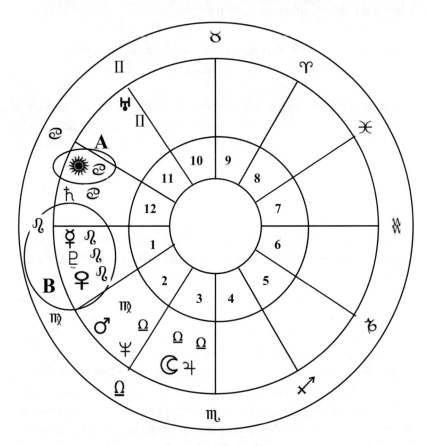

FIGURE 27.
THE BIRTH CHART OF GEORGE W. BUSH[62]

suggesting a possible power complex. But because the conjunction falls in the First House in Bush's chart, it has even greater force.

Bush's chart mirrors, in an almost uncanny way, the emotional reaction of the American people to the September 11 attacks. Fear and insecurity reigned, at least for a few months, and there was a natural desire to defend the homeland and strike back aggressively at the attackers. Bush was able to ride a wave of national sentiment that coincided exactly with his most basic instincts. After a few months, when the shock and trauma of the attacks had begun to wear off, the nation settled back into a more balanced view of the need to defend itself. But the president, living in a perfect storm of anger and denial, remained mobilized and on the alert. He was able to persuade the nation to invade and conquer Iraq because his impulse to attack and defend still resonated to some degree with the national mood.

From September 11 on, Bush's powerful Wood energies, exaggerated by imbalanced Water, drove both his attitudes and policies. Although born under a Water sign, the Wood and Fire energies of his rising sign had always dominated his behavior. The events of September 11 converted George W. Bush into a full-blown Wood type, and the self-proclaimed "War President" made aggression and conflict a virtual signature of his presidency.

THE SIGN OF PISCES: IN THE FOOTSTEPS OF JESUS

Pisces, whose symbol is the fish, is a complex blend of mainly Water, Earth and Fire. Pisces is ruled by the planet of Neptune and is associated with gentleness, creativity, humility and spiritual awareness. There is an innocence and vulnerability about the Piscean that can make the stresses of everyday life hard to bear. Pisceans are often deeply loving people, a sign of strong Earth energies, and their innate creativity is indicative of strong Fire as well as Water. At their best, Pisceans embody the connectedness of Earth, the depth of Water and the inspiration of Fire. Some of the world's great artists have had Pisces prominent in their charts.

The Age of Pisces, which lasted from roughly 1 A.D. to the year 2000, is often associated with the life of Jesus and the dawning of Christianity. Jesus and his disciples' many connections with the Sea of Galilee, with fish and fishing signify the link between spiritual awareness and the sign of Pisces. I discuss the important historical connection between Christianity and the Age of Pisces in Chapter 7.

One of America's greatest presidents was a Water type with strong Piscean energies who lived with a burden of melancholy, and who presided over the greatest crisis the nation has ever faced. He ultimately triumphed with the help of personal qualities that transcended the ordinary and crossed over into the realm of Spirit. In energy terms, his life and the quality of his presidency recall the words of Tao Cheng, an 11th century Chinese scholar: "The Sage who makes himself as Water is distinguished for his humility."

Vision, Inspiration and Faith: the Birth Chart of Abraham Lincoln

Lincoln's emergence at a time of maximum national danger was a pattern that has repeated itself over and over again in American history. In every century great figures have appeared to lead the nation through war and other major national crises. But of all of America's great presidents, Lincoln's memory remains more powerful than perhaps any other. His enduring legacy is probably due, not to his political skills or other personal talents, though he had many, but to the profound spiritual quality of his being. It gave his life and work a resonance that can still be felt today. The energies that made Lincoln such an extraordinary figure are evident in his birth chart (Figure 28).

Lincoln's chart is notable, first, because his birth and rising signs are the same. His birth sign is Aquarius and Aquarius is on the eastern horizon (oval A). This doubling of signs happens whenever a person is born at or around daybreak.

Since the rising sign represents the outer public persona and the birth sign the inner core of personality, there was no inherent conflict in Lincoln—as there was with Bill Clinton, George W. Bush and other presidents—between the inner and outer man. That may help explain why Lincoln is remembered as a person of such authenticity and integrity.

Aquarius is, among the twelve signs, the preeminent sign of change, progressive ideals and humanitarian vision. Lincoln was, in effect, a "double Aquarius"—a fitting title for a man whose presidency would see the abolition of slavery and the reshaping of American society. But though his humanitarian instincts ran deep, Lincoln, unlike many Aquarians, was not a man of cool, dispassionate temperament—a Metal type. The deep emotion and prophetic power in his words convey far more than simply a rational

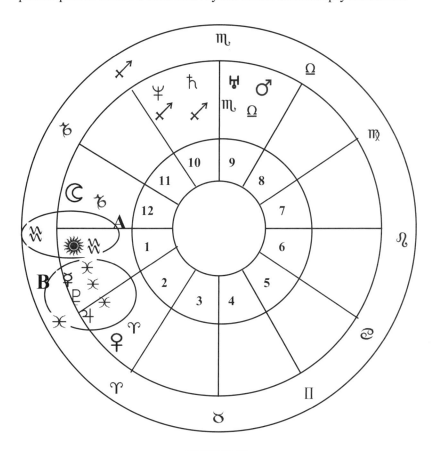

FIGURE 28.
THE BIRTH CHART OF ABRAHAM LINCOLN[63]

vision for a more just society. Lincoln was moved by deep compassion and a strong sense of spiritual connection. He thus expressed the finest qualities and deepest awareness of the Water type. Those energies are represented in Lincoln's chart by the prominence of both Pisces and Capricorn.

"With Malice Toward None:" the Spirit of Pisces

Lincoln's chart has three planets—Mercury, Jupiter and Pluto—in Pisces and all are in the First House, making Pisces' influences exceptionally strong (oval B). This repeats a familiar pattern in which prominent personalities often have several plancts in a single sign and all are in the First House. Lincoln's Moon is in the Twelfth House, the House of Pisces, strengthening the sign's influences even more.

Lincoln's innate gentleness and humility, his emphasis on forgiveness and reconciliation as the war ended, and his spirituality all testify to his deep immersion in Piscean energies. They contributed to his fondness for scripture and lay behind the Biblical quality of his writings. One of the most familiar phrases from his Second Inaugural Address—"With malice toward none, with charity for all"—could serve as a motto for the Piscean spirit.

The Capricorn Factor

One of Lincoln's greatest strengths, astrologically speaking, was one of his heaviest burdens. The Twelfth House, the house of prayer, meditation and spirituality, is the house of seclusion, withdrawal and emotional suffering as well. Lincoln's Moon in the Twelfth House strengthened his connection to Spirit but increased the risk of withdrawal and depression. That was a particular problem for Lincoln since his Moon fell in the sensitive sign of Capricorn. That placement, as we saw earlier with Napoleon, can be an indicator of depressive tendencies and helps explain the sense of melancholy that surrounded Lincoln. At the same time, Capricorn's powerful connections with Spirit undoubtedly contributed to the depth and power of Lincoln's vision.

THE METAL TYPE PERSONALITY

Metal is the energy of structure, organization and values. It forms the backbone of both character and intellect. Metal types tend to be morally upright, intelligent, analytical and well-organized. They see the world mainly through ideas rather than emotion. Typically calm and composed, they believe in principle and in careful, rational decision-making.

Metal types are often dignified with a reserved or even formal personal manner. Because of their natural restraint, they tend to suppress or even repress certain feelings. When threatened, Metal types can retreat into ideas and rules, showing a stubborn insistence on order and procedure. Metal types tend to set high standards for themselves as well as others. When they fail to meet those standards, they can harbor conscious or unconscious guilt or feelings of inadequacy. When others disappoint them, they can be moralistic, self-righteous and condescending. Metal types are often tall and lean, with a wiry, ectomorphic body type.

THE METAL SIGNS: GEMINI, LIBRA AND AQUARIUS

Each of the Metal signs expresses in its own way the structure and organization of Metal. Aquarians are often interested in ideas and the life of the mind; Librans have a gift for balance, organization and harmony; Geminians have a talent for oral or written communication or both.

Virgo, a traditional Earth sign, has a particularly strong Metal component; in fact, Virgo expresses the Metal type's strong sense of duty more clearly than perhaps any other sign. Virgos tend to be highly organized and to pay close attention to detail—both Metal qualities. Although I discuss Virgo in the section on Earth energies, it could just as easily be classified as a Metal sign.

THE SIGN OF GEMINI: COMMUNICATION AND DUALITY

Gemini, which is ruled by the nearby, rapidly rotating planet of Mercury, is the most dynamic of the Metal signs, a curious blend of Metal and Fire. The two energies, though naturally in tension with one another, are compatible in some ways. Fire, the energy of speech and expressiveness, complements the structure and organization of Metal, helping explain why so many journalists are born

under the sign of Gemini. In other respects, Fire and Metal are almost direct opposites. The Fire type's passion, spontaneity and
love of life directly challenge the carefulness and restraint of
Metal. That conflict may help explain the Geminian's well-known
duality, represented by the sign's symbol, the Twins.

One recent president displayed both the strengths and weaknesses of the sign. He and his family represented a rare blending of
highly developed Fire and Metal energies. Their remarkable combination of dynamism and detachment created a unique charm and
charisma that helped launch a political dynasty.

Passionate Detachment: the Birth Chart of John F. Kennedy

The 35th president was born under the sign of Gemini and had both
the Sun and Venus in that sign (Figure 29, oval A). Kennedy had
the fondness for communication that is Gemini's hallmark. He had
a gift for oratory as well as a talent for spontaneous give and take.
He especially enjoyed press conferences where he could show off
his quick and agile mind, his ability to think on his feet and his
delightful off-the-cuff sense of humor. Kennedy's charm and verbal skills, so typical of the Fire type, illustrate the strong Fire component in the sign of Gemini. Gemini's duality expressed itself in
Kennedy's personal behavior, discussed earlier in the section on
former President Bill Clinton.

Although his vibrant, charismatic personality—a Fire quality—
was a major political asset, Kennedy had other, more subtle traits
that revealed the strength of Metal. There was a curious detachment, even remoteness, about him that showed in his manner, his
voice and even his eyes. Kennedy seemed at once engaged and disconnected, as if he could enjoy and participate in life while at the
same time viewing it from a distance.

That quality may have been an invaluable asset when, in October of 1962, the Cuban missile crisis took the world to the brink of
nuclear war. Kennedy was urged by several of his advisors to
bomb the missile sites in Cuba, which could have triggered all-out
war with the Soviet Union. Kennedy alone had the calm, vision

and judgment to agree to remove American missiles from Turkey. The Soviets then agreed to remove their missiles from Cuba, the crisis ended and the world stepped back from the nuclear abyss.

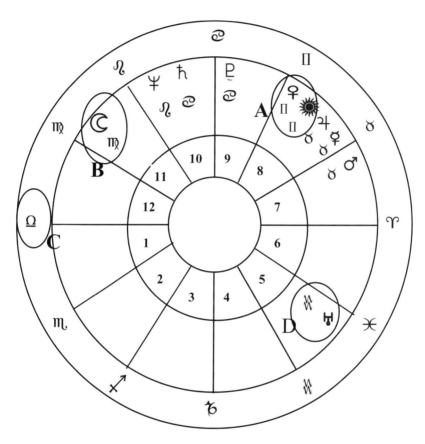

FIGURE 29.
THE BIRTH CHART OF JOHN F. KENNEDY[64]

The source of Kennedy's unusual detachment is hinted at in his chart. The three most important influences—the Sun sign, Moon sign and rising sign—are all heavily Metal in character. The Sun is in Gemini, the Moon in Virgo (oval B) and the rising sign is Libra (oval C). Uranus, the ruler of the Metal sign of Aquarius, is in its own sign (oval D).

Intelligence, objectivity and judgment are all associated with

Metal, but so are sadness and a sense of loss. Tragically for John Kennedy and the whole Kennedy clan, sadness and loss have been all too frequent companions. The same energies that were so central to the Kennedy mystique, and to the family's many triumphs, were intimately bound up with their tragedies as well.

THE SIGN OF LIBRA:
GRACE, HARMONY AND BALANCE

Libra, a harmonious blend of Earth, Metal and Fire, is one of the more grounded of the twelve signs. Librans are warm and gracious people who seek above all to preserve harmony and balance in relationships. They favor conciliation and compromise as ways of insuring a pleasant life for themselves and those around them.

The Libran's stability and love of comfort is indicative of prominent Earth energies. Libra's ruling planet, Venus, rules both Libra and the Earth sign of Taurus. Libra's Metal qualities are evident in the Libran's dignity and reserve and in her well-developed sense of honesty and fair play represented by the sign's symbol, the scales of justice. The Libran's warmth and social skills reflect the influence of Fire. The sign's major vulnerabilities are indecisiveness and a tendency to try to satisfy everyone's needs and   desires.

When Libra appears in the charts of prominent people, it tends, as we have seen, to be as the rising sign. One president whose Libran qualities were more central to his nature was a military man with a decidedly unwarlike temperament.

The Gentle General: the Birth Chart of Dwight D. Eisenhower

Dwight D. Eisenhower, the Supreme Allied Commander in Europe during World War II, directed the planning and execution of the D-Day landings in Normandy in June of 1944. That invasion led a year later to the German surrender and the end of the war in Europe. Eisenhower, a national hero, went on to win election as president in 1952 and again n 1956. He presided over a period of relative peace and prosperity in the U.S.

Eisenhower's temperament, unlike that of many generals, was notably mild, even bland. He rose to prominence, not through daring military exploits (he never saw combat), but through an uncommon talent for planning and administration. When war broke out he was plucked from relative obscurity by General George C. Marshall and placed in charge of the greatest amphibious invasion force in history.

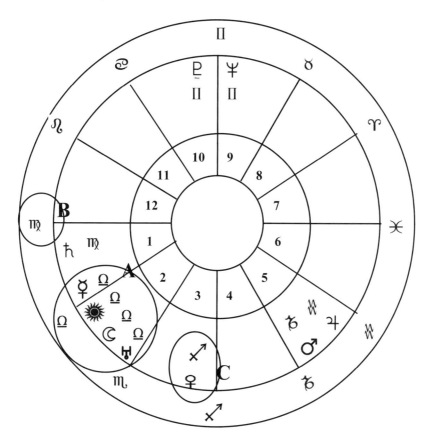

FIGURE 30.
THE BIRTH CHART OF DWIGHT D. EISENHOWER[65]

Eisenhower's birth chart (Figure 30) contrasts dramatically with those of Napoleon, Mussolini and even George W. Bush, all of whom had powerful Wood and Wood-Fire energies in the forefront of their personalities. In fact, Eisenhower's chart has not a single planet in a Wood sign—no Aries, no Scorpio, no Leo. Instead he has a remarkable seven planets in Metal Signs, four in Libra (oval A), two in Gemini and one in Aquarius. To seal his identity as a Metal type, Eisenhower's rising sign is Virgo (oval B).

Eisenhower's gift for planning and organization, as well as his strong sense of duty, were a direct reflection of his dominant Metal energies. His four planets in Libra in particular, including both the Sun and Moon, gave him a natural skill for negotiation and an ability to balance the competing interests within large and diverse groups. Those talents were invaluable in coping with the outsized egos of Churchill, Montgomery and other wartime allies, and in hammering out an invasion plan that was acceptable to all.

Eisenhower's mild temperament was a reflection of a lack of Fire as well as Wood. The only Fire in his chart is Venus in Sagittarius (oval C), but Venus is the planet of love, not war. Venus in Sagittarius suggests an adventurous attitude toward romance, perhaps explaining Eisenhower's wartime affair with his secretary. The absence of both Fire and Wood in Eisenhower's chart may help account for the somewhat passive and even absent-minded quality that overtook him as he grew older.

The one hint of real aggression in Eisenhower's nature was in his temper, which had a tendency to flare up suddenly then subside quickly. That quality is typical when Mars is in Capricorn, a sign that tends to restrain any planet that comes under its influence. It is ironic that Mars, the planet of weapons and war, had only limited power in the man who commanded one of the greatest military forces in history.

The Germans knew nothing of Eisenhower's birth chart but they must have been keenly aware of his name. Dwight Eisenhower was descended from German stock and his name (probably originally Eisenhauer) means "Iron Striker" in German. More than a few German soldiers must have pondered that fact as the Allied war machine drove across Europe in 1944-45, smashing its way into the heart of Germany.

THE SIGN OF AQUARIUS:
INTELLECT, HUMANITY AND DISTANCE

Aquarius is a sign of primarily Metal and Water energies. Aquarians tend to be intelligent and forward-looking with an interest in progressive causes and a genuine concern for the human condition. In personal relations Aquarians often display a certain emotional coolness and distance characteristic of dominant Metal or Metal-Water energies. Aquarius is ruled by the planet Uranus.

The third president, one of the great figures in American history, illustrates the inner depth and outer detachment of the Aquarian personality.

Genius and Paradox: the Birth Chart of Thomas Jefferson
.

Thomas Jefferson, a Renaissance Man, embodied the highest expression of Aquarian qualities—a broad and deep humanitarian vision, exceptional intelligence and a brilliantly inventive mind. He was a statesman, politician, writer, philosopher, educator, architect and inventor. President John F. Kennedy, at a White House dinner honoring Nobel laureates in 1962, welcomed his guests with the following comment: "I think this is the most extraordinary collection of talent, of human knowledge, that has ever been gathered at the White House, with the possible exception of when Thomas Jefferson dined alone."

Jefferson's birth chart is shown in Figure 31. His vision for a new nation and a new kind of human freedom are beautifully symbolized by his rising sign, Aquarius, and by Uranus, Aquarius' ruling planet, rising with it on the eastern horizon (oval A). Uranus is in Capricorn, a limiting influence on the emotions but often an indication of unusual mental gifts. Jupiter is in Virgo (oval B), another common sign of scientific or technical talent and, like Uranus in Capricorn, a restraining influence on the emotions.

These placements help explain both Jefferson's extraordinary intelligence and his lack of emotional intensity despite abundant Fire energies elsewhere in his chart. One writer describes Jefferson's strange combination of inner passion and outer coolness as follows:

> There was grace, nevertheless, in his manners; and his frank and earnest address, his quick sympathy (yet he seemed cold to strangers), his vivacious, desultory, informing talk gave him an engaging charm. Beneath a quiet surface he was fairly aglow with intense convictions and a very emotional temperament. Yet he seems to have acted habitually, in great and little things, on system.[67]

The Aries Factor

Jefferson's birth sign, Aries (oval C), gave him the energy, boldness, confidence and courage to make full use of his talents. All of those qualities were important for the man who, among many other accomplishments, wrote the Declaration of Independence; completed the Louisiana Purchase; designed the University of Virginia and wrote its first curriculum; invented new archeological techniques; was president of the American Philosophical Society; and was the architect of Monticello, his home, where he invented many novel and ingenious devices.

Aries may help account, too, for the disparity between Jefferson's public ideals and his private behavior. The man who was perhaps the foremost spokesman for human liberty and equality was himself a slaveholder until the day he died. His 187 slaves included Sally Hemmings, with whom he apparently had a long-time sexual relationship and by whom he apparently fathered several children.

Slavery was the order of the day in 18th century Virginia and Jefferson may have felt, rightly or wrongly, that he could not free his own slaves even if he believed in principle that slavery was wrong. Whether his relationship with Sally Hemmings was entirely an exploitation or something else is not known. But if Jefferson kept slaves even though he could have freed them, and if he misused his power over Sally Hemmings for his own sexual gratification, he was like other presidents whose outer behavior concealed a

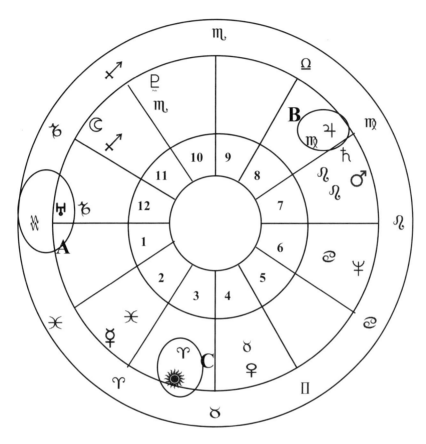

FIGURE 31.
THE BIRTH CHART OF THOMAS JEFFERSON[66]

dark inner secret. Like Clinton, Kennedy, Bush and others, Jefferson's birth and rising signs are a clue to his paradoxical behavior. Aquarius, Jefferson's rising sign, embodies the values of equality and humanity that Jefferson championed throughout his life. Aries, his birth sign, carries, along with many positive associations, the energies of selfishness and an impulse for control and domination. To the extent that Jefferson's private life conflicted with his public ideals, the energies of Aries and Aquarius help explain those inner contradictions.

THE EARTH TYPE PERSONALITY

Earth types are affectionate, supportive, good-natured and reliable. Earth, a primary energy of connection, is the foundation of parental and family love, friendship and a sense of community. Earth types enjoy giving and sharing and, because of their gift for empathy, take pleasure in the happiness and well being of others.

Earth types are sensual and have strong appetites and they are continually balancing their own considerable needs and desires against those of the people around them. If an Earth type's dominant energies are not well developed or become imbalanced, Earth types can be, paradoxically, one of the more selfish and manipulative of the five types.

THE EARTH SIGNS: VIRGO, TAURUS AND CAPRICORN

Most of the signs, as we have seen, represent a dominant energy blended with one or more secondary energies. For one and possibly two of the Earth signs, however, Earth may not be the dominant energy at all. Virgo has an extremely strong Metal component and is ruled by Mercury, the same planet that rules the Metal sign of Gemini. Capricorn has strong Water and Wood components, both of which rival the power of Earth. Taurus is the only Earth sign in which Earth is clearly the dominant energy, but even Taurus is a complex blend of most and possibly all of the five energies.

THE CONTRADICTORY SIGN OF CAPRICORN

Capricorns are grounded, conservative and practical—all Earth qualities. They tend to be ambitious and focused on work, achievement and recognition—Wood qualities. But a key to the Capricorn's nature, and perhaps an explanation of the sign's contradictions, is its prominent Water energies.

Capricorn can be associated with both the most profound awareness and with a somewhat plodding and uninspired attitude. One writer uses the sign's symbol, the goat, to illustrate Capricorn's extremes.

[There are] two kinds of goat: the giddy mountain goat, stepping neatly from crag to crag, always moving on to nibble greener grass further up the mountain; and the domestic goat restricted to the small patch of grass within the circle allowed him by a post and chain.[68]

Capricorn's duality may be partially explained by the enigmatic energy of Water, which embodies both fear and depth, both caution and a gift for the transcendent. As I noted in Chapter 3, Water represents life's infinite possibilities but carries with it the potential for disabling fears. If the domestic goat has given into those fears and submitted, symbolically or literally, to the constricting rings of Saturn—Capricorn's ruling planet—the mountain goat faces fear willingly as it climbs steadily toward the summit. The following examples illustrate both the dangers and the opportunities presented by the powerful sign of Capricorn.

Fear and Constriction: The Birth Chart of Richard Nixon

Nixon was a gifted politician who made significant contributions as president including the historic breakthrough to China in the early 1970's. He was undone by his own fear, suspicion and paranoia combined with an inherently ruthless nature. He committed criminal acts in trying to help cover up the Watergate scandal and resigned the presidency in 1974 rather than face impeachment and removal from office. His birth chart is shown in Figure 32.

Nixon was a near-caricature of the Water type. He had black hair and dark eyes with black eyebrows and a dark, swarthy complexion. His habitual frown, along with the dark suits and ties he favored, gave him a brooding, shadowy appearance. His forced smile and awkward manner were those of a man who was clearly uncomfortable in his own skin.

Nixon was born under the sign of Capricorn and, besides the Sun, had two important planets, Jupiter and Mercury, in that sign (oval A). If Nixon had been blessed with strong Fire energies to help lighten and counterbalance his powerful Water, he might have channeled his behavior into more positive directions. Unfortunately

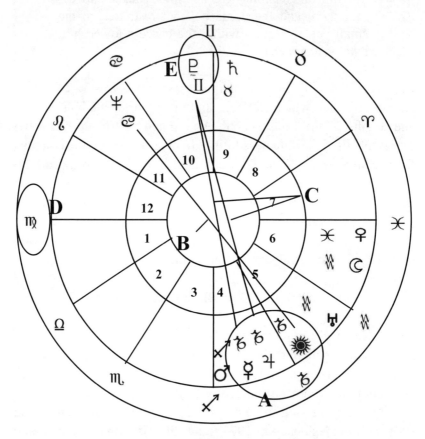

FIGURE 32.
THE BIRTH CHART OF RICHARD NIXON[69]

his chart has only a single planet, Mars, in a Fire sign. To make matters worse, each of the planets in Capricorn is in a tense relationship with other planets, an indication of chronic psychological stress. The Sun is in direct opposition to Neptune (line B) which, according to one authority, can indicate emotional difficulties or weakness of character.[70] Both Mercury and Jupiter are in opposition to Pluto (lines C), which can indicate emotional blockages and sometimes a tendency to exploit people.[71]

The constricted quality of Nixon's personality may be partially explained by his rising sign, Virgo (oval D). Virgo, as I noted, has an important Metal component and well-balanced Metal is necessary for the free expression of emotion. When Virgo rises but the person has other significant energy imbalances, the result can be a cramped, inhibited personal style. Virgo is often associated with an instinct for service, which may have been one of Nixon's original motivations for going into politics. Unfortunately, those instincts were distorted by other negative forces in his personality.

Pluto's placement sheds light, not only on Nixon's character, but on his legendary stamina and endurance. Pluto, a Wood planet of energy and dynamism, is associated with the ability to rebound from adversity and make new beginnings. Its placement near the Midheaven (oval E), combined with the natural tenacity of the Water type, helps explain Nixon's remarkable resiliency and ability to reinvent himself. It helps account, too, for his attachment to fine living and his habit of associating with super-wealthy friends. Pluto is associated, among other things, with great wealth and, if Nixon was not a Plutocrat himself, he may have felt that spending time with them was the next best thing.

The great irony about Richard Nixon is that, like many Water types, he was keenly perceptive and had a natural gift for reading people and their motives. His fatal blind spot was in failing to understand himself and in projecting his own shortcomings onto other people. When, on August 9, 1974, he was about to leave the White House for the last time, Nixon gave a farewell speech to his White House staff. He made a comment at the end—ostensibly about the press and others who had been critical of him—in which he unknowingly summed up the reasons for his own downfall:

> Always give your best, never get discouraged, never be petty; always remember others may hate you, but those who hate you don't win unless you hate them, and then you destroy yourself.

Another man who was born under the sign of Capricorn, and who expressed the sign's deepest and most transcendent qualities, was an illumined yogi who dedicated his life to the spiritual well-being of others.

Capricorn Exalted: the Birth Chart of Paramahansa Yogananda

Paramahansa Yogananda was born in India in 1893 and came to the United States in 1920. One of his goals was to help unite East and West by bringing the spiritual teachings of India to the West. He founded Self Realization Fellowship, an international organization with world headquarters in Los Angeles, and lived in the U.S. for over 30 years. Besides teaching, lecturing and overseeing the activities of SRF, Yogananda wrote extensively about his experiences. He is best known as the author of the spiritual classic *Autobiography of a Yogi.*

After Yogananda's passing in 1952, Self Realization Fellowship continued to flourish and today provides spiritual guidance and instruction to thousands of followers around the world.[72] Its message is the universal teaching of Hinduism: that Spirit resides within every person and that every individual has the inborn capacity to experience God directly through meditation. The technique Yogananda taught is Kriya Yoga, an ancient practice based in part on *pranayama,* the conscious control of life energies. I discuss *pranayama* in Chapter 7.

Yogananda's birth chart is shown in Figure 33. His birth sign, Capricorn (oval A), is complemented by his Moon in the Twelfth House, the House of Pisces, a place of inwardness and spirituality. Like Lincoln, Yogananda's depth and spiritual capacities can be traced in part to the combined energies of Capricorn and Pisces.

Although he spent much time in deep meditation, Yogananda was far from a recluse who sought only solitude. He had an outgoing, charismatic personality that made him an inspiring public speaker and enabled him to found, organize and oversee a large and active worldwide organization. Yogananda's dynamism and love of life can be seen in his rising sign, Leo, and in his Moon rising in Leo on the eastern horizon (oval B).

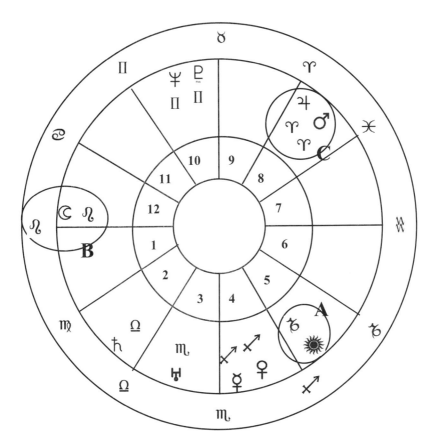

FIGURE 33.
THE BIRTH CHART OF PARAMAHANSA YOGANANDA[73]

Like Capricorns the world over, Yogananda had an earnest, purposeful attitude and took great satisfaction in achieving practical goals. He worked tirelessly to spread the teachings of yoga, eventually returning for a time to India to help oversee a second major center there called the Yogoda Satsanga Society.

Yogananda, like many Capricorns, was a talented musician. He wrote a number of devotional songs and chants which are still performed today by devotees around the world.

As a Capricorn, and one who chose to be a mountain goat who

would scale the heights of spiritual awareness, Yogananda needed a generous helping of courage to face the inevitable challenges that would come his way. That courage came, as it did with Martin Luther King, Thomas Jefferson and others, in part from the sign of Aries. Yogananda's chart has two important planets in Aries, Jupiter and Mars, the latter being Aries' ruling planet (oval C).

Like several of the personalities discussed above, Yogananda's birth and rising signs represent strongly contrasting energies. Leo and Capricorn are opposites in much the same way as, for example, Leo and Cancer in George W. Bush's chart or Leo and Libra in Bill Clinton's. But Yogananda, unlike the others, had resolved the inner contradictions that the birth and rising signs often represent. He was able to use his dynamic outer energies for purely positive purposes—to complement rather than conceal his inner feelings and impulses.

THE SIGN OF VIRGO: PURITY AND SERVICE

Virgo's symbol, the virgin, captures the sense of purity and perfection that represent Virgo at its best. Virgo's two primary impulses, to love and to serve, express the Earth and Metal energies of the sign. Virgos have a strong sense of duty and right behavior, are careful and meticulous and pay close attention to detail—all expressions of strong or even dominant Metal energies. Virgo's ruling planet, Mercury, rules the Metal sign of Gemini as well.

When the energies of Virgo are imbalanced or poorly developed, they can lead to a variety of ills ranging from fussiness, excessive criticism and condescension to obsessive or compulsive behaviors, guilt, inhibition or anxiety. People with strong Virgoan influences often take an active interest in health and hygiene. This recalls the discussion in Chapter 3 of Freud's Anal Stage and the development of Metal energies in the growing child. The Sixth House, the House of Virgo, is known as the House of Health.

One woman who expressed the highest qualities of Virgo decided on her life's work as a child. She went on to found a charitable order that continues its work even after her death.

Love and Sacrifice: The Birth Chart of Mother Teresa

Mother Teresa was born Agnes Bojaxhiu in Macedonia on August 27, 1910. She felt a call to the religious life at the age of twelve. She left her family home at the age of 18 and joined the Sisters of Loreto in Ireland. From there she went to India where she became a teacher in Calcutta. In 1948 she requested permission to leave her teaching duties and go to work among the poorest of the poor in Calcutta's slums. In 1950 she founded her own order, the Missionaries of Charity, which now has branches throughout the world.

For her work Mother Teresa received the Nobel Peace Prize in 1979. On her death in 1997 the government of India gave her a state funeral to honor her life and work.

Mother Teresa's birth chart is shown in Figure 34. Its focus is the conjunction of the Sun and Mars in the sign of Virgo (oval A). The Sun-Mars conjunction confers tremendous energy and its placement in Virgo encouraged Mother Teresa to direct those energies toward a life of service. Her Sun in the Ninth House, associated with foreign languages and foreign travel, is consistent with a person who left her native country at an early age never to return.

The Gift of Sagittarius Rising

To spend her life working among the poorest and most needy people on earth, Mother Teresa needed more than an instinct for service and even more than faith—she needed an unshakably positive and optimistic nature. Without it she would surely have sunk eventually into depression. Mother Teresa was able to do the extraordinarily difficult work she did, and do it for so long, because she was blessed with the rising sign of Sagittarius, a sign of optimism, happiness and good feeling (oval B). The energies of Sagittarius helped her maintain her spirits even in the most difficult and trying of circumstances.

The power of Sagittarius rising is evident in the career of another prominent personality whose career took him in a very different direction: former president Ronald Reagan. Reagan's optimism and high spirits were legendary, and in fact his critics accused him of ignoring the uglier realities of American life and seeing only the pleasant façade on the surface. I discuss Reagan and his vision of the City on a Hill later in this chapter.

The Darkness

There is a puzzling feature in Mother Teresa's chart that may have had a different meaning for her than for some other people. Her Sun and Moon are in a tense Square relationship—a 90° angle separating them (line C). This is believed to represent a conflict between the conscious mind or Ego, represented by the Sun, and the Unconscious represented by the Moon. In many people it appears to create a powerful drive for outward success, possibly to compensate for some perceived inner deficiency.

Mother Teresa was as highly motivated as many successful people but her goals were far more unselfish, and required far more sacrifice, than is usually the case. Even so, her Sun-Moon square could represent an ordinary emotional conflict that drove her to a life of service to make up for some inner sense of inadequacy. On the other hand, it may have represented a different kind of conflict between the conscious mind and the Unconscious—one between ordinary daily life and the awareness of God. Mother Teresa had a continuing, deeply painful inner experience that she called "the darkness" and that one source described as follows:

> Hidden from all eyes, hidden even from those closest to her, was her interior life marked by an experience of a deep, painful and abiding feeling of being separated from God, even rejected by Him, along with an ever-increasing longing for His love.... Through the darkness she mystically participated in the thirst of Jesus, in His painful and burning longing for love, and she shared in the interior desolation of the poor.[75]

Mother Teresa, like many saints and near-saints, was given an inner cross to bear that reflected both her own humanity and the human condition. On a personal level, the tension between her Sun

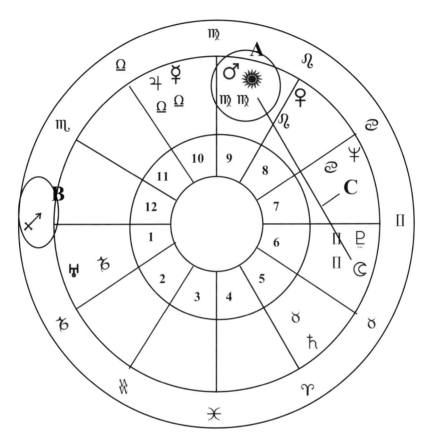

FIGURE 34.
THE BIRTH CHART OF MOTHER TERESA[74]

and Moon—her conscious and unconscious awareness—may have represented her separation from God, a painful experience for someone as spiritually attuned as she. More generally, it may have symbolized human suffering and society's indifference to it—and her duty to experience the pain and rejection of the poor even as she was working so hard to overcome it.

THE SIGN OF TAURUS: HUMANITY AND THE ARTS

Taurus' symbol is the bull, a domestic animal associated with farming and with a life lived close to the land. The sign's dominant Earth energies are evident in the Taurean's agreeable, affectionate disposition, strong appetites and equally strong need for stability and security.

Taurus' ruling planet, Venus, is closely associated with love, beauty and the arts. Taurus, along with Capricorn, is one of the traditional musical signs and Taureans are drawn not only to music but to the arts in general. Tchaikovsky, Leonardo da Vinci and Shakespeare were all born under the sign of Taurus.

The Taurean's Achilles Heel is his sometimes deficient or imbalanced Wood and Water energies. They can cause laziness, stubbornness or a tendency to fall into ruts or routines. One explanation may be the Taurean's dominant Earth energies, which tend to suppress and weaken Water, the energy of drive and will power, through the Controlling Cycle.

At their best, Taureans are both caring and creative people. One of the 20th century's most beloved violinists expressed the finest qualities of Taurus. He was a child prodigy whose musical career spanned nearly 75 years.

Signs of a Musician: the Birth Chart of Yehudi Menuhin

In his autobiography, *Unfinished Journey*, Yehudi Menuhin acknowledged the direct, straightforward pattern of his career. He was born in 1916 in New York City and, after his family moved to California, began to study violin at the age of four. He made his professional debut at age seven with the San Francisco Symphony. Four years later he appeared at Carnegie Hall in New York City and his performance of the Beethoven Violin Concerto made him an international star. When Albert Einstein heard him play, he is reported to have said, "Now I know there is a God in heaven." Menuhin went on to have one of the longest and most distinguished careers of any modern musician.

Menuhin's birth chart is shown in Figure 35. The source of his musical gifts, like his career, is clear and straightforward. The two musical signs, Taurus and Capricorn, are his birth sign and rising

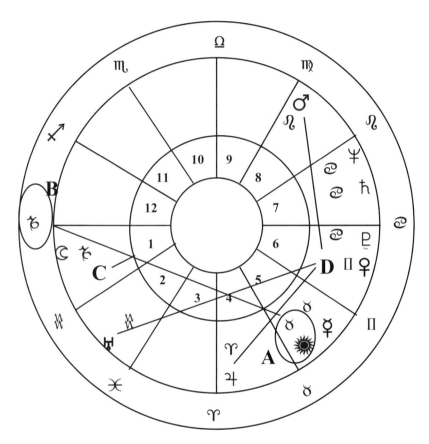

FIGURE 35.
THE BIRTH CHART OF YEHUDI MENUHIN[76]

sign respectively (ovals A and B). The Sun in Taurus is in a harmonious Trine relationship with the Capricorn rising sign (line C), magnifying the effects of both. Mercury is in Taurus as well. Venus, the ruler of Taurus and of the arts, has harmonious connections with three other planets—Uranus, Mars and Jupiter (lines meeting at D). These placements suggest not only artistic talent but exceptional charm and sensitivity—all hallmarks of Menuhin's playing.

Menuhin's birth and rising signs, Taurus and Capricorn, are both Earth signs and his life exemplified the caring and concern typical of the Earth type. Besides his concerts and recordings, Menuhin was a conductor and educator, founding music schools for young people and participating in many charitable and philan-thropic causes around the world. He was multilingual and multicul-tural and his musical tastes reflected those broad understandings. He made a number of innovative recordings, including work with the Indian master Ravi Shankar combining the sounds of the violin and sitar. He was knighted by Queen Elizabeth, received the Legion of Honor from France and many other international awards. He died in Berlin in 1999 at the age of 82.

Menuhin's seriousness as a musician, and as a human being, are reflected in his Capricorn rising sign. His Moon in Capricorn, like that of Napoleon and Lincoln, subjected him to occasional bouts of depression. Uranus, befitting a man who was both an innovator and a humanitarian, is in its own sign, Aquarius.

PART 2. LIFE ENERGY AND RELATIONSHIPS

Chapter 3 showed that some of the most basic emotional conflicts in the individual are represented by tensions within the Controlling Cycle. Those same tensions play themselves out in virtually every relationship. For example, Fire and Metal compete in the individ-ual to make a person relatively fun-loving and spontaneous or more restrained, responsible and controlled. In a relationship between a Fire type and a Metal type, the same conflict is almost certain to be present. When he wants to spend money on a new car but she wants to save for college tuition or retirement; or when she wants to go out of town for the weekend but he feels obliged to stay home and take care of responsibilities, the struggle is between the im-pulses of Fire and Metal. If the couple can find a healthy balance between their competing dominant impulses, the relationship is more likely to thrive; if not, problems are almost inevitable.

Even for people who are the same type or complementary

types, conflicting energies will occasionally clash. The Five Elements can serve as a model for understanding, and possibly correcting, some of those conflicts. To illustrate, I give two examples—the first a virtually universal struggle as old as the human race, and the second a variation on the same theme featuring a common pairing of Enneagram types.

WOOD, EARTH AND THE BATTLE OF THE SEXES

In Chapter 3 I described the natural tensions between Wood and its Controlling Cycle neighbors, Earth and Metal, as a portrait of civilization. An important part of that portrait——the natural tension between Wood and Earth—plays itself out every day in the age-old struggle between men and women. In Part 1 we saw that the traditional male qualities of strength and aggressiveness are rooted in Wood energies—in the Wood signs of Aries and Scorpio, the Wood-Fire signs of Leo and Sagittarius and the Wood planets of Mars and Pluto. The traditional female qualities of love, compassion, sensitivity and service are grounded in Earth energies—in the Earth signs of Virgo, Taurus and Capricorn, the Metal-Earth sign of Libra and the Earth planet of Venus and the Moon.

Although society is changing rapidly today, men are still to some extent the aggressive breadwinners who venture out into the world and wrest a living from it. Many women still stay at home and take care of the home and children. As the relationship between men and women continues to evolve, that process can be better understood if it is seen in terms of the interplay, and gradual development and integration, of Wood and Earth energies.

Men and Women, Mars and Venus

John Gray's popular book, *Men are from Mars, Women are from Venus*, is an insightful analysis of the personality differences between men and women. Gray shows how a greater understanding of those differences can lessen conflict and improve relationships. Although Gray does not discuss life energy or astrology directly, the tongue-in-cheek title of his book refers to the planets that most clearly represent Wood and Earth energies. In introducing the male and female traits that he believes best illustrate gender differences, Gray describes men as follows:

> Martians value power, competency, efficiency, and achievement. They are always doing things to improve themselves and develop their power and skills. Their sense of self is defined through their ability to achieve results. They experience fulfillment primarily through success and accomplishment.[77]

Women, on the other hand, have the following qualities, according to Gray:

> Venusians have different values. They value love, communication, beauty and relationships. They spend a lot of time supporting, helping and nurturing one another. Their sense of self is defined through their feelings and the quality of their relationships. They experience fulfillment through sharing and relating.[78]

These words could, without changing a line, have been written to describe the qualities of Wood and Earth energies and the primary traits of the Wood and Earth personality types. Power, success and accomplishment are hallmarks of Wood while love, nurturing and support define the essence of Earth. Gray's overall message could be restated in energy terms as follows: The natural tensions between men and women come about because men are dominant in Wood energies while women are dominant in Earth. If women learn to better understand men's Wood qualities, and men learn to better understand women's Earth qualities, the sexes will get along much better.

The Mothers of Wood and Earth

The relationships of the Nurturing Cycle can help flesh out the natural polarity between men and women. Women tend to build and sustain relationships primarily through sharing feelings and experiences—that is, by talking with one other. For women, process is as important as content. Knowing that her companion is interested and paying attention is essential for a woman, a way of validating both herself and her feelings.

The Nurturing Cycle confirms the natural connection between communication and support. Fire, the energy of speech and expressiveness, nourishes Earth, the energy of caring and relationships. In Chinese terminology, Fire is the Mother of Earth. Women as a gender have traditionally embodied the truth of that leg of the Nurturing Cycle. In their historic roles, women can be described generally as Earth energy nourished by Fire.

Men as a gender have been, not surprisingly, the traditional energetic opposites of women. Whereas women have found emotional nourishment through the verbal sharing of feelings, men have tended to keep their feelings to themselves, insisting on a certain zone of privacy. John Gray refers to that habit as a man "going into his cave." In relationships, men have long found meaning, not primarily through talking with other men, but by doing things with them—fishing, hiking, playing sports or sitting quietly around a campfire.

Water is the energy of listening and silence and Wood is the energy of action and accomplishment. In the Nurturing Cycle, Water nourishes Wood—it is the Mother of Wood. Men as a gender have embodied the truth of that leg of the Nurturing Cycle. Men can be described, in historical terms at least, as Wood energy nourished by Water. The traditional male and female patterns are shown in Figure 36.

Avoiding Stereotypes

Not every man, of course, is a Wood type and not every woman is
an Earth type. Many men today have strong, well-developed Earth
energies. They include counselors, therapists, nurses, social workers, workers in charitable and religious organizations and many
others. Many women today have strong and well-developed Wood
energies—lawyers, politicians, business people, athletes and soldiers among others.

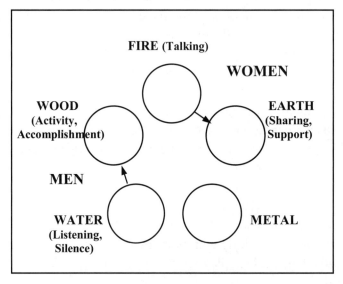

FIGURE 36.
THE TRADITIONAL ENERGY PROFILES
OF MEN AND WOMEN

Women have not only entered the work force in large numbers,
they now occupy positions of great power and influence. In the
U.S. women now run major corporations and hold senior political
posts. A women currently serves as Secretary of State and another
is being widely touted as a future presidential candidate. Interna-
tionally there have been recent women heads of state in Great Britain, Ireland, Israel, the Philippines, India and Pakistan. To the extent that classifying men and women as Wood and Earth has

become an inaccurate stereotype, it illustrates how rapidly society has evolved in recent decades and how quickly men and women are developing their non-dominant energies.

Energy principles suggest that the growing parity of men and women is an important part of the overall process by which individuals and society are becoming more whole. Earth, the dominant female energy, is, as we have seen, at the center of both the original Five Elements diagram (Figure 2) and the chakra system (Figure 4). The longstanding subjugation of women represents the denial of a fundamental truth— that love and compassion are at the center of the human organism, and that developing those qualities is a key to growth at every level.

In Part 3 below I describe the development of American society in terms of the gradual evolution and balancing of Wood and Earth energies. It is no coincidence that society's dramatic progress since the beginning of the 20th century has coincided with the rise of women during the same period.

Love and Growth: the 2-5 Enneagram Couple

Even when a man is not a Wood type or a woman is not an Earth type, traditional male and female energies can be a kind of background influence that affects relationships in important ways. The relationship between the Enneagram Two and Five is an example.

Spiritual teachers often say that people meet and form relationships with those who can teach them important life lessons. If so, the pairing of the Enneagram Two and Five surely illustrates that principle. The Two and Five are as close to polar opposites as one is likely to find among the nine types. The Two, often described as the Lover, is an unambiguous Earth type: caring, affectionate, relatively sociable and extroverted. Giving and sharing define the Two and provide much of her sense of identity and self-worth. Material things matter to her and give her a fundamental sense of well being. In a relationship, a sense of emotional connection to her partner is vital. In talking with him, process is as important as content—she must feel that he shares, or at least understands and supports, her feelings whether she clearly expresses them or not.

The Five lacks the very qualities the Two most values—empathy and a sense of emotional connection. The Five, often called the Observer, is the most emotionally disengaged of the nine types. He is an introverted Metal-Water Head type who, perhaps by repressing difficult emotions such as fear or grief, has to some extent lost touch with his body and therefore with his feelings. While the Two relates to the world, and to her partner, mainly through emotion, the Five experiences life mainly through ideas. What the Five most needs (or at least thinks he needs) is for his partner to behave rationally and consistently—to support his life strategy of succeeding by figuring things out and staying one step ahead by using his wits. To make matters worse, the Five often has a streak of asceticism or self-denial that directly conflicts with his partner's love of comfort and material pleasure.

Given their radical differences, it may seem unlikely that the Two and Five would ever get together, but they often do. Although conflicts are inevitable, each partner gets something of value from the other. The Five, who lacks vibrancy and emotion in his life, is energized by his partner and by others whom she brings into their circle. The Two, who as an Earth type is vulnerable to feelings of neediness and insecurity, is attracted to her partner's self-sufficiency and inner strength. Whether the two ever succeed in growing beyond their personal limitations or not, the relationship itself makes them both, in a sense, more whole.

The natural tensions between the Two and Five are illustrated by the conflict between Earth and Water in the Controlling Cycle. The Two, an Earth type, might be said to control the Five through her greater energy, expressiveness and sense of connection. The Five, however, has developed an effective strategy for holding his own in the relationship. Anger is a powerful tool for maintaining control and the Five, although nominally a Metal-Water type, often possesses a considerable reservoir of the Wood energies of frustration and anger.

The Five is on the same general continuum as the schizoid type discussed in Chapter 3. As I noted there, the schizoid type tends to react to a sense of disconnection with frustration and anger. In the Two-Five pairing, the Five feels even more disconnected than usual when he compares himself with his relatively well-integrated partner. He may get angry at her for behaving inconsistently or irrationally, but the real problem is that he cannot relate to or understand her feelings because he has so few of his own. He justifies his attitude by saying, and believing, that he is standing up for principle—but principle is so important to him only because he has so few other resources to rely on. Therefore the Five uses anger to take the moral high ground, throw his partner on the defensive and maintain the balance of power in the relationship.

Thus, even for a couple whose dominant energies are not Wood and Earth, the male's Wood energies and the female's Earth energies are never far out of sight. The natural tension between them can be one of the commonest sources of conflict in the relationship.

Energy Insights for the Two and Five

The Two and Five tend to get stuck in negative patterns because what they need is the opposite of what they want or what feels natural to them. The Five wants to analyze the relationship and tell his partner where she is going wrong—but what he needs is to find his own feelings and talk about them with his partner. The act of doing so will help create the Earth energies of connection, precisely what the Five lacks. To help get in touch with his feelings, the Five may want to try energy or body-centered techniques, concentrating on freeing up the hidden or blocked Earth energies of empathy and compassion.

The Two, who is good at expressing feelings but not so good at explaining them, needs to be clearer with her partner about how she feels and take advantage of his natural ability to understand and apply those understandings. If she learns to verbalize her feelings rather than simply expecting him to guess or sense them—something that is extraordinarily hard for him to do—she may be surprised at how caring he can be.

PART 3. LIFE ENERGY AND SOCIETY

If life energies underlie the attitudes and behaviors of every individual, and if they influence every relationship, they must ultimately shape society itself.[79] The cumulative energies of thousands or millions of people, expressed in opinion polls, focus groups, at the ballot box and elsewhere, elect public officials and bring about policies that express the will of the majority.

The connection between society and the dominant energies of the people within it is fairly clear in a democracy. It is harder to see when a dictator frustrates the will of the people. When a Saddam Hussein or Kim Jyong Il takes power, the combined desires of millions of individuals can be ineffective to overcome the aggressive intentions of a few. Even then, however, familiar energy principles can be instructive.

In Chapter 3 we saw how, in the schizoid personality type, the Water energies of fear and the Wood energies of frustration and anger can overwhelm the Earth energies of connection, causing a split in consciousness. An authoritarian government creates a kind of mass version of the schizoid pattern—an unhealthy society in which people's feelings and desires are disconnected from their everyday reality. Oppressed peoples, like the schizoid type, may want to be connected both to their fellow citizens and to society as a whole—that is, they may want democracy—but they can only have it when some combination of factors overcomes the fear, intimidation and aggression that are preventing it. The energy relationships are identical to those in the schizoid pattern and are shown in Figure 37.

Earth Energy and the Social Contract

Democracy in the modern world began with the French and American revolutions in the late 18th century. A major inspiration was the French philosopher Jean Jacques Rousseau and his groundbreaking essay, "The Social Contract," published in 1762. In it Rousseau described the condition of mankind before civilization,

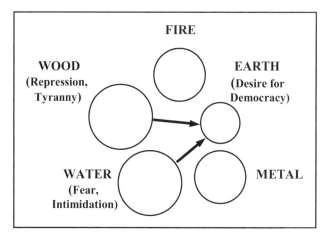

FIGURE 37.
THE ENERGY PROFILE IN AUTHORITARIAN REGIMES:
SOCIETY'S VERSION OF THE SCHIZOID PATTERN

and even to some extent in his own day, as a "state of nature" in which force was the ruling principle.

Rousseau's proposal, revolutionary for its time, was that a civil state be established based on the principle of human freedom. In return for giving up certain "natural rights," people would be given the protections and privileges of membership in the state. Rousseau summarized the Social Contract as follows:

> Each of us puts his person and all his power in common under the supreme direction of the general will, and, in our corporate capacity, we receive each member as an indivisible part of the whole.

Rousseau's vision of a community in which each person would be an indivisible part of the whole was equivalent to saying that Earth energy was assuming a new importance in human affairs. Rousseau's own words confirm the link between Earth, the energy of parental and family love, and the new civil state he envisioned:

> The most ancient of all societies, and the only one that is natural, is the family. The family then may be called

the first model of political societies: the ruler corresponds to the father, and the people to the children;
and all, being born free and equal, alienate their liberty
only for their own advantage.

Democracy and the Holistic Impulse

Rousseau's vision, and its acceptance by large numbers of people
as a new principle in human affairs, was a major turning point in
human development—a dramatic illustration of the Holistic Impulse at work. Less than thirty years after the publication of "The
Social Contract," revolutions in France and the United States gave
birth to the first modern democracies. In the 200+ years since, the
Wood energies of the state of nature have gradually given way to
the evolving Earth energies of democracy and equality. Today
democracy is in the ascendant with over 100 functioning democracies in the world by one count,[80] and with strong democratic pressures being brought to bear where it does not yet exist.

In spite of democracy's dramatic progress over the last two
centuries, it is still not clear when or if Rousseau's vision of the
civil state as a kind of extended family will be fully realized. Almost since the beginning, strong opposing forces have tried to prevent the circle of empathy from growing so wide that it includes all
members of society. In the U.S. as elsewhere, opponents have been
motivated generally by the Wood energies of independence, self-
reliance and self interest.

A Split in the American Psyche

The democratic impulse is more than just an undiluted expression
of Earth energies. Democracy represents the Earth qualities of
sharing, equality and concern for other members of society but it
expresses, too, a desire for independence and a certain amount of
personal control and autonomy. The latter are Wood qualities and
the patriots who went to war for freedom and independence were
expressing a powerful combination of Earth and Wood. Although

their ultimate goal was peace, that goal was attainable only because the patriots were willing to make war to achieve it. Their success was a measure of how strong and well-developed the Wood energies of the early Americans were. Therein lies a clue to the strange split in the American psyche that has lasted for over two hundred years and that persists today.

From its earliest days, American society has been sharply divided over what democracy means and who is entitled to its full benefits. On the one hand, Americans have set a high standard of freedom and equality for the rest of the world, and the U.S. has been among the most open and generous nations on earth. On the other hand, there has always been a clear dividing line between those who, in Rousseau's phrase, are "indivisible parts of the whole" and those who have been consigned to the margins of society to be neglected and forgotten.

In the beginning, the only full citizens were adult white males, and even they received widely varying treatment from government depending on their wealth. There was slavery in the U.S. for 90 years after independence and women were denied the vote for nearly 150 years. Men, women and children alike were often forced to work under inhumane conditions until reforms were enacted in the 1930's. Only since the 1960's has government begun to address the medical needs of the elderly and indigent. Today, 230 years after independence, there are still strong remnants of racism and other forms of prejudice and inequality. The U.S., the world's richest nation, lags behind other developed countries in the resources it devotes to a number of basic human needs.

The circle of empathy has steadily widened in the U.S. over the last two centuries, but progress has been slow and uneven because, in spite of Americans' strong and continuously developing Earth energies, their powerful Wood energies remain a potent counterweight. Nowhere was the power of Wood more evident than in the westward expansion that began in the early 19th century.

Manifest Destiny and the Archetype of Wood

The Revolution proved that Americans were a brave and determined people but war was not something they wanted—it was more or less forced on them by the King's oppressive policies. The westward expansion was different; Americans enthusiastically embraced the challenge of exploring and settling an entire continent.

The spirit of the early Americans embodied all the qualities of the Wood-type personality—boldness, initiative, bravery, vision, a willingness to take risks and a sense of life as a great adventure. Two writers on Chinese medicine have given the Wood type a revealing name: "the Pioneer."[81] Recalling Jung's discussion of symbols and their meanings, they suggest that the term has near-archetypal importance. If so, the early American pioneers were virtual symbols of dominant Wood energies.

Wood—the Energy of Expansion, Weapons and Aggression

The westward expansion began, actually and symbolically, with the Lewis and Clark expedition in 1804. It was commissioned by President Thomas Jefferson who, as we saw earlier, was himself born under the Wood sign of Aries. Jefferson's boldness and sense of unlimited possibilities for the new nation helped set the tone for the Era of Discovery. It was Jefferson who, even though he lacked constitutional authority, completed the Louisiana Purchase in 1803, buying over 800,000 square miles of territory from France— stretching from the Mississippi River to the Rocky Mountains and from Louisiana to Canada—for $15 million. The Louisiana Purchase is one of history's most dramatic examples of the Wood impulse for growth and expansion.

Physical aggression is another hallmark of Wood and the early Americans did not shrink from making war if it helped them achieve their objectives. They battled the Indian tribes for decades, killing many thousands and finally moving the others to reservations. They fought the Mexican army and took Texas away from

Mexico. Even wildlife were not spared. The buffalo, which once covered the prairies in the tens of millions, were cruelly slaughtered almost to the point of extinction. Then, as the Era of Discovery was coming to an end, it gave way to the Era of the Cowboy, when a man's six-gun became his best friend. Today, 150 years later, Americans' love affair with their guns is as passionate as ever.

Whether one believes the westward expansion represented the fulfillment of God's plan—Manifest Destiny—or of man's ambitions, or both, it proved beyond doubt the extraordinary power of Americans' Wood energies.

Abolition: a Great Holistic Leap Forward

After Americans achieved democracy, the next great holistic advance was the abolition of slavery in the 1860's. It was a result of the greatest collision of Wood and Earth energies in American history—the Civil War. The Earth forces of union and abolition were arrayed against the Wood forces of slavery and secession. Slavery was a long-standing, home-grown institution that formed the basis, not only of the Southern economy but of Southern culture itself. To overcome it the Union forces had to struggle for four years against a fierce and passionately dedicated Confederate army.

The scale of the war, and the tragedy of countrymen killing one another, recalls other epic battles in history. One of those was the struggle on the fields of Kurukshetra recounted in the Bhagavad Gita, the great spiritual classic of India, sometimes referred to as the Hindu Bible. In the opening chapter of the Gita, the warrior-prince Arjuna, who is about to go into battle, ponders the futility of war as he sees his own relatives and friends lined up on opposing sides.

> Seeing that these stand here, ready to die, For whose sake life was fair, and pleasure pleased, And power grew precious:- grandsires, sires, and sons. Brothers, and fathers-in-law, and

> sons-in-law, Elders and friends! Shall I deal
> death on these Even though they seek to slay
> us?[82]

The Bhagavad Gita uses the tragedy of war and senseless destruction as a metaphor for the suffering in life that is dictated by the
Law of Karma. The Civil War was caused by the evil of slavery
and, before it was over, it inflicted untold suffering on both sides.
The cosmic workings of the Law of Karma are particularly clear
and poignant in the Civil War. That fact was not lost on Abraham
Lincoln, the most spiritual of our presidents. Although Lincoln was
a Christian, he saw the war in distinctly karmic terms. In his
Second Inaugural Address, delivered shortly before the end of the
war and his own death, Lincoln said the following:

> Fondly do we hope, fervently do we pray, that this
> mighty scourge of war may speedily pass away;
> Yet, if God wills that it continue until all the wealth
> piled by the bondsman's two hundred and fifty
> years of unrequited toil shall be sunk, and until
> every drop of blood drawn with the lash shall be
> paid by another drawn with the sword, as was said
> three thousand years ago, so still it must be said
> "the judgments of the Lord are true and righteous
> altogether."

From an Asian perspective, Lincoln was attuned, not only to the
Law of Karma, but to the inscrutable workings of the Tao. Like all
great leaders, he sensed the flow of history and was wise enough
not to resist it but to let the current carry him at its own pace. He
bided his time throughout the war, issuing his Emancipation
Proclamation in 1863, freeing slaves in some states, and finally
sending the 13th Amendment to Congress at the end of the war,
abolishing slavery in all states forever.

The cosmic significance Lincoln saw in the Civil War reinforces the idea that it was a watershed moment in American history. In Rousseau's terms, it meant that the state of nature, or rule

by force, would no longer be allowed to coexist alongside the Social Contract. In energy terms it meant that the Wood energies of oppression and cruelty had shrunk to the point where, domestically at least, military force would no longer be needed to overcome it. The holistic battles of the future would be fought, for the most part, in less dramatic settings, and between more subtle forms of Wood and Earth energies.

The Early 20th Century, Robber Barons and the Bully Pulpit

The end of the Civil War did not, of course, mean the end of racial violence in the U.S. Some refer to Reconstruction, the period in the South following the war, as the Second Civil War. It was an ugly period that saw lynchings, rapes, murders, cross burnings and the rise of the Ku Klux Klan. In the North, racial as well as religious and gender discrimination were widespread. White male Protestants were still, in many ways, the only Americans with full civil rights.

As the 20th century dawned and violence and direct physical oppression were on the wane, aggressive business practices became a kind of substitute outlet for excess Wood energies. Employment abuses were widespread, and the labor movement would develop as a way of balancing the rights of employers and workers. There had always been unscrupulous business people but, during the Gilded Age at the turn of the century, the expanding economy allowed them to thrive as never before. J.P. Morgan, Andrew Carnegie, John D. Rockefeller and others were brilliant, but often ruthless, men whose dubious tactics helped make them fabulously wealthy, in part because government made so little effort to stop them. The Robber Baron became a symbol, like the warrior of earlier times, of the bold, all-conquering dominant Wood type.

At that moment in history, Teddy Roosevelt emerged as the most compelling political figure of his time. Roosevelt owed his success, in energy terms, to an exceptional blend of all five basic energies. His Wood qualities were among the most dominant. A veteran of the Spanish-American War where he had led his Rough Riders on the charge up San Juan Hill, Roosevelt was aggressive, loved a good fight and had a vision of the country's greatness and the energy to match it. He boldly launched the Panama Canal project and saw it through to completion. Building on the Monroe Doctrine of the previous century, he announced that the United States had the sole right to intervene in Latin American affairs. To reinforce his message, he sent the American fleet on a very public "good will tour" of the world's ports. His term "the Bully Pulpit " referred to the presidency as a platform for forcefully urging action on important issues. The term suggested that, while the time for real bullies might be passing, the power of Wood energy was still vital for mobilizing people and getting things done.

Another of Roosevelt's mottos—"Speak softly and carry a big stick"—was a highly effective blend of Earth and Wood. It expressed a desire for peace and conciliation but always supported by the implied threat of force. Indeed, Roosevelt's Earth energies were as vital and well-developed as his Wood. He mediated the Russo-Japanese War in 1905 and was awarded the Nobel Peace Prize for his efforts. He took a firm stand against the excesses of big business and led antitrust efforts to protect the public against railroad monopolies and other abuses. He took an active role in conservation and the environment, establishing many new national forests and insuring that certain lands would forever be free from development.

Roosevelt's rare combination of Wood and Earth energies—of forcefulness and compassion, boldness and sensitivity to society's more vulnerable interests—was a key to his greatness. His other energies were equally well developed and balanced. He had the vibrancy and enthusiasm of Fire, the intelligence and discipline of Metal and the depth and tenacity of Water. Since TR's day, perhaps only his cousin Franklin and Bill Clinton, among the presidents, have even approached Teddy Roosevelt's exceptional blend of personal qualities and skills.

Women's Suffrage and the Liberation of Earth

As the 20th century was getting underway, the steady growth of Earth energies in society was moving the nation toward another major holistic advance. The opponent this time was not foreign domination or physical enslavement but gender discrimination rooted in the dominant Wood energies of men. Those energies had kept women in a subservient role since the nation's founding nearly a century and a half earlier.

In 1920, following decades of agitation under the leadership of Susan B. Anthony, Katy Stanton and others, the 19th Amendment to the Constitution was ratified, giving women the right to vote. Women's suffrage was a first step toward recognizing women's full equality in society.

When men finally released women from their political bondage, they made it possible for Earth energies to begin playing a far more prominent role in society. The results began to be felt within a few years. Much of society's growth since the 1920's has been due to the greater political power of women—either directly through the vote or indirectly through the power of public opinion. The rise of women, as I noted earlier, is an indication that human energies as a whole are beginning to come into better balance. Everyone can see the damage that the distorted Wood energies of war, conquest, bigotry, domestic violence, greed and other forms of aggression and selfishness have done. If society is to continue reversing those trends, it is essential that women, the primary bearers of Earth energies, play an increasingly prominent role at every level.

Society as a Family: FDR and the New Deal

The economic excesses of the 1920's helped cause the stock market crash of 1929, plunging the nation into the longest and deepest economic decline in its history. Banks failed, credit dried up and business activity slowed to a crawl. Unemployment soared to record levels and tens of millions were without work, money or the

means to feed themselves or their families. Bread lines and soup
kitchens sprang up everywhere. There was widespread misery and
no clear way to put an end to it.

In 1932, during the darkest days of the Depression, Franklin D.
Roosevelt, Teddy's cousin, was elected President. He replaced
Herbert Hoover, a believer in the *laissez-faire* philosophy that
government should play the most limited role possible in the lives
of its citizens. Hoover had tried a few indirect measures to relieve
the economic crisis but they had largely backfired.

FDR, like his famous cousin, was a man of action. Though he
came from a wealthy, patrician upbringing, he had known personal
hardship—he had been crippled by polio—and he had an instinctive sympathy for the poor and the downtrodden. In the first 100
days of his administration, Roosevelt enacted a whole series of
new government programs designed to stimulate the economy and
put people back to work. The federal government became a major
nationwide employer, hiring citizens to build roads, bridges, dams
and bring electricity for the first time to rural areas, mostly in the
South.

The New Deal addressed, not only people's present needs, but
their future concerns. The FDIC was created, guaranteeing that
bank deposits would not be lost and reducing the chances of
another major economic crash. One of the New Deal's lasting lega-
cies was the Social Security system, which assured citizens for the
first time that they would not be left penniless when they grew old.

The New Deal stimulated the economy, helped businesses and
banks get back on their feet and reduced the length and severity of
the Depression. Although the country's economic troubles would
continue for several more years, Roosevelt's policies greatly
reduced the hardships and improved the living conditions of millions of Americans. Roosevelt became one of the most popular
presidents in history and was elected to an unprecedented four
terms.

The New Deal, like democracy itself, redefined the role of government in the lives of its people. Roosevelt's direct intervention in
the economy was in the spirit of Rousseau and his vision of society

as an extended family. Like a caring father, Roosevelt reached out to help those who could not help themselves. His sympathy and compassion were the embodiment of Earth energies—the antithesis of Hoover's belief that individuals should be left, even in the harshest of circumstances, to fend for themselves.

Roosevelt understood, however, that kindness and generosity are not enough, that the Earth energies of compassion must be balanced, whenever possible, by the Wood energies of personal responsibility and individual effort. The Works Progress Administration, or WPA, was based on that principle. Americans were given, not handouts but jobs, helping preserve their sense of dignity and self worth while improving the nation's infrastructure.

Wood and Earth, Republicans and Democrats

Roosevelt's policies, though hugely popular, were not universally admired. People of wealth in particular tended to see the president and his New Deal as a threat to the dominance of business in American life. The conflict between the Earth energies of the New Deal and the Wood energies of unregulated free enterprise were the forerunners of the modern Democratic and Republican parties.

Throughout the 1950's, 60's and 70's, the Earth-Wood balance would shift several times as Republican and Democratic administrations traded power. In 1952, Dwight D. Eisenhower brought a military background and a conservative world view to the White House. Eisenhower's *laissez faire* domestic policies, which had been so disastrous under Hoover, were better suited to the 1950's, which were a time of relative peace and prosperity. Still, Eisenhower, in essentially ignoring important social problems, especially race relations, until he was forced to address them, simply postponed a gathering crisis and insured that it would be worse when it did come.

The 1960's brought a violent end to the surface tranquility of the 1950's. The Vietnam War abroad and racial unrest at home were a dark echo of the 1860's a century earlier. The defeat of the Confederacy had been a crushing blow to the Wood energies of slavery and oppression. A hundred years later, the defeat in Vietnam was equally devastating to the war hawks who believed in the absolute supremacy of the U.S. military. The nation learned, at the cost of 58,000 lives, that it could not simply have its way anywhere in the world. Tragically, that lesson would be forgotten thirty years later with the invasion of Iraq.

At home, the Wood energies of racial discrimination were continuing to weaken as Earth energies grew stronger. Almost exactly a century after the end of the Civil War, the Civil Rights Act of 1964 and the Voting Rights Act of 1965 guaranteed African-Americans certain basic rights that had been denied them for almost 200 years. The circle of racial empathy, which had widened dramatically in the 1860's, expanded a bit further in the 1960's.

The U.S. felt the influence of evolving Earth energies in other ways in the 1960's. President Lyndon Johnson orchestrated the passage of landmark Medicare and Medicaid legislation, providing health coverage for the first time for the elderly and indigent. His Great Society program, a well-intentioned effort to fight poverty and improve education, was less successful. U.S. society had grown more complex, and government bureaucracies more bloated and unwieldy, than in the 1930's. Unlike the New Deal, which had focused heavily on short-term relief, Johnson's Great Society tried to address deeper, more systemic social problems and it did so with very mixed results. The waste and inefficiency of government programs in the 1960's harmed the progressive cause and showed that, even if Rousseau's vision of society as a family is attainable in principle, it will be an exceptionally difficult task for a nation as large and diverse as the U.S.

In the late 1960's and 70's, the presidencies of Richard Nixon and Jimmy Carter were, in part, reactions to the failures of previous administrations. Nixon was elected at the height of the Vietnam War and Carter in the aftermath of the Watergate scandal. Although Nixon was a Republican and Carter a Democrat, both held office while Democratic majorities controlled Congress. The mood of the nation, as it had been since the early 1960's, continued to be relatively liberal.

A Hard Turn to the Right:
Ronald Reagan and the City on a Hill

The pattern changed abruptly with the election of Ronald Reagan in 1980. Although Reagan was elected in part because of Carter's failures, both domestically and in the Iranian hostage crisis, his huge margin of victory signaled the coming of a far more conservative period in American politics. In energy terms, the growing influence of Earth, which had brought about profound improvements in society since the Civil War, was being challenged again by a powerful resurgence of Wood. Just as it had since the nation was founded, Americans' belief in personal independence, self-reliance and self-interest was still at war with their instinct for caring, sharing and community. The Reagan presidency opened a new chapter in that struggle and, at least temporarily, saw Wood energies regain the upper hand.

Reagan exuded the confidence, high spirits and positive attitude that Americans like best in their leaders. He used his tremendous charm and gift for simple, effective images to sell both the American people and himself on his policies. He joked that trees cause pollution, implied that all poor people are lazy and irresponsible, and—while increasing the national debt to record levels—complained that government was a major cause of society's ills.

Reagan chose an extraordinarily ironic image to represent his vision for society. Whether it was because he had originally been a Democrat or for some other reason, his favorite phrase came from the writings of a liberal Christian thinker. John Winthrop, an Englishman who would become the first governor of Massachusetts, sailed to the New World in 1630 with a group of Christian pilgrims. While aboard ship he wrote an essay entitled "A Model of Christian Charity" which foresaw the establishment of a compassionate community in Boston, the city the pilgrims were about to found. Winthrop wrote:

> We must be willing to abridge ourselves of our superfluities for the supply of others' necessities....

> make others' conditions our own....for we must
> consider that we shall be as a City upon a Hill, the
> eyes of all people are upon us; but if our hearts
> shall turn away so that we will not obey, but shall
> be seduced and worship other gods our pleasures,
> and profits, and serve them, it is propounded unto
> us this day, we shall surely perish out of the good
> land whether we pass over this vast sea to possess
> it.

The whole tone and tenor of Reagan's presidency directly contradicted Winthrop's message. In making tax cuts the centerpiece of his domestic agenda, Reagan showed that he and others were not "willing to abridge ourselves of our superfluities for the supply of others' necessities." In cutting funds for important social programs, he showed that he was unwilling to "make others' condition our own." And in failing to condemn the economic excesses of the 1980's, Reagan allowed himself to be "seduced and worship other gods our pleasures, and profits, and serve them..."

Reagan appropriated and used Winthrop's image to persuade Americans to ignore the very ideals Winthrop stood for. It was leaders like Reagan, in fact, whom Winthrop was warning against. If a mark of leadership is a gift for encouraging and bringing out the best and most generous instincts in people, Ronald Reagan was, at least in the domestic sphere, not a good leader.

In international affairs Reagan went about his job like a high-stakes poker player. He succeeded, as gamblers sometimes do, through a combination of skill, audacity and sheer good luck. In dealing with the Soviet Union and the threat of nuclear war, he took extraordinary risks by aggressively confronting the Soviets, vastly increasing military spending and placing nuclear missiles in Europe. Years later, after the Soviet Union had been dismantled, it was learned that the Soviets had feared a first strike by Reagan and had felt compelled to consider a first strike of their own.

As luck would have it, Mikhael Gorbachev became head of the Soviet Union, dramatically changing the dynamics of U.S.-Soviet relations. Reagan's skill in negotiating with Gorbachev was undeniable but it was Gorbachev's conciliatory and statesmanlike approach which, in the end, tipped the balance toward peace. With Gorbachev's approval, the Berlin Wall came down, the Soviet Union was dissolved and the nuclear arms race ended. Reagan was vindicated in his aggressive approach and received joint credit with Gorbachev for ending the Cold War. As they had all his life, Reagan's skill and determination had combined with his unfailing good luck to create the ingredients for success.

Ronald Reagan was born under the sign of Aquarius but his rising sign was Sagittarius—a sign of optimism, confidence, talent and good fortune. Reagan was literally born under a lucky star and, until he developed Alzheimer's disease in old age, it guided him almost unerringly throughout his life. Even in one of his unluckiest moments—when he was almost assassinated shortly after taking office—the bullet that might have killed him missed his heart by inches. He recovered and went on to serve eight full years as president. Fortunately for the United States—especially considering the stakes in the Cold War—Ronald Reagan's good luck was the nation's as well.

Hints of Integration: the Presidency of Bill Clinton

Ronald Reagan was followed in office by another Republican, George H.W. Bush, then by Bill Clinton, a Democrat. Although Clinton was an avowed liberal, some of his major successes represented a creative blending of conservative and liberal ideas. While extending a hand to the less fortunate, Clinton balanced the federal budget for the first time in memory. His welfare reform legislation tempered generosity with a requirement that needy people take more responsibility for their own well being.

Whether based on conviction, political necessity or both, Clinton's approach represented a balancing of the Wood energies of self-reliance, firmness and discipline with the Earth energies of sharing and compassion. Like Franklin Roosevelt and his WPA, Clinton showed that government, like a supportive parent, could be both kind and firm. Clinton's approach suggested that liberals and

conservatives, rather than simply overreacting to each other's excesses, might take positive elements from both sides and synthesize
them into a more balanced and comprehensive political philosophy.

The 21st Century and a Resurgence of Wood

The presidential election of 2000 was less an endorsement of conservatism than it was proof of how evenly divided the U.S. electorate had become. It was the closest election in history and was
decided by the U.S. Supreme Court and 537 votes in the state of
Florida.

After the attacks of September 11 and the U.S. response in Afghanistan, George Bush had two choices—attack the terrorist problem at its roots by reaching out to the Muslim world in a spirit of
reconciliation, or use force to destroy more suspected enemies.
The president, of course, chose the latter course. In energy terms,
he chose Wood over Earth. As of this writing, over 2,500 American soldiers have been killed in Iraq, tens of thousands have been
wounded, and tens of thousands of Iraqis have died. Both England
and Spain have been attacked by terrorists in retaliation for their
role in the war. Violence continues in Iraq and is increasingly described as the beginnings of a civil war. Whether stability eventually comes to Iraq or not, the growing consensus is that the war
there has deeply alienated the Muslim world, created a haven for
terrorists and made the worldwide terrorist problem worse rather
than better.

George W. Bush's policies and the widespread support he received for them, at least in the beginning, illustrate again how powerful and persistent the Wood energies of Americans can be. The
Iraq war, however, and the tilt toward aggression it represented,
were to some extent a distortion of Americans' true attitudes. If
only a few hundred more people in Florida had voted for Al Gore,
there probably would have been no Iraq war. That war illustrates
how the Holistic Impulse can be temporarily derailed, sending
society in the opposite direction; sooner or later, however, society

begins to correct its course, responding again to the larger patterns that are guiding it.

Change and the Widening Circle of Empathy

I have described society's progress several times as a widening circle of empathy. In the U.S. the circle began to expand with the coming of freedom and self government. It took another major step forward with the abolition of slavery. Since then it has continued to grow, slowly and unevenly, but ultimately in the direction of greater compassion and inclusiveness. Now, more than two centuries later, the circle encompasses all the laws, customs and institutions that make the U.S. the free, open and relatively civilized society it is today. The circle of empathy, and some of the major advances that have helped expand it, are shown in Figure 38.

Most if not all of society's major advances met fierce resistance when they were first proposed. That resistance often continued until the very moment of change. But strangely, once change occurs it quickly begins to feel natural and right, not only to its supporters but often to its former opponents. How many Americans today could imagine living in a society where women were denied the vote, where working people had no voice in their job conditions, where people were left entirely on their own in old age, or where African-Americans and other minorities were denied basic human rights? Yet each of these changes was highly controversial at the time it was proposed and each was condemned, often by large numbers of people, as a radical departure from the status quo.

Part of every person's education should include the systematic study of change. Holistic change in particular has brought us civilization, democracy and a relatively enlightened society. The study of change might encourage people to place greater value on the changes that have improved their lives, and to anticipate and welcome further change rather than instinctively resisting it. If there is a basic flaw in the conservative political philosophy, it is in its belief in the status quo as a guiding principle. Custom and tradition are useful and important, and change often requires giving up something of value in return for something of even greater value. But resisting change on principle is ultimately self-defeating because it amounts to swimming against the tide of history.

The Strange Decline of Liberalism

All of the advances shown in Figure 38 represent the adoption of liberal ideas. The coming of democracy, the abolition of slavery, women's suffrage, Social Security, Medicare, civil rights legislation and many other fundamental changes have expressed the essence of the liberal philosophy—a greater sense of equality and a deeper concern for the well being of all of society's members. Given that distinguished record, it is astonishing that liberals in the U.S. have allowed themselves to be thrown so completely on the defensive, and that many liberals today shrink from even using the word liberal to describe themselves.

Liberals are largely to blame for their own problems. The wasteful spending programs of the 1960's opened them up to charges of trying to solve society's problems by throwing money at them. Jimmy Carter in the 1970's appeared soft and unfocused both on the economy and in the Iranian hostage crisis, fueling the reputation of liberals as weak and indecisive. Bill Clinton reversed the trend somewhat in the 1990's but, after the events of September 11, Americans had a new reason to embrace politicians with a proven track record of strength, resolution and, above all, a willingness to use force. Finally, in the run-up to the Iraq war, Democrats utterly abdicated their responsibility to stand up to the president's unjustified calls for war.

The challenge for liberals is to stop running away from their beliefs and to stand up and fight for them instead. Doing so is not easy; Earth energy, the force behind the liberal impulse, is the energy of love, compassion and community but Wood is the energy of boldness and courage. Conservatives have a natural advantage over liberals in their willingness to acknowledge their beliefs openly and take the consequences. Liberals need to cultivate their non-dominant Wood energies and demonstrate the courage of their

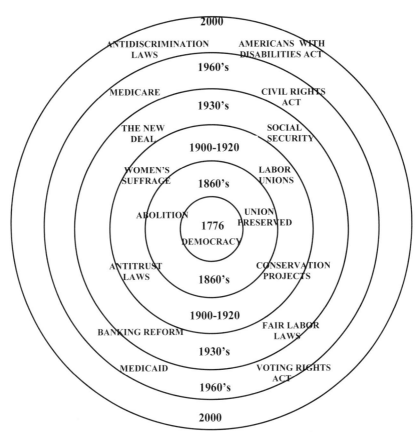

FIGURE 38.
THE WIDENING CIRCLE OF EMPATHY IN THE U.S.

convictions as forthrightly as conservatives do.

Equally important, liberals need to explain why their values are so important to society's growth and well being. Conservatives may have a natural advantage over liberals in their political temperament, but liberals have an even greater advantage in the power of their ideas. As the circle of empathy clearly shows, history is on the side of the liberal point of view. Thanks to the Holistic Impulse, one or more liberal ideas is now percolating in the consciousness of millions of people. Whatever society's next major advance may be—universal health coverage, a more creative effort to reconcile the West with the Muslim world, criminal justice reform or some other innovation—it is certain to represent a greater sense of inclusiveness and a greater concern for humankind as a whole. Liberals should take comfort from that fact and work to bring those half-formed ideas to the surface.

As the Holistic Impulse continues to do its work, Wood energy, rather than controlling or even stifling Earth as it did in Rousseau's day, is likely to assume more of a supporting role—balancing generosity and kindness with the firmness and discipline that healthy individuals and societies need. As that process continues, liberals and conservatives may ultimately find the common ground that has eluded them for over 200 years. If so, the United States may yet be the City on a Hill that John Winthrop envisioned.

CHAPTER FIVE
INTUITION AND THE BODY BRAIN

Life energy links things that seem on the surface separate and unconnected: mind and body, the human body and natural forces, human personality and the heavens above. As we saw in Chapter 4, life energy connects individuals with the political forces that shape society itself, creating patterns of growth that are apparent from the perspective of history.

Life energy is, too, the linking principle behind the mysterious kind of knowing we call intuition. Intuition can be defined in various ways but is often described as a direct knowing, or the direct perception of reality, without ordinary thinking or the evidence of the five senses. Intuition makes use of some unseen but tangible channel of communication. Energy healers and other intuitives, some of whose work is described below, generally agree that life energy is the medium through which intuition works. I define intuition here as a direct knowing made possible by the sensing of life energies—in another person, in time and space or in the mind of God.

Intuition, Perception and Judgment

One of the difficulties in discussing intuition is that it almost never occurs by itself; it is usually blended with an element of thinking or emotion or both, and it is easy to confuse the different factors. Because intuitions are often spontaneous and more or less effortless, some writers tend to view any knowledge that comes unbidden into awareness as an intuition. But ordinary thinking and memory can seem effortless, too. One writer gives the following examples in an attempt to show that intuitions are not always reliable:

> My geographical intuition tells me that Reno is east of Los Angeles, that Rome is south of New York, that Atlanta is east of Detroit. But I am wrong, wrong, wrong.[83]

These examples show how misleading our perceptions and possibly our judgments can be, but not our intuitions. We may think Reno is east of Los Angeles but not because of intuition. We know L.A. is on the West coast while Reno is well inland, so we assume incorrectly that Reno is east of Los Angeles. New York seems to be north of Rome because New York is in the far northern part of the U.S. while Rome is in the far south of Europe. A similar perceptual illusion may apply to Atlanta and Detroit, but in each case it is not intuition—it is our knowledge, memory and experience, combined with quirks of geography—that trick us. Intuitions may not always be reliable but it is important, in trying to understand them better, not to confuse intuition with other kinds of knowing.

PART 1. THREE KINDS OF INTUITION

The three kinds of intuition discussed below represent three categories of information that come to us through intuition: about people, about things that happen in time and space, and about God. Because intuition is by nature a deep phenomenon that sometimes touches on or crosses over into the realm of Spirit, this chapter introduces a theme that will continue to the end of the book: that life energy is the unseen link, not just between mind and body, but between mind, body and Spirit.

MEDICAL INTUITON: SENSING THE ENERGIES OF MIND AND BODY

One of the most important uses of intuition is in detecting the energies of health and illness. Those who can do so are known as medical intuitives, and they consistently agree that intuition is not an exotic or magical process but a concrete skill that anyone can learn. One prominent healer, teacher and writer, Barbara Brennan, refers to the reading of life energies as High Sense Perception and describes it as an extension of the work of the five senses. She describes her intuitive work as "a type of 'seeing' in which you perceive a picture in your mind without the use of your normal vision. It is not imagination. It is sometimes referred to as clairvoyance."[84]   In her book *Hands of Light: A Guide to Healing Through the Human Energy Field,* Brennan makes the following suggestion to those who wish to develop their intuitive skills:

> The [energy] information coming to you comes through your five senses. These have been labeled traditionally as sight, touch, taste, hearing and smell…You may know whether or not you think primarily in pictures, sounds or feelings. I recommend that you find out, because the way you access through the normal senses is the way that I would recommend that you begin learning to develop your High Sense Perception.[85]

Brennan, who was a physicist with NASA's Goddard Space Center before becoming a healer, has created a detailed and systematic guide to what she calls the Human Energy Field, or HEF, commonly known as the aura. For her, the aura is a primary tool in reading the energies of health and illness. She describes the aura as a multi-layered sheath of life energies that surrounds the body, interacting with the chakras and embodying all the functions of mind and body. According to Brennan, the energies of the aura make up a complete template, or energy duplicate, of the human body:

> The structured layers [of the aura] contain all the forms the physical body has, including internal organs, blood vessels, etc., and additional forms t h a t the physical body does not contain. There is a vertical flow of energy that pulsates up and down the field in the spinal cord….I call this the main vertical power current. There are swirling cone-shaped vortexes called chakras in the field. Their tips point into the main vertical power current, and their open ends extend to the edge of each layer of the field they are located in.[86]

By reading the color, form, density and other qualities of the aura's energies, Brennan and others like her can literally see the underlying energetic roots of illness. The body's energies often contain specific information about the person's life history that can be essential to the healing process. The information can come in various forms—"in either a symbolic picture in my mind, a concept or a direct verbal message."[87] Brennan gives the following example of a person whose persistent anger is a threat to her health:

> With HSP, you will be able to see a red haze around the angry person. To find out what is happening with her on a deeper level, it is possible to focus on the cause of the anger, not only in the present, but also on how it relates to childhood experience and to her relationship with her parents. Under the red haze will appear a thick, gray fluid-like substance that conveys a heavy sadness. By focusing in on the essence of the gray substance, you will probably even be able to see the childhood scene that caused the deeply rooted pain. You will also see how that anger is harming the physical body... Using HSP, you will be able to find the words that will help that person let down, connect to the deeper reality, and help her find a solution.[88]

Brennan stresses that most illnesses originate in the energy system—often, as in the above example, through emotional stresses that take a toll on the body by disrupting energy flow for long periods. Brennan points out that, while a healer may be able to identify the energy patterns that are undermining health, changing those patterns is not the work of healer alone. It often requires an honest self-examination by the client and a willingness to address deeper life conflicts. That process often crosses over into the domain of Spirit. In Brennan's words:

> To deal with the source [of illness] usually requires a life change that ultimately leads to a personal life more connected to the core of one's being. It leads us to that deeper part of ourselves that is sometimes

called the high self or the spark of divinity within.[89]

Barbara Brennan thus sees energy healing ultimately as a spiritual activity. The human energy field, she says, "becomes the medium through which we find ways to reach inside to our deepest being. It becomes the bridge to our soul..."[90]

Symbolic Sight and the Language of Energy

Caroline Myss is another well-known medical intuitive who, like Barbara Brennan, regards energy healing as essentially a spiritual process and intuition as a tool for promoting it. Myss, like Brennan, believes that anyone can acquire intuitive abilities, or what she calls symbolic sight, through practice. In her book *Anatomy of the Spirit: the Seven Stages of Power and Healing,* she describes intuition as follows:

> ...I firmly believe that intuitive or symbolic sight is not a gift but a skill—a skill based in self-esteem... think of learning to use intuition as learning to interpret the language of energy.[91]

Myss interprets energy influences mostly in terms of the chakras, but she describes the overall energy field in much the same way that Barbara Brennan describes the aura:

> Your physical body is surrounded by an energy field that extends as far out as your outstretched arms and the full length of your body. It is both an information center and a highly sensitive perceptual system. We are constantly "in communication" with everything around us through this system, which is a kind of conscious electricity that transmits and receives messages to and from other people's bodies. These messages from and within the energy field are what intuitives perceive.[92]

Myss, like Brennan and other energy intuitives, inevitably speaks of her work and its deeper importance in spiritual terms. She describes the link between everyday life, life energy and Spirit as follows:

> In these early days the impressions I received were mainly of a person's immediate physical health and the related emotional or psychological stress. But I could also *see* the energy surrounding that person's body. I saw it filled with information about that person's history. And I saw that energy as an extension of that person's spirit. I began to realize something I had never been taught in school: that our spirit is very much a part of our daily lives, it embodies our thoughts and emotions, and it records every one of them, from the most mundane to the visionary…It participates in every second of our lives. It is the conscious force that is life itself.[93]

The inner seeing of medical intuitives like Caroline Myss and Barbara Brennan helps confirm life energy's central role in human life. As a force that "embodies our thoughts and emotions," it is the stuff of our conscious and unconscious minds. As an "an extension of…Spirit" it is our tangible link with the Divine. I explore those connections further in Chapters 6 and 7.

SENSING A PAST, PRESENT OR FUTURE EVENT

The energy connections that make medical intuition possible can help explain more common, everyday intuitions as well, the kind we call hunches and sometimes dismiss as coincidences. Sensing that a friend, relative or spouse might call just before the phone rings; feeling that someone's eyes are on you only to turn and see a stranger staring from across the room; deciding to go to a movie or take a walk at the same time your friend or partner has the same idea—these are simple intuitions in which one person senses the thoughts, feelings or simply the presence of another person through connections in their respective energy fields.

Other, more important intuitions are based on the same principle but include the added dimension of time. A store owner or CEO hires a new manager because she has a gut feeling the applicant will do a good job; a family moves to a new city because it feels like the right time for a change; a lawyer accepts a new case because it feels like a winner. Decisions like these usually involve an element of knowledge or judgment, but the deciding factor is often an indefinable sense of rightness—an intuition.

Intuitions like these, about what a person ought to do, are in a sense ways of predicting the future. They are usually less dramatic than what we call visions or premonitions but they are similar in that they represent a direct inner knowing about things that have not yet happened. Such experiences raise an important question: If intuition is the sensing of life energies, where are the energies of the future and how is it possible to gain access to and read them?

Spacetime and Energy's Four Dimensions

Even before Einstein, it was known that time is a relative phenomenon with no absolute existence. Spiritual masters teach that we experience the forward movement of time as a way of making sense of our everyday lives. The feeling of time passing, according to those who have had the experience, can evaporate entirely and become timelessness or what is sometimes referred to as the Eternal Now.

Einstein showed in a different way that time is subjective—that it can speed up, slow down or run at different rates for people in different circumstances. Einstein's genius was in proving scientifically what mystics have known intuitively for centuries.

In the four-dimensional realm of Spacetime, everything that ever happened or will happen already exists and can, in principle, be known. Energy principles suggest that the events of the past and future, like those of the present, are encoded in life energies and that sensing past or future events represents the accessing and reading of those energies wherever they may be. Thus the medical intuitive who sees a person's early life traumas in the aura, and the medium who gives past life readings are both accessing the energies of Spacetime past. Seers and visionaries like Nostradamus and the Biblical prophets are able to read the energies of Spacetime future.

Confidence as a Form of Intuition

A trivial example of knowing the future is the athlete who has a sudden intuition of success: the basketball player who, as he receives the ball, *knows* he is going to make the last minute shot at the buzzer, or the golfer who, as she stands over the ball. *knows* she is going to sink the final putt to win the tournament. These kinds of experiences suggest a relationship between confidence and intuition. A person who is confident of success feels, by definition, a positive connection between the present and the future. It may not be as specific as the athlete's sudden flash of certainty but it is a connection nevertheless.

We know that life energies flow, not only in the body, but back and forth between and among individuals. We experience time as something that flows from the past into the present and on into the future. In some cases at least, the confident person, like the golfer or basketball player, may sense the flow and momentum of life energies surrounding her. Like the athlete with a sudden certainty of victory, she expects success because she can feel those energies leading her onward toward her goal.

Visions, Premonitions and Warnings

People who have had premonitions or warnings, or whose close family members have had such experiences, tend to take intuitions more seriously. There is a history of such intuitions in my family.

My maternal grandfather, to whom I was very close as a child, lived for many years with my grandmother and their eight children in a small town in southeastern Arizona. My grandfather told a story of how, when he was a young man, he had to drive to another town one day on business. To get there he had to travel through mountainous country. As he was climbing a hill he suddenly had a vision of his deceased mother hovering over the highway ahead of him. She looked extremely concerned and was frantically waving her arms toward him and crying, "Go back! Go back!" The image was so powerful that my grandfather, stunned, instantly stopped the car, turned around and drove home.

Later, a news report came over the radio that there had been a rockslide on the highway, covering the road with large boulders. It had happened at the same time, and in the same area, where my grandfather had his vision.

Another story from my childhood, told to me by my mother, concerned her Aunt Riva for whom my mother was named. Riva was in her later years and lived quietly with her husband. One night Riva awoke to the sound of a group of women weeping and wailing outside her bedroom window. She was sure no one could be outside at that time of night, but the eerie sounds continued for several minutes. Finally they stopped and Riva went back to sleep. A few days later, Riva's husband suddenly and unexpectedly died.

Many years later my mother reminded me of that story and told me another one. In 1972, after my father had had a heart attack and was not feeling well, my parents drove from their home in Arizona to California for a vacation. They rented a comfortable apartment in the beautiful seaside town of La Jolla. Their time together that summer, my mother said, was like a second honeymoon after an extremely happy 34 year marriage. One night, my mother awoke to a noise outside. It sounded like a group of women weeping and wailing. After a few minutes the sound stopped and my mother tried as best she could to go back to sleep. A few days later, at a family wedding in San Francisco, my father had a second heart attack and died.

Powerful experiences like these suggest that past, present and future are indeed linked, and they hint at an underlying spiritual reality that shapes our lives. Spirit's presence becomes even more explicit in a third kind of intuition.

SPIRITUAL INTUITION

The awareness of God is, by definition, the deepest form of intuition. Whether it is feeling God's presence in everyday life, sensing His wishes in guidance or merging oneself with God in deep meditation, spiritual intuition represents the meeting and blending of human and divine energies.

The techniques of classical yoga meditation make practical use of the link between life energy and spiritual intuition. *Pranayama,* a Sanskrit word meaning life energy control, refers to a group of techniques that have been a part of Indian spiritual practice for thousands of years. I discuss *pranayama* and its role in spiritual growth in Chapter 7.

Guidance and the One-Way Mirror

Guidance is the sense that God, or another higher being, is subtly directing the pattern of one's life through some form of internal communication. Guidance is relatively common, not only among those who follow a religious calling, but among energy healers and others who work with life energies. In their books, both Barbara Brennan and Carolyn Myss describe important patterns of guidance that have helped shape their careers as healers.

My view is that everyone's life, from the most mundane detail to the most important life-changing decision, is invisibly guided by God. Everyday life is thus like a one-way mirror in which God sees and influences us but we can't see Him. When a person begins to feel guidance, the one-way mirror becomes a kind of window through which we can feel God's presence or at least sense His wishes. Guidance is important, not because there is anything unusual about God's role in our lives, but simply because one becomes aware of that role. The person becomes, in effect, a partner with God in shaping the pattern of his or her own life. Guidance, more than anything else, represents a new responsibility as well as a chance to grow closer to God.

Guidance is, too, at least in my experience, to some extent a test of faith. Following guidance is no guarantee that life will be smooth or trouble-free or even that it will always make sense. Accepting guidance, in the end, is just one more way of expressing confidence and trust that God has one's long-term best interests at heart.

For me, guidance feels very much like having a conversation with another human being. We take for granted, after all, that one of life's most common daily experiences—feeling the conscious presence of another person—is an intuitive experience. We know we are not alone in the world, not because we can see and hear other people, but because we can feel their awareness directly. When that happens, two minds literally merge and become, to some extent, one. The experience is so clear and unambiguous that we accept it unquestioningly as a basic life truth. No amount of evidence could convince us to the contrary and in fact any such evidence would seem strangely irrelevant. In Chapter 6 I discuss Western science and materialist philosophy and how their failure to consider intuitive forms of knowing makes it impossible for them to address consciousness in a meaningful way.

The Five Elements and Types of Spiritual Awareness

Barbara Brennan describes intuition as an extension of the five senses and teaches that a person's dominant sense, such as seeing or hearing, may be that person's most natural way of experiencing intuition. In a similar way, one's dominant energy type may suggest the most natural way to experience Spirit. Fire types, for example, who are naturally joyful and exuberant, may find that cultivating a deeper and more transcendent kind of joy is, for them, the most rewarding pathway to spiritual growth. The development of spiritual awareness through Fire energies is called Ananda Yoga or the Yoga of Joy.

The Indian master Paramahansa Yogananda referred to the ecstasy of God-communion as "ever-new joy." Yogananda, whose name itself means Joy through Yoga, described ever-new joy as an ever-changing, constantly renewing experience which, no matter how many times it is repeated nor how long it might last, one can never grow tired of.[94] The term suggests that, in heaven as on earth, Fire is the energy of both joy and creativity. Just as the works of painters, writers, composers and other human artists can evoke unique, indescribable emotions in us, the experience of God's infinite creativity can be an inexhaustible source of joy for those who are attuned to it.

People with other dominant energies have their own characteristic forms of spiritual intuition. Earth types, for whom love and compassion are primary, may experience the truth, embodied in Christianity and other faiths, that God is love. The yoga of transcendent, unconditional love and devotion to God is known as Bhakti Yoga.

Metal types, who tend to experience life primarily through the intellect, may practice Jnana Yoga, the Yoga of Wisdom, discovering God through a profound intuitive understanding of the nature of reality. Metal types tend to gravitate toward asceticism and the principle of non-attachment to worldly things. The Buddha was an outstanding example.

Water types, who have a gift for listening, solitude and peace, may practice Mantra Yoga, the yoga of sound and its vibrations, perhaps including the Om meditation in which one listens internally for the cosmic sound of creation. The spiritual intuition of the Water type recalls the peace that passeth understanding referred to by the apostle Paul.

For Wood types, who tend to be busy and active, the path of service, or Karma Yoga, is a natural choice. Great karma yogis in recent history have included Mahatma Gandhi and Mother Teresa. Because the impulse to serve is grounded in part in the same Earth energies that embody love and compassion, karma yogis may experience, and express, Spirit in the form of unconditional love. Mother Teresa, for example, was born under the sign of Virgo, a blend of Earth, Metal and Wood energies, helping explain both her deep compassion and her affinity for an active life of service (see Chapter 4).

Paramahansa Yogananda is another example of spiritual diversity. He was known as a Premavatar, or Incarnation of Love, and, like Mother Teresa, was powerfully motivated toward a life of service. For Yogananda, the complex sign of Capricorn helped account for the range of his spiritual talents. Capricorn, one of the musical signs, embodies among other things the Water energies of listening, and Yogananda prescribed the Om, or listening, meditation as a daily part of spiritual practice for his students. Finally, Yogananda, as I noted above, experienced God through the ever-new joy of divine Fire energies. It was natural for him to do so, since the Fire sign of Leo was both his Moon sign and rising sign.

Mind, Body and Spirit: Expanding the Human Diagram

In Chapter 3 I described mind, body and energy system as the three basic components of the human organism. That three-part scheme was helpful in identifying life energy's role in physical and emotional health, personality, relationships and society.

The link between life energy and spiritual intuition makes it clear that mind, body and energy system cannot fully explain human experience. Spiritual intuition represents a natural connection, via life energies, between the everyday world and the realm of Spirit. For a complete picture of a human being, the natural link to Spirit must be included.

Figure 39 illustrates the full breadth and depth of life energy's connecting power. As the force or process at the intersection of mind, body and Spirit, life energy is the fundamental linking principle at every level of life.

If the shape of the diagram is vaguely familiar, it may be because it resembles the well-known Peace Symbol of the 1960's (Figure 40). That symbol, which some say represents an inverted crucifix or "Nero's Cross" and was meant to mock Christianity, was, according to one source, actually designed as a protest against the nuclear arms race.[95] The symbol combines the semaphore signals for the letters N and D, representing Nuclear Disarmament.

Whatever the origin of the Peace Symbol, its resemblance to a simple diagram representing the unity of mind, body and Spirit—

the core of the holistic philosophy—is a happy coincidence, or at least a happy correspondence.

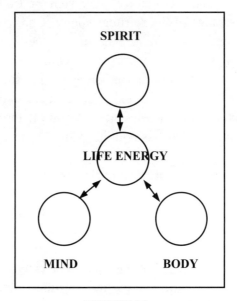

FIGURE 39.
THE COMPLETE HUMAN ORGANISM

PART 2. THE BODY BRAIN,
INTUITION AND MOVEMENT

Science and everyday experience agree that the brain is a primary seat of consciousness. It not only feels like the center of our awareness, it has by far the largest concentration of nerve cells in the body. The firing of neurons in the brain is associated with, and may be a requirement for, many if not most kinds of human experience.

Still, we know that awareness is not confined exclusively to the brain. Physical sensations are proof that many experiences are shared between the head and body. We feel an itch in the foot, a tickle in the side or a pain in the stomach even though we feel it "from" the head—and even though the nerve impulses for those experiences are all processed in the brain. The ability to have an experience in both the head and body at the same time is a natural outgrowth of the structure of the life energy system. The chakras begin at the root of the body and have major substations in the

FIGURE 40.
THE 60'S PEACE SYMBOL

lower abdomen, at the solar plexus level and near the heart. Since those centers represent a network of energies that process daily experience, it would be surprising if they did not represent a network of awareness as well.

There is evidence that we experience emotions, like physical sensations, in both head and body. Some of the evidence, though admittedly unscientific, is so universal that it is part of folk wisdom. We feel love in our hearts and fear in our bellies; we have a gut feeling that something will happen or that something is true. Recent scientific research supports these everyday perceptions. Candace Pert, whose work I referred to in Chapter 3, has shown that neuropeptides, the body chemicals associated with emotion, are produced not only in the brain but in the body, and that they latch onto receptors in many places, especially in the gut.

Further evidence comes from the work of body-centered psychotherapists who find that people who lose touch with their bodies tend to lose touch with their feelings as well. At the far end of the spectrum, body energies may be essential to the normal awareness of physical reality. In Chapter 3 I discussed the schizoid pattern and suggested that perceiving the world in three dimensions requires that head and body energies work together like a kind of human stereo system.

The Enneagram, discussed in Chapter 4, takes a similar approach. The three Enneagram categories—Head, Heart and Gut types—are distinguished in part by their ability, or inability, to feel and process emotion. Head types are both the least emotional of the three types and the least in touch with their own bodies.

The energies of the body, and especially of the abdomen, are viewed as central in a number of Asian teachings. In Japan the *hara,* or abdomen, has an almost mystical significance that goes back at least to medieval times. The ritual suicide known as *hara kiri* ("belly cutting") was practiced by samurai warriors centuries ago and, in modern times, even by some Japanese military officers at the end of World War II. The 20th century Japanese shiatsu master Masunaga developed a system for assessing the body's energies by palpating areas in the abdomen. The technique, known as *hara* diagnosis, will probably join the traditional Chinese art of pulse diagnosis as a standard method for assessing the energy system.

In the Asian martial arts the lower abdominal area known as *dantien* ("dahn-tee-EN"), or "reservoir of life energy," is crucial to body awareness, strength and agility. I discuss d*antien* in the next section.

Further work will show whether the energies of the body deserve to be called a brain in the true sense. Whether they do or not, they are so fundamental to life and normal awareness that they should be seen as a major, distinct part of the energy system. I use the term body brain in that general sense—to stress that most if not all human activities depend on a partnership between head and body energies.

Two activities where body energies appear to be especially important are intuition and movement. Both depend less on thinking, a traditional head function, than on feeling and sensing, which are more often associated with the body. Identifying some of the body energies of intuition and movement may lead to techniques for developing those energies and improving the skills associated with them.

BODY ENERGIES AND INTUITION

People with intuitive gifts are able to penetrate the surface appearance of things and sense the life energies that lie beneath. In terms of *yin* and *yang,* intuition is a *yin* activity—one of receptiveness, sensitivity and depth.

Each of the chakras, like each of the meridians, is viewed as primarily either *yin* or *yang.* In general, the odd-numbered chakras—one, three, five and seven—are *yang* while the even numbers—two, four and six—are *yin.*[96] Therefore we might expect to find the energies of intuition mainly in the second, fourth and sixth chakras. The second and fourth are body chakras while the sixth is a head chakra. The differences in the kinds of intuition associated with the three *yin* chakras illustrate some of the differences between head and body energies.

The Second Chakra, the Moon and Female Intuition

The lower chakras are usually described as the processing centers for ordinary thoughts, feelings and desires, while the upper chakras are viewed as the abode of higher and purer feelings and experiences. That view tends to portray human beings as a kind of Centaur—the mythical creature whose lower half was a horse and upper half was a human being.

Donna Eden sees a nobler role for the lower chakras, especially the second, which lies a couple of inches below the navel. The second chakra's responsibility for the sex drive and the elimination of wastes is, in her view, "only the basement of a very large mansion." At a deeper level, she says, the second chakra

> ...is a sacred vessel, a womblike container of imagination and creative impulse...It holds a world of joy, freedom and laughter, removed from the traumas and pain of life. It is a protected domain, where the creative force can flourish. Within the second chakra, babies grow, imaginative projects germinate, and the boundless creativity of the

universe flows into each of us.[97]

For Donna Eden the second chakra is a center for intuition as well, and for the energies of intuitive healing:

> The energies of the second chakra reflect a person's natural healing abilities....a protective womblike vibration extend[s] outward that people can almost sit in, as if sitting in a large lap. A blue or indigo color will be strong in the second chakra of such individuals. Indigo is traditionally the color of the sixth chakra, which has to do with psychic ability. Having indigo in the second chakra is like being psychic at the body level. It is more than a gut knowing. It is as if the energy of the umbilical cord is still active and somehow receives information from the cosmos.[98]

Eden's image of the second chakra as a umbilical cord connected to the healing energies of the universe recalls the qualities of Earth energy: its fundamental connecting power and its association with parenting, love, compassion and friendship. It is perhaps natural that the same Earth energies that embody these values should facilitate their expression through healing.

The second chakra is associated with Earth energies in other ways. It is located next to the womb and carries a woman's reproductive energies. Its name in Sanskrit, *Svadhisthana,* can be translated in three ways—as "one's own abode," "sweetness" or "to taste with pleasure."[99] All of these meanings are strongly suggestive of Earth, the energy of home and hearth, appetites and sense pleasures. In physiology Earth energy, and specifically spleen energy, regulates blood sugar—"sweetness"—in the body. Some authorities even refer to the second chakra as the spleen chakra and the spleen meridian, as we have seen, is a bearer of love in the energy system.

Folk wisdom has it that women are more intuitive than men and that there is something called women's intuition. The explanation may lie in the fact that Earth energies embody certain kinds of intuition and that women are the gender embodiment of Earth. That would help explain why so many medical intuitives, including the three quoted in these pages—Donna Eden, Barbara Brennan and Caroline Myss—are women.

Finally, in the Kabbalistic Tree of Life, the energy center Yesod, which corresponds to the second chakra, is associated with the moon, which has strong feminine/Earth associations in several traditions. In Western astrology the moon rules Cancer, the most domestic of the twelve signs. Cancer is a highly intuitive sign and when the moon falls in Cancer in the birth chart, it virtually guarantees that the person will have strong intuitive capacities.

In the Indian tradition the second chakra is associated with Water, not Earth, and the first chakra is the traditional Earth chakra. One reason, as I noted earlier, is that each of the two lower chakras has a heavy concentration of both Earth and Water energies. The Indian system chooses to emphasize the Earth qualities of the first chakra and the Water qualities of the second. In the next section I discuss the importance of the Water energies of both the first and second chakras in body control and movement.

Intuition and the Heart Chakra

The other *yin* body chakra is the fourth chakra or heart chakra. As a primary center for love, it is, like the second chakra, an important reservoir of Earth energies. The heart chakra is the central point in the chakra system and a gateway to spiritual awareness. The kind of love it embodies gives a clue to the kind of intuition it contains. One writer argues that the love of the heart chakra is different in kind from second chakra love. She describes it as follows:

> The love we experience at the level of the heart chakra is distinctly different from the more sexual and passionate love of the second chakra. Sexual love is object-oriented—the passion is stimulated by the presence of a particular person. In the fourth

chakra, love is not dependent on outside stimula-
tion, but experienced within as a state of being.[100]

The universal, unconditional love referred to here is the love of
saints and sages and perhaps of God's love for us. It is more than
an emotion—it is a guiding principle of reality and a form of spiritual intuition.

The Third Eye and Pure Understanding

The final *yin* chakra is the sixth chakra, which is not a body chakra
at all but is located in the forehead, between the eyebrows. It is often referred to as the Third Eye or Spiritual Eye and is more
frequently associated with intuition than any other chakra. Unlike
the body chakras, which have a strong Earth component and are
heavily weighted toward the emotions, the Third Eye's energies are
more abstract and concerned with pure understanding. The sixth
chakra has more to do with transcending everyday life than with
addressing ordinary human problems. In the healing context, the
sixth chakra may relate more to diagnosing than treating illness.

For some people, the lack of emotion in intuition is not only
normal and natural—it is essential for the intuition to be considered
reliable. In *Anatomy of the Spirit,* Caroline Myss describes the development of intuitive sixth chakra energies through what she calls
"detachment—a state of mind beyond the influences of the
'personal mind.'" Because detachment is so essential to her work,
Myss evaluates her own intuitions as follows:

> I learned from experience to discern the difference
> between personal and impersonal impressions; my
> indicator of an accurate intuition is a *lack* of emo-
> tion. For me, a clear impression has *no* emotional
> energy connected to it whatsoever. If I feel an
> emotional connection to an impression, then I con-
> sider that impression to be contaminated.[101]

The striking difference between Donna Eden's "protective, womblike vibration" and Caroline Myss' "impersonal impressions" with "no emotional energy connected to [them] whatsoever" illustrates the wide range of intuitions that are possible even within the domain of healing. It illustrates, too, a fundamental difference between head and body energies.

BODY ENERGIES AND MOVEMENT

Intuition and body control are very different phenomena but they have certain important things in common. Both are forms of knowing that depend on the flow of life energies, and both rely less on thinking than on sensing and feeling. Intuition is knowing that something is true, while body control is knowing how to do something—swing a tennis racket or golf club, do Tai Chi or Karate, ski, dance, bowl or swim—with strength, coordination and agility.

In intuition the energies of knowing come from beyond the self—from other people, the environment or sometimes the mind of God. In movement the energies come from within—from the personal Unconscious, which contains a blueprint for rhythmic, coordinated motion. When a person is fully attuned to those energies, a kind of automatic, effortless process takes over. The person is "in the zone," "in a groove" or "locked in." The feeling is reminiscent of intuition, which rises up naturally out of the Unconscious and flows without conscious effort.

Head and Body Energies: a Delicate Balance

Movement is more complex in some ways than intuition because it combines conscious will, or head energies, with unconscious, instinctive knowing or body energies. Whether you are in a tennis match, golf game, on the ski slopes, baseball field or elsewhere, you must constantly coordinate your conscious movements with the impulses coming out of the Unconscious. If the connection is broken even for a moment, you may hit a bad shot, drop the ball or slip and fall. The mistake may cause you to tense up, start trying too hard or start analyzing your movements instead of letting them flow naturally.

Anyone who has played or competed in sports knows the frustration of having the conscious, analyzing mind try to take over for the body's instinctive knowing. Try as we might, it simply doesn't work. We start performing well again only when we find a way to relax and reestablish the balance between conscious and unconscious forces—between head and body energies.

There are many new and innovative techniques for improving sports performance. Some come out of the growing field of sports psychology and include methods for improving concentration, building self confidence and removing emotional blocks. Some techniques, like visualization, make use of life energy principles. Since images, attitudes and emotions are embodied by both positive and negative energies, visualizing positive outcomes creates helpful influences in the energy realm that can tip the balance toward success.

The "Zen of" books take another approach to tapping into the body's unconscious knowing. Whether in archery, swimming, tennis or another sport, the Buddhist principle of trusting the universe and opening oneself to experience can lead to a deep state of relaxation and awareness akin to meditation. That state encourages the deeper energies of the Unconscious to rise to the surface and play a greater role in outer activities.

Targeting the Mind-Body Connection Directly

The most direct way to influence movement through the mind-body connection is by working consciously with life energies. Life energy, as we have seen, is the meeting place of mind and body and is highly responsive to attention and will. Focusing mentally on the energy centers that govern movement can be a powerful tool for improving physical performance.

Life energy control is the explicit principle behind the Asian martial arts, from combat techniques like Karate and Jujitsu to more meditative activities like Tai Chi and Chi Gong. Cultivating body awareness through life energies affects the organism on every level—physical, mental, emotional and spiritual.

In the martial arts, mind, body and energy system are in constant and close communication. A well-known Tai Chi text, *Chen Style Taijiquan*, points out that physical strength depends not only on body conditioning but on mind-body interaction through the energy system:

> At the instant in which the waist rotation stops, the hands should also stop. This requires the mind to be focused totally upon the movement. For generations practitioners have been instructed to use the mind (*yi*) rather than muscular strength (*li*) to lead their energy. '*Yi* leading the *qi, qi* moving the body, *qi* swelling like a drum, and *qi* circulating in the whole body.'[102]

The area known as *dantien,* between the navel and genitals, is perhaps the body's primary center for movement and control. *Dantien* is described as follows in *Chen Style Taijiquan:*

> [*dantien*] is the most important center in the body....It is the body's center of gravity as well as the energy   center....The *dantian* stores qi [*chi*] and drives it throughout the body.[103]

Dantien's location helps explain its importance to body awareness and movement. It coincides with a large ganglion, or collection of nerve tissue, called the sacral plexus (Figure 41). The sacral plexus is the terminus for a number of important nerves that control sensation and movement in the legs and feet, including the sciatic nerve which is the largest nerve in the body. The sciatic nerve is almost an inch thick and extends from the buttocks to the toes. Its branches crisscross the legs from top to bottom (Figure 42).

Dantien appears to be the energy support for the sciatic nerve and the impulses that travel through it. That helps explain why developing and learning to control *dantien* energies is so essential to mastery in the martial arts.

Life Energy and Sports

Life energy control, whether conscious or unconscious, is essential in any activity where strength, agility and coordination are important. In many Western sports, good technique reflects an instinctive awareness of energy flow. Golf is a good example because a good golf swing has a number of things in common with good martial arts technique.

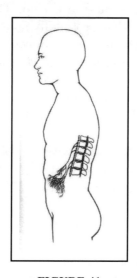

FIGURE 41.
THE SACRAL PLEXUS

In golf, as in certain styles of Tai Chi, the core movement is rotating the body around a central point. In golf the body rotates on the backswing, then returns to exactly the same position before striking the ball. In Chen style Tai Chi, the emphasis is on rotating at the waist around the central point *dantien:*

> The waist acts as the central link connecting the
> upper and lower body. It is the "dominator"
> that controls circular movements...Dantian rota-
> tion is the essence of Chen style Taijiquan.[104]

Golf, like Tai Chi, is relatively unforgiving—it requires precise movements and leaves very little room for error. That precision depends on conscious or unconscious attunement to the life energies emanating from *dantien* and circulating throughout the body. Each part of the lower body has important energy centers associated with it—*dantien* in the lower abdomen, minor chakras in each of the knees and minor chakras and other energy points on the bottoms of the feet. The feeling of unity and effortless rhythm in a good golf swing reflects a corresponding unity in the flow of energies.

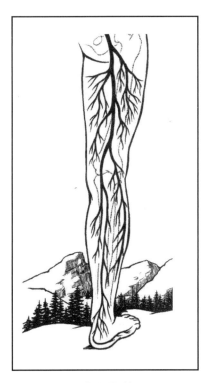

FIGURE 42.
THE SCIATIC NERVE AND ITS BRANCHES

Even before swinging the club, an experienced golfer takes a stance that encourages energies to move as freely as possible. Relaxing the muscles, bending the knees and shifting the weight slightly forward all encourage optimum energy flow. Some com-

mercial golf shoes even come with soft rubber lifts that can be
placed under the heels. They move the weight forward onto the
balls of the feet, which helps in two ways. First, it encourages the
body to rotate rather than sway from side to side. Equally important, it brings a major energy point into solid contact with the
ground. Kidney 1, known as Gushing Spring, is the first point on
the kidney meridian and a major source for the grounding energies
that flow from the earth into the body. Kidney 1 is located on the
sole, just behind the balls of the feet (Figure 43).

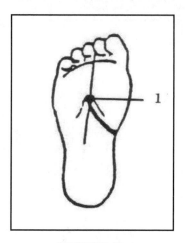

FIGURE 43.
"GUSHING SPRING"

The kind of energy that flows upward from Kidney 1 is a further clue to its importance in body control and movement. Kidney
energy, as we have seen, is a form of Water energy and Gushing
Spring is a fitting name for the point where Water energy enters the
body. Water, as we have seen, is a subtle and mysterious force
associated, among other things, with silence, listening and music.
Musicians and composers tend to have prominent Water energies
in their birth charts.

Without rhythm there can be no music and Water is a primary
energy of both. Water energy helps musicians make better music
and it helps athletes, dancers and martial artists move more
smoothly and gracefully. Gushing Spring is one source of the

Water energies of rhythm; *dantien* may be another. *Dantien,* as I noted earlier, is in the same area as the second chakra and some believe the two are simply different names for the same energy center.

The second chakra, as I noted earlier, is the traditional Water chakra in the Indian tradition. In her book *Energy Medicine*, Donna Eden describes the second chakra as a focal point, not only for the Earth energies of compassion and healing, but for creative energies including those of music:

> Musicians and artists often have an extraordinary second chakra, expansive and rich in colors and textures and complexity.[105]

Thus it appears that Water energies not only flow upward from the feet but are concentrated in the lower abdomen and flow downward from there. The whole lower part of the energy system, it seems, is filled with the Water energies of rhythm. Any exercise or technique that strengthens or develops those energies can be expected to improve physical coordination and performance.

Energy Exercises to Improve Body Control

Life energy, as we have seen, is highly responsive to human attention and will. Paying attention to energy flow is, to use a sports metaphor, a kind of spectator sport that has certain mild benefits. Focusing on those energies and willing them to move and change is a more dynamic activity—a way of participating actively in the game.

One of the simplest ways to begin is to place the attention on *dantien.* Stand up, relax, bend the knees and visualize the energies of the lower abdomen flowing downward through the pelvis, legs and feet, then back again to *dantien.* Continue visualizing energy flow as you move. Take a step forward or back, do a dance step or simply walk across the room. Then stand still and become aware of the weight distribution in your feet. Move your weight forward until you almost lose your balance. Feel the tension in your knees that is required to keep you upright. Feel the connection between the earth and the bottoms of your feet and visualize energies flowing upward from the earth through Gushing Spring. To become more stable, try shifting your pelvis forward and, as you do, visualize *dantien* opening and energies flowing out and down through the legs and feet.

To move from passive attention to active will, try following the instructions in *Chen Style Taijiquan*. As you move, "use the mind rather than muscular strength to lead [the] energy." Visualize the energies in your limbs moving in response to your mental commands, with your body following their lead. In doing so you are recreating what is actually happening below the conscious level. The exercise is a first step in making the unconscious conscious.

With practice you will begin to feel a greater connection, or unity, in your movements. You may begin to feel life energies themselves—a slight tingling sensation in the hands, feet or elsewhere, or a feeling of flow or vibration like an electric current. Energy awareness, like any activity, is a skill that can be learned and that improves with practice.

You can apply these principles to any sport or other physical activity. It is easiest to do in individual sports like swimming, golf, skiing or bowling where you move at your own pace and are not distracted by an opponent's movements. But since these techniques were developed to enhance the combat skills of martial artists, they can be applied to basketball, football, soccer, baseball or any competitive sport.

The Paradox in Sports and Spirituality

For all their obvious differences, there are some intriguing similarities between sports and spirituality. In sports, relaxation is essential. If you tense up, try too hard or think too much, things almost always go badly. No matter how much you want to win, you can only do so if you can convince your body, in effect, that it really doesn't matter.

A similar principle applies to spiritual growth. The Asian peoples discovered centuries ago that overcoming desire was a key to getting what one really wants. The Tao Te Ching captures this paradox in its opening verses:

> Ever desireless, one can see the mystery.
> Ever desiring, one can see the manifestations.
>
> Work is done, then forgotten.
> Therefore it lasts forever.[106]

Physical movement and agility are thus a kind of metaphor for spiritual growth. In Tai Chi and the other martial arts, the two actually merge. Success comes when the most intense effort combines with the deepest relaxation. The result can be a transcendent state of peace in which, in the words of one Tai Chi instructor, the world stops moving and time comes to a halt.

Whether you apply energy principles to sports in the spirit of the martial arts—practicing what might be called the Tao of Sports—or simply to become a better ball player, swimmer, skiier or dancer, moving with an awareness of life energies is a way of touching a deeper and more complete part of yourself.

CHAPTER SIX
LIFE ENERGY, SCIENCE AND PHILOSOPHY

Chapters 2 and 3 showed that the Western medical and psychological models are incomplete without the life energy system included. I gave many examples in those chapters of life energy's central role in both physical and emotional health.

Because every living thing has a life energy system that is essential to its existence, all of the life sciences are, by definition, incomplete without the energy system included. Biology, biochemistry, genetics, neuroscience, veterinary medicine and other disciplines will all become richer and more complete systems when life energy is finally incorporated into their models. That process will begin when instruments are developed that can detect and measure life energies and perhaps distinguish one energy type from another. That will mark the beginning of the study of life energy as a science.

In this chapter I am concerned, not with how science will one day harness and use life energies as a tool, but with how life energy principles can help clarify the boundaries of science itself, and shed light on science's relationship to philosophy and even spirituality.

One of the main points of intersection, and conflict, between science, philosophy and spirituality is in the debate over evolution. Conventional Darwinism illustrates the materialist view that life is the product of a blind, mechanical process. That view is contradicted by major philosophies from both East and West which hold that mind, not matter, is the first principle of life. Recent findings in science itself—in our understanding of the Big Bang and in the strange behavior of matter at the subatomic level—further undermine the materialist view.

In this chapter I suggest a solution to the apparent conflict between science and faith over evolution. Mind, I argue, and specifically God's mind, guides evolution by influencing the life energies that drive mutations. Some of the main points in the argument are as follows:

1. Materialism is a contradictory and self-limiting philosophy because it is unable to answer, or even meaningfully address, the question of consciousness and how it arises.
2. Consciousness is the basic principle of life and matter is a product of consciousness, not the other way around.
3. There is evidence of two kinds of design in nature—Engineering Design and Aesthetic Design. Together they provide persuasive evidence that life is the deliberate creation of a conscious Designer who is both Engineer and Artist.
4. The life energy realm—where physical, mental, emotional and spiritual energies meet—is a natural vehicle through which God can guide the processes of evolution. Whether natural selection completely explains life's origins or not, God is the ultimate architect of evolution and of living things.

PART 1. THE LIMITS OF SCIENTIFIC MATERIALISM

Science, as everyone knows, deals with events in the physical world. The laws of physics, biology, chemistry and other sciences describe physical processes and the behavior of physical objects and forces. From the stars and galaxies above to the rich chemical soup within the human cell to the tiny universe of particles and waves inside every atom, science theorizes and predicts based on physical observation and measurement.

Science's spectacular success has encouraged some to believe that the tools of conventional science might one day explain virtually all of life's mysteries. Even in the relatively intangible field of psychology, researchers have shown that mental events have physical counterparts, not only in the brain but in specific protein molecules that circulate throughout the body. Research in neuroscience and genetics continues to uncover ever more detailed connections between body processes and mental and emotional events. On the surface, these findings support the materialist view that life arises from non-life, encouraging scientists to believe that the mind itself might ultimately be understood in physical terms.

In spite of these advances, large chinks have been appearing in the armor of science for some time, and certain stubborn questions continue to prevent scientists from fully explaining life as a physical phenomenon. One of the main stumbling blocks is consciousness itself—what it is, where it comes from and how it relates to matter and physical processes. Some of the most perplexing riddles concern the workings of the Unconscious. As I noted in Chapter 3, science has made little if any progress since Freud's day in answering the most basic questions about the Unconscious: What is it? What is it made of? How does it manage to organize our mental lives so effectively? There is good reason for these failures. Because science is based on physical observation and measurement, it can only give answers in quantitative, physical terms. Whenever life or consciousness is involved, the best science can do is show a relationship between the body and the mind, between the physical and the non-physical. Identifying relationships is useful and important but it leaves the basic "What is it?" questions unanswered. For those, philosophy, not science, is needed.

Materialist Philosophy: Clinging to a Slender Reed

Materialist philosophy is the attempt to give ultimate answers to life's questions using the methods and models of science. Not surprisingly, those who favor materialism tend to place a high value on the scientific method, and they assign a lesser value to other, non-scientific kinds of knowing. But as I suggested, science cannot address consciousness directly; it can only describe relationships between mental events and physical structures and activities—the brain, DNA, cellular processes and so on. By limiting themselves in advance to the kinds of knowledge they are willing to consider, materialists deny themselves the very tools they need for a deeper understanding.

And Computers Created Man in Their Own Image?

Daniel Dennett is one of the better known writers and advocates for the materialist view of consciousness. He is the author of a number of books, including the imposingly titled *Consciousness Explained*. In his book, he freely admits his allegiance to the scientific point of view and his unwillingness to consider other kinds of evidence:

> I will try to explain every puzzling feature of human consciousness within the framework of contemporary physical science; at no point will I make an appeal to inexplicable or unknown forces, substances or organic powers.[107]

Dennett begins by attacking dualism, the philosophical school associated with Descartes which holds that the mind is made of something different from matter. Dennett argues that the laws of physics make that impossible, since the mind could not influence the body if it did not contain physical energy.

> A fundamental principle of physics is that any change in the trajectory of any physical entity is an acceleration requiring the expenditure of energy, and where is this energy to come from? It is this principle of the conservation of energy that...is apparently violated by dualism...and is widely regarded as the inescapable and fatal flaw of dualism.[108]

In falling back on the laws of physics to try to explain how mind and body interact, Dennett illustrates the self-imposed limitations of materialism. Life energy principles, which have been known and studied for centuries, can readily explain how the mind influences the body—not through physical energies but through a force that unites the two at a higher level of organization. Mind and body, as we have seen, are unified at the life energy level, a non-physical but entirely real dimension of reality.

Because of the ultimate unity of mind and body, the so-called dualistic view that Dennett criticizes is not dualistic at all. Descartes was on the right track in sensing that the mind was not made of matter. What he did not anticipate was that the body itself is ultimately non-physical—that both mind and matter are reflections of a deeper reality grounded in life energies.

Dennett, even though armed with only the quantitative tools of science, is not content to show that there are relationships between the brain and the mind. His goal is far more ambitious—to resolve what he calls the mystery of consciousness itself. He says:

> What, then, is the mystery? What could be more obvious or certain to each of us than that he or she is a conscious subject of experience, an enjoyer of perceptions and sensations, a sufferer of pain, an entertainer of ideas, and a conscious deliberator? That seems undeniable, but what in the world can consciousness itself be? How can living physical bodies in the physical world produce such phenomena? That is the mystery.[109]

Dennett give a number of interesting examples of how conscious activities correspond to certain structures and relationships within the brain and nervous system. His examples lead to his ultimate conclusion: that the brain is a kind of elaborate computer, and that the mind's activities are like software programs operated by the brain's hardware. The system, Dennett says, creates what computer scientists refer to as a "virtual machine."

After much discussion, and after having raised the question several times as to whether his argument really amounts to a theory of consciousness, Dennett finally says on page 281:

> ...at last it is time to grasp the nettle, and confront consciousness itself, the whole marvelous mystery. And so I hereby declare that YES, my theory is a theory of consciousness. Anyone or anything that has such a virtual machine as its control system is conscious in the fullest sense, and is conscious because it has such a virtual machine.

Dennett's conclusion is a stunning anticlimax. Contrary to his claim, he has not explained what consciousness is at all nor how it could ever arise out of lifeless matter. Instead he has told us, like a good scientist, what some of the technical requirements for consciousness may be and who he thinks has it—"anyone or anything that has such a virtual machine as its control system." In describing rather than explaining consciousness, Dennett reveals the inadequacy of scientific tools to give any real insight into what consciousness is.

In dwelling on the parallels between computers and people, Dennett both trivializes and obscures the real mystery of consciousness. Because he sees the computer as a suitable model for the human mind, he argues that, at some point, computers themselves might become conscious.

> ..In principle, a suitably 'programmed' robot, with
> a silicon-based computer brain, would be con-
> scious, would have a self. [110]

Even Dennett does not claim that the computer on his desk—or any real computer—is conscious, only that it is possible "in principle." He gives no evidence for his conclusion nor any way to verify it directly, in spite of his claimed allegiance to the scientific method. He argues, in effect, that mechanical devices like computers can be conscious because they are like us and we are conscious. At the same time, he urges us to model ourselves after computers because, in certain limited ways, we are like them. The argument is not only circular, it turns the creative process on its head. Human beings created computers, not the other way around, and a hallmark of creation is that the creator invests something of himself, but not everything, in his creations.

In most ways, computers and people couldn't be more different. The most obvious is that computers aren't alive—they are not the natural offspring of conscious beings but are mechanical devices powered by electricity. Equally important, computers, for all their speed and power, are strictly quantitative devices. Although

Dennett claims that computers could be programmed to duplicate every detail of human experience, he fails to explain, even in principle, how anyone could reduce human emotion, or other non-rational, non-quantitative experiences, to digital form and code for them in any programming language.

The lesson to be drawn from computers is not how alike humans and computers are, but how different. Computer software is encoded on magnetic discs in the form of digital electronic signals. Human software, the stuff of the Unconscious, is written in the far more subtle language of life energies. A computer's "life" depends on being plugged into an electrical outlet, but life energy both embodies human consciousness and is its own power source. Unlike Dennett's hypothetical computer with "consciousness in the fullest sense," real living things don't risk having their richly satisfying lives abruptly ended if, for example, a four-year-old child decides to pull the plug.

Genesis 1:27 tells us that God created man in His own image. One of the ways we resemble God is in our power to create but our creations, like God's, are only pale echoes of the original. We may contain the seeds of divinity within us but most of us, unlike our Creator, are far from divine. Similarly, our creations, computers, have some of our attributes but are decidedly non-human. They lack both life energy and the consciousness that depends on it. Like God, we have the power to create; unlike God, we cannot do so with life energies. Therefore we cannot give the gift of life.

PART 2. IT'S AN ETHEREAL WORLD: IRISH PHILOSOPHY, QUANTA AND THE WISDOM OF ASIA

Reality is merely an illusion, albeit a very persistent one.
—Albert Einstein

In the Western world, non-materialism is often seen as an exotic philosophy that was transplanted from faraway places like India and China. In fact, major philosophers from both East and West have agreed that life is ultimately grounded, not in matter, but in consciousness.

George Berkeley was an 18th century Irish philosopher and Catholic bishop, and was a prominent figure in the philosophical school known as Empiricism. He advocated the famous theory of Subjective Idealism. Its main idea is quite simple: that in the deepest sense, the physical world has no independent existence of its own but is a projection of our minds and the mind of God. If there were no observer to see it, the world would literally cease to exist. Berkeley summarized his view in the following famous quotation:

> All the choir of heaven and the furniture of earth, in a word all those bodies which compose the mighty frame of the world, have not any subsistence without a mind.

The gist of Berkeley's idea is illustrated by a well-known riddle. If a tree falls in the forest and nobody is there to hear it, does it make a sound? The riddle is effective because it tricks us into visualizing a tree falling in an empty forest, and the image of a tree falling silently seems like a contradiction. In fact, it is a contradiction. As soon as we imagine ourselves watching the tree, our imaginary forest is no longer empty—we are there watching (and listening) and when the tree falls, we both see and hear it.

The real point of the riddle is Berkeley's point—that it is impossible to separate things or events from our experience of them. A tree only looks like a tree because that's how it looks to us. The sound of a tree falling is only a sound because we hear it. Things only exist to the extent that somebody, somewhere experiences them existing.

Berkeley's argument is hard to take seriously because everyday experience seems to contradict it. We know that, when we go to bed at night, things will be the same in the morning as they were the night before. The sun will rise in the east, the little pile of coins we left on the night table will still be there—everything simply picks up from where it left off. If, as Berkeley says, things are so dependent on someone observing them, why is the world so stable and reliable?

Berkeley's answer is that God makes the world stable by holding it in His mind and paying constant attention to it. Just as a tree ceases to exist, at least for us, when we stop looking at it, the world would cease to exist if God stopped thinking about it. All of the things in nature that we take for granted are reliable and consistent only because God keeps them that way. The Indian concept of *maya* expresses the same idea—God creates the illusion of an independent physical reality by making things so stable and dependable that we see no good reason to believe otherwise.

The Observer Effect and Other Scientific Evidence

In earlier times, Berkeley's view, no matter how insightful, would have been easier to dismiss because there was no solid evidence to support it. Things have changed since Berkeley's day. We now know many things about nature that cast serious doubt on the claim that matter, not consciousness, is the primary stuff of life. Some of the evidence is as follows.

1. Our experience of the world is utterly dependent on the equipment we use to perceive it. If our eyes, ears and nervous systems were made differently, our surroundings would look, sound and feel like a very different place.

2. We know that the Big Bang was the origin of the universe. Before that there was no space, no time and no matter. Whatever existed then could not have depended on matter because there was no matter to depend on.

3. Relativity theory shows that matter has no absolute existence but can be converted into energy. Even the framework that matter exists in—space and time—is plastic and changeable and the two are dependent on each other and on the observer experiencing them.

4. The most direct confirmation of Berkeley's view comes from recent discoveries in quantum physics. The Observer Effect, in which matter literally comes into being when someone looks for it, is described as follows by the physicist Paul Davies:

> None of the foregoing really gets to grips with the central paradox of the quantum theory, which is the unique role played by the mind in determining reality. As we have seen, the act of observation causes the ghostlike superposition of potential realities to cohere into a single, concrete reality.[111]

Thus at the most basic level, science has confirmed that physical objects are not only dependent on our minds, they are created by them. This discovery undermines and perhaps destroys the basic premise of materialist philosophy. At the quantum level, matter is not the source of consciousness—consciousness is the source of matter. Berkeley's insight, applied at the subatomic level, has become an established principle of modern physics.

Rene Descartes, the French philosopher who preceded the Empiricsts, is credited with what is probably the most famous phrase in Western philosophy—*Cogito ergo sum*: I think, therefore I am. Consciousness, Descartes said, is existence. After that basic principle, everything else is secondary.

THE ASIAN PERSPECTIVE: LIFE AS A PLAY OF IDEAS

Many centuries before the Western philosophers, the saints and sages of Asia had realized the same truths, not through philosophical insight but through direct experience. The great philosophy-religions of India and China agree that mind, not matter, is the foundation of existence.

Hinduism and the Eternal Spirit

Swami Sri Yukteswar Giri (1855-1936) was an Indian spiritual master and guru of Paramahansa Yogananda. In his book *The Holy*

Science, he described the physical world from the perspective of Hinduism:

> Through *Avidya* [ignorance] man believes that the material creation is the only thing that substantially exists...forgetting that this material creation is substantially nothing and is a mere play of ideas on the Eternal Spirit. [112]

Sri Yukteswar's words echo those of Bishop Berkeley. The image of creation as a "play of ideas on the Eternal Spirit" hints at God as a kind of cosmic Storyteller, and at earthly life as a drama spun out of God's imagination.

Taoism and the Gate to Mystery

Taoism, as we have seen, is the origin of the concepts of *yin* and *yang* and of the idea that everyday life is a play of opposites. Like Hinduism, Taoism teaches that the source of life is eternal and transcends time, space and matter. The Tao Te Ching introduces that idea in its opening verse:

> The Tao that can be told is not the eternal Tao.
> The name that can be named is not the eternal name.
> The nameless is the beginning of heaven and earth.
> The named is the mother of ten thousand things.
> Ever desireless, one can see the mystery.
> Ever desiring, one can see the manifestations. [113]

Taoism teaches that matter, which manifests itself as the "ten thousand things" of everyday life, is only a surface appearance. Giving in to its seductive power limits one's perspective—"Ever desiring, one can see the manifestations." Overcoming the lure of the material can lead to a deeper understanding—"Ever desireless, one can see the mystery."

Buddhism and the Great Illusion

Buddhism, like its sister religions, teaches that a deeper awareness of life means transcending the realm of the material. By accepting the Buddha's Four Noble Truths and following the Eightfold Path to Enlightenment, one can achieve Nirvana, the joyful awareness of spiritual truth. Nirvana signifies that one has conquered the Great Illusion—the erroneous idea that the everyday material world is the ultimate reality.

PART 3. EVIDENCE OF DESIGN

If mind, not matter, is the foundation of life, and if life is but a play of ideas on the Eternal Spirit, the development of life on earth must be far more than just an automatic, mindless process. Even if Darwin's theory of natural selection is correct, or partly correct, the accumulating evidence from both philosophy and science suggests that consciousness is the active, creative force behind evolution.

Before presenting my view of evolution and how life energy principles can help clarify it, I discuss below some of the current arguments for and against what is called Intelligent Design.[114] The mystical philosophy-religions of Asia are like eyewitness testimony in a court case. They say, in effect, "I know that God exists because I have seen Her." The search for design in nature is more indirect. Like a case based on circumstantial evidence, the Argument from Design tries to prove God's existence from the long trail of clues She left behind.

There are two kinds of possible design in nature. The current debate over what I call Engineering Design centers on the claim that living things are too complex to have been produced by a mindless, automatic process. A second kind of design—I call it Aesthetic Design—represents my view that there are beautiful symbolic patterns in nature that have no practical utility at all, and therefore could not have been produced by natural selection.

ENGINEERING DESIGN: FROM PALEY'S WATCH
TO THE MACHINERY OF THE HUMAN CELL

Although the mainstream scientific community still largely accepts orthodox Darwinism, there are growing doubts in many quarters as to whether chance natural selection alone can fully explain the diversity of life we see on earth. Most authorities agree that Darwin's theory does a good job of explaining small changes in organisms, but no one has yet explained, much less proven, how natural selection can account for larger and more important innovations, including the appearance of entirely new species. Two researchers have expressed the problem as follows:

> It is now approximately half a century since the neo-Darwinian synthesis was formulated. A great deal of research has been carried on within the paradigm it defines. Yet the successes of the theory are limited to the minutiae of evolution, such as the adaptive change in coloration of moths; while it has remarkably little to say on the questions that interest us most, such as how there came to be moths in the first place.[115.]

The Argument for Irreducible Complexity

Michael Behe is one of the more controversial recent writers on evolution. He is a professor of biochemistry at Lehigh University and author of *Darwin's Black Box: the Biochemical Challenge to Evolution.* He argues that Darwin's theory falls far short of fully explaining how complex living things came into being.

Behe argues that natural selection may account for some of the simpler changes in living things, but that for many highly complex structures—especially the immensely complicated systems within the living cell—random individual mutations could not have produced them. Behe gives many detailed examples and coins the term "irreducible complexity" to describe them. An irreducibly complex structure is one made up of a number of interdependent parts suited for a particular purpose, and that will not work if even a single part is missing.

One of Behe's examples is the cilium, a tiny hairlike structure that certain cells, including sperm cells, use as a kind of paddle to "swim around" inside the body. The cilium is so small that it took the invention of the electron microscope to see its details. But in spite of its tiny size, the cilium is, in Behe's words, "a swimming system...[that].....requires a paddle to contact the water, a motor or source of energy, and a connector to link the two. All systems that move by paddling—ranging from my daughter's toy fish to the propeller of a ship—fail if any one of the components is absent."[116]

Behe describes each of the three parts of the cilium in detail. Each is made of a different chemical material and all of the parts must be assembled properly and work together in order for the cilium to function. Behe argues that the cilium and other irreducibly complex structures could not have developed from the gradual, piecemeal changes that are the product of individual mutations. How, then, did they develop?

> Clearly, if something was not put together gradu-
> ally, then it must have been put together quickly or
> even suddenly. If adding individual pieces does
> not continuously improve the function of a system,
> then multiple pieces have to be added together.[117]

Behe describes two current, non-Darwinian theories of how organisms may have developed quickly rather than gradually, but he finds each unsatisfactory. He settles on a third explanation called Intelligent Design. He traces the Argument from Design back to pre-Darwinian times, noting that, before the theory of evolution, both scientists and philosophers often accepted the idea that the world was the product of a conscious Designer.

To illustrate how the Argument from Design was framed in the days before the electron microscope, Behe cites the famous example given by the 19th century Anglican minister William Paley in his book *Natural Theology*.

> In crossing a heath, suppose I pitched my foot upon a stone, and were asked how the stone came to be there. I might possibly answer, that for anything I knew to the contrary it had lain there forever...But suppose I had found a <u>watch</u> upon the ground, and it should be inquired how the watch happened to be in that place, I should hardly think of the answer which I had before given...[118]

Paley describes how the inner workings of a watch "are framed and put together for a purpose" and that "if the different parts had been differently shaped from what they are, or placed after any other manner or in any other order....either no motion at all would have been carried on in the machine, or none that would have answered the use that is now served by it."[119]

Paley goes on to describe various biological structures, such as the heart, which he believes illustrate the same principle of irreducible complexity that Michael Behe is now advancing two centuries later. Although Behe's 21st century examples are far more complex than Paley's, his argument is essentially the same as Paley's.

Like Paley, Behe's views have received a mixed reception. Those who disagree with him claim that Behe underestimates the creative power of natural selection. Some of the opponents of Engineering Design attack Behe's ideas directly; others do so indirectly. One of the most vocal contemporary critics takes a mechanistic, computer-inspired approach reminiscent of the views of Daniel Dennett.

Evolution as Information Processing

Richard Dawkins is an evolutionary biologist and author of several books, including T*he Blind Watchmaker: Why the Evidence of Evolution Reveals a Universe Without Design*. The title refers to the Reverend Paley and his famous watch analogy. Dawkins emphatically believes that the "watchmaker" in nature is not an

Intelligent Designer at all but simply the blind, automatic processes of natural selection.

Dawkins, like Dennett, sees the computer as a useful model for understanding life processes, including human consciousness. Both men see humans as essentially machines come to life and evolution as a process governed by the same data processing rules that make computers work. Like Dennett, Dawkins takes the radical view that we can use one of our own creations as a model for understanding our own far more complex and subtle makeup.

Dawkins uses a variety of arguments to advance his thesis. In one chapter he describes three computer programs he wrote to illustrate how complex things can be built up from simple ones. The first is a program that tries out different combinations of letters from the alphabet and, within forty or fifty "generations," is able to come up with the phrase "Methinks it is like a weasel." The example correctly illustrates the power of what Dawkins calls cumulative selection—building on successive small improvements to speed up the process of change.

Dawkins' second example is a program that starts by drawing a single straight line, which branches into two lines, then into four, and so on, simulating what happens when cells divide. The result, after a number of repetitions, is a shape that looks something like a tree. Dawkins then varies the program to simulate what would happen if different "genes" were involved. For instance, one version might cause the branching lines to diverge by twenty degrees, another by thirty degrees, and another by forty degrees. The result, as Dawkins shows, is a whole series of different line drawings of "trees," each of which has a somewhat different shape.

Dawkins' final example is a program that simulates random mutations by arbitrarily adding or subtracting a value before drawing a line. The result is an "evolving" series of shapes that end up looking something like a bunch of insects drawn on a sheet of paper.

Dawkins's programs are excellent teaching tools for illustrating some of the basic mechanics of evolution. They cleverly illustrate how genes affect development and how mutations cause small changes which eventually become large changes over many generations. But as a device for persuading the reader that simple organisms like bacteria, given three or four billion years, could have evolved into you or me, they are highly misleading. Dawkins' computer programs are, in the end, nothing more than mathematical formulae that give instructions for carrying out quantitative, mechanical tasks. They ignore the central and most important fact of life—consciousness—and the remarkable subtlety and variety of human experience that are associated with it.

Dawkins, like Dennett, fails to address the qualitative, non-rational parts of ourselves—emotion, intuition, creativity—and how any set of digital instructions could ever represent those experiences in a meaningful way. How could one write a computer program, for example, that would capture the essence of the following experiences?

> The emotions one felt on the day one's first child
>   was born
> The inspiration that moved Bach to write his 3rd
>   Brandenburg Concerto
> The taste of chocolate

Dawkins ignores these kinds of questions because he has no choice. Only by reducing life to ideas that can be expressed as numbers can he model human beings after computers. He tellingly describes his understanding of the essence of life as follows:

> There is nothing special about the substances from which living things are made: living things are collections of molecules, like everything else...Maybe they do vibrate and throb and pulsate with "irritability" and glow with "living" warmth, but these properties all emerge incidentally. What lies at the heart of every living thing is not fire, not warm breath, not a "spark of life." It is information, words, instructions. If you want a metaphor, don't think of fires and sparks and breath. Think instead,

of a billion discrete, digital characters carved in
tablets of crystal.[120]

Dawkins' words are not only chilling, they are contrary to
everyday experience. To argue that human warmth is an incidental
part of life is to say that love, compassion and the other emotions
that make civilization possible are of no value either to us person-
ally or to evolution itself. When Dawkins extols "information,
words, instructions" and claims they are life's essence, he gives an
extreme example, a virtual caricature, of the analytical bias of science.

Dawkins' treatment of religion is another example of his
extreme materialist bias. Whether there is design in evolution—the
stated theme of his book—is a two-part scientific-religious question. To address it in a serious way, one would expect a discussion
of both the scientific and religious arguments, including the pros
and cons for each. Since Dawkins is a biologist, not a clergyman or
philosopher, he might be forgiven for making his scientific arguments somewhat longer and more detailed than his discussion of
religion. But at a minimum, we can expect more than the following on the question of God's possible role in designing life:

> To explain the origin of the DNA/protein machine
> by invoking a supernatural Designer is to explain
> precisely nothing, for it leaves unexplained the ori-
> gin of the Designer. You have to say something
> like, "God was always there," and if you allow
> yourself that kind of lazy way out, you might as
> well just say "DNA was always there," or "Life
> was always there," and be done with it.[121]

This is the sum and substance of Dawkins' discussion of the religious argument for design. In two sentences he dismisses the collected wisdom of 4,000 years of spiritual history and rejects the
fundamental teaching of every great world religion. When
Dawkins calls the belief that God is eternal the "lazy way out," he
not only trivializes a deep spiritual insight, he ignores an issue that

has important scientific implications. The Big Bang, which Dawkins' fellow scientists have identified as the origin of the universe, marked the beginning of time, space and matter. It is difficult even to talk about what happened before the Big Bang since time did not yet exist. The notion of timelessness, and of an eternal, timeless reality, are no longer just philosophical ideas—they are concepts that are bumping up against the outer frontiers of science itself.

Dawkins concedes that his book is, to some extent, a work of advocacy rather than a straightforward presentation of ideas. But even in a book intended to persuade, a writer has an obligation to present competing ideas in a fair and balanced light. Dawkins has praised Darwin's *Origin of Species* for having "...made it possible to be an intellectually fulfilled atheist."[122] Dawkins is entitled to his personal beliefs but his book makes it clear that those beliefs are based on a distorted view of both science and religion.

Challenging Irreducible Complexity Directly

Another prominent critic of Intelligent Design, Kenneth Miller, attacks Michael Behe's theory head-on. Miller, a professor of biology at Brown University and the author of *Finding Darwin's God,* argues that the structures within the living cell, although highly complex, evolved gradually in a series of step-by-step changes.

Miller attacks irreducible complexity in several ways. He argues that the individual parts of complex systems—for example, the sonar system that bats use to locate insects—may have evolved through the cooperative actions of several genes working together. Miller argues that bats may have used such a process to convert a crude, barely workable system into the highly sophisticated echolocation system that bats have today.

Although cooperative genes are a popular topic in evolutionary biology today, Miller does not explain how or why such genes may have mutated at just the right time, and in just the right ways, to bring about the echolocation system in bats.

Miller discusses, and tries to refute, some of Behe's specific examples of irreducible complexity. The cilium, he argues, is not irreducibly complex because there are many different kinds of cilia, some more complicated than others, and the more complex varieties may have evolved from the simpler ones. Again, however, Miller fails to give details that might explain how any cilium could have evolved all of its working parts through a series of individual random mutations.

Another of Behe's examples that Miller criticizes is the human blood clotting mechanism. The clotting cascade, as it is called, is, in Behe's phrase, a kind of "Rube Goldberg machine"—a long series of complex and improbable chemical interactions that must be perfectly timed and coordinated for the system to work. Behe claims the system could never have evolved through piecemeal mutations; Miller argues that it could and gives a number of technical reasons why.

The clotting cascade illustrates, not just the complexity of the human body, but of the argument over Intelligent Design. As a scientific argument, it is too technical for anyone but specialists to resolve. The continuing disagreement between Behe, Miller and others illustrates that even specialists can be passionately divided on the issue.

Miller, however, seriously weakens his own argument when he admits, at least indirectly, that mutations may not occur by chance after all. Miller, a man of faith, is intent on showing—as the title of his book suggests—that God's will can somehow be reconciled with the workings of evolution. He says:

> Since chance—and for that matter, free will— played such an important role in bringing me to life, does this mean that I cannot view my own existence as part of God's plan? Of course not. Any clergyman, very much in the Christian tradition, would caution me that God's purposes do not always submit to human analysis. God's means are beyond our ability to fathom, and just because events <u>seem</u> [emphasis added] to have ordinary causes, or <u>seem</u> [emphasis added] to be the result of

chance, does   not mean they are not part of that Divine plan.[123]

Miller is clearly trying to have it both ways—to argue on the one hand that evolution is a truly random, mechanistic process, and on the other that it is part of God's plan. How that could be possible Miller does not say. In effect, he throws up his hands and says, "I don't know—but God surely does." But in acknowledging that events may only "seem" to have ordinary causes and may only "seem" to be the result of chance, Miller concedes there could be a hidden mechanism that makes events appear to be random while they are actually part of God's design. That mechanism, I argue, is the mutation process, which God invisibly guides by influencing the life energies at the level of individual cells.

Further study will one day show whether Behe or Miller is right—whether living things required whole clusters of simultaneous mutations to evolve as they did, or whether separate individual mutations were sufficient. Whichever explanation is correct, God, I argue, is the creative intelligence behind evolution. The argument over irreducible complexity is, in the end, a side argument—a debate, not over God's presence or absence in creation, but over the engineering details of God's design.

AESTHETIC DESIGN: SYMBOLIC PATTERNS IN NATURE

The long and fierce debate over evolution shows, among other things, how difficult it can be to prove Engineering Design. No matter how complex living things are, and no matter how persuasive the evidence may be that they were designed, natural selection always provides a respectable counterargument. Because useful changes in living things give them a clear survival advantage, any process that preserves those improvements demands to be considered. Natural selection argues that usefulness, not design, explains the ever-growing complexity of living things.

Aesthetic Design is different. There are beautiful patterns in nature that do not give living things a survival advantage of any

kind; in fact, they have no practical use at all. Therefore natural selection cannot explain them. For that reason Aesthetic Design may
be more persuasive than Engineering Design as an argument for
God's role in creation.

Some people see beauty itself as evidence of God's invisible
hand. Philosophers disagree on that point but in any case there is a
stronger argument for Aesthetic Design. The symbolic relationships between human beings and natural forces, and between
human personality and the heavens above, are more than just beautiful things. They are complex and beautiful patterns that strongly
point to a Designer whose creative vision embraces, not just planet
earth, but the solar system and the stars beyond.

The Artistry of the Five Elements

I described the Five Elements system and its beautiful symbolism
in Chapter 1. Fire energy nourishes Earth energy as the sun warms
the earth; Earth energy controls Water energy as a riverbank contains a river's flow; Water energy nourishes Wood energy as water
makes plant grow; and so on. These and other correspondences
exist, it is true, because human beings named the five energies, but
they were able to do so only because the correspondences were
already there, waiting to be discovered.

The five energies correspond to the four seasons as well, and to
a fifth quality that transcends the *yin-yang* duality of everyday life.
Fire and Water, the energies of extroversion and introversion,
correspond to summer and winter, the seasons of peak vitality and
maximum dormancy. Wood and Metal, the energies of expansion
and contraction, correspond to spring and autumn, the seasons of
growth and decline. The fifth energy, Earth, bears the transforming
emotion of love and symbolizes the human capacity to rise above
the tensions and conflicts of earthly life.

The meridians too, have their own inner poetry. Several of the
sister meridians embody physical and emotional qualities that
mirror one another. The Earth meridians carry the energies of the
physical need for food and its emotional equivalent, the need for

love. The Metal meridians process both physical waste and the emotional residues of grief and guilt. Wood energy nourishes the eyes and makes vision possible; in the psyche, Wood is an energy of growth and inner vision, and of visionaries like Thomas Jefferson and Martin Luther King.

There is no survival value in these patterns. Their value is entirely aesthetic—in the beautiful symbolism that connects human life with the natural world. Because natural selection cannot account for them, the most likely explanation is that an Intelligent Designer created them in order to make the universe a more beautiful place. That conclusion is even more likely when we consider the even grander unity and symbolism that links human life with the stars and planets.

Astrology as God's Art

I described the artistry that links human life and the heavens in Chapter 4. It begins with the familiar duality of male and female. The solar system's two most prominent bodies from our point of view, the Sun and Moon, are a cosmic mirror of men and women. The Sun is *yang* and rules the sign of Leo, which embodies the traditional male qualities of strength, leadership, dominance and control. More generally, the Sun represents the Freudian Ego, and the birth sign, the single most important influence in the chart, is the sign in which the Sun is traveling at the moment of birth.

The Moon, which is *yin* to the Sun's *yang*, strongly affects a person's emotional and intuitive makeup—traditional female qualities. The Moon rules the sign of Cancer, the most domestic of the twelve signs. If the Moon is in its own sign, a person will have well-developed family instincts and strong intuitive capacities.

The rising sign—the sign on the eastern horizon at the moment of birth—symbolizes the dawning of consciousness and carries the energies of the outer public persona. The First House adjoins the horizon and any planet in that house "dawns" in consciousness and has special prominence. The Twelfth House, by contrast, lies just on the other side of the horizon and any planet in the Twelfth

House strongly affects the Unconscious.

Jupiter and Saturn, the two largest planets, bear contrasting energies. Jupiter and the sign it rules, Sagittarius, embody optimism, confidence, high spirits and good luck. Saturn, a planet of limitation and struggle, is girdled by rings that symbolize its constricting influence on the human psyche.

Each of the planets, signs and houses mirrors, in its own way, some aspect of personality or behavior. Mercury, the closest planet to the Sun and the most rapidly rotating of the planets, is associated with quickness, movement and communication. Venus and Mars, the planets of love and war, can tip personality in the direction of kindness and compassion or toward anger, aggression and conflict. Uranus is an influence for change, Neptune a faraway, nebulous planet of softness and spirituality, and Pluto a dynamic and sometimes disruptive force.

Some students of astrology, as I noted earlier, believe that the relationships between personality and the heavens are purely symbolic; others see a causal connection between planetary energies and human behavior. Whichever view is correct, astrology is, in the end, a spiritual teaching whose truth is powerful evidence of an underlying unity in all of creation—and of a God for whom beauty and symbolism are as important as science and engineering.

PART 4. EVOLUTION, LIFE ENERGY AND GOD

If God designed the world as a combined work of engineering and art, what tools did He use? We know from the laws of physics, chemistry and other sciences that nature follows definite laws. The organization we see everywhere suggests that God has a preference for natural, orderly processes. The beauty of the universe, like that of a symphony, a painting or a well-designed novel, comes in part from the order and structure that give it shape and form. The pattern suggests that, in creating living things as in creating the universe as a whole, God chose a natural rather than a supernatural process. Mutations are the natural mechanism through which living things change, adapt and develop.

God's hand can be seen in evolution, I argue, if we make a single, simple change in our understanding of how mutations work. By removing the element of chance—which is not scientifically provable and is not a part of Darwin's theory *per se*—and substituting the conscious will of God, evolution becomes both a natural and a divine process. Life energy, which connects body and mind with Spirit, is a crucial link in the chain.

Darwin's Fateful Assumption

Charles Darwin's groundbreaking book, *On the Origin of Species*, was published in 1859. The main elements of his theory are quite simple:

1. Living things, including humans, evolved gradually over millions of years through a process called natural selection.
2. In natural selection, individuals undergo slight changes and pass them on to their offspring. Beneficial changes give the offspring a better chance of survival so those changes tend to become permanent in the population. Over long periods, natural selection leads to major improvements in species and, eventually, in the appearance of entirely new kinds of living things.

Because the science of genetics did not yet exist when Darwin developed his theory, he could not have known that mutations lay behind the changes in living things. He freely admitted his vague understanding of how variation and natural selection worked:

> The result of the various, quite unknown, or dimly seen laws of variation is infinitely complex and diversified.

> The laws governing inheritance are quite unknown; no one can say why the same peculiarity in different individuals of the same species, and in individuals of different species, is sometimes inherited and sometimes not so.[124]

Darwin concedes, in the opening paragraph of Chapter 5 of "The Origin of Species," that his theory does not claim, or prove, that chance lies behind natural selection:

> I have hitherto sometimes spoken as if the varia-
> tions—so common and multiform in organic beings
> under domestication, and in a lesser degree in
> those in a state of nature—had been due to chance.
> This, of course, is a wholly incorrect expression,
> but it serves to acknowledge plainly our ignorance
> of the cause of each particular variation.

Darwin reserved his personal beliefs for his private correspon-
dence. Darwin is sometimes described incorrectly as an atheist. In fact, he was a religious man whose writings suggest he was a kind of Deist: that he saw the hand of a cosmic Designer, if not in the events of daily life, at least in the overall laws of nature. In his response to a letter from the Harvard botanist Asa Gray, who was both a supporter of Darwin and a devout Christian, Darwin con-
fessed how troubled he felt by some of the implications of his own theory:

> With respect to the theological view of the ques-
> tion. This is always painful to me. I am bewildered.
> I had no intention to write atheistically...[but]...I
> am inclined to look at everything as resulting from
> designed laws, with the details, whether good or
> bad, left to the working out of what we may call
> chance. Not that this notion at all satisfies me. I feel
> most deeply that the whole subject is too profound
> for the human intellect. A dog might as well specu-
> late on the mind of Newton. Let each man hope and
> believe what he can.[125]

Science and Non-Science

Darwin's private conflict foreshadowed the long public debate that would follow. His belief that chance governed natural selection, and the acceptance of that view by others, spawned a controversy between science and faith that has lasted for almost 150 years and that shows no sign of abating.

As Darwin's writings show, his belief in chance was neither a part of the theory of evolution itself nor was it even science. It was apparently based, at least in part, on Darwin's reluctance to hold God responsible for the cruelty and suffering he saw in nature.[126] But whatever Darwin's reasons, his belief in chance was no more scientific than, for example, the creationist notion that the world was made in six days. There was then, and is now,[127] no scientific proof that genetic mutations are due to chance. Nevertheless, the idea managed to attach itself to the legitimate scientific ideas of Darwinism and came to be accepted as a *de facto* part of the theory itself.

The Discovery of Mutations: the Gap Widens

When the new science of genetics showed that mutations lay behind variations in living things, the gap between science and religion grew even wider. The advocates for randomness and chance now had a specific mechanism to point to which, they claimed, had all the earmarks of a mindless, accidental process. Mutations, it turned out, were not only as common as fleas but almost as predictable. They often occurred through a simple error in copying the DNA sequence during cell division, a kind of "clerical error" in the cell. Scientists today can estimate about how often a mutation will occur for a given organism—the mutation rate. The vast majority of mutations are of little or no consequence and end up getting lost in the evolutionary soup. Does this not show that mutations are merely random, accidental events?

Unfortunately for the materialist view, it does not. Mutations may be common, predictable and mostly unimportant, but that merely shows that evolution is an extremely inefficient and even wasteful process; in other words, it is very much like life itself. Mankind's long, slow, painful struggle up out of the swamp and into the modern world has been a monument to messiness and inefficiency. The list is a long one—war, conquest, cruelty, barbarism, slavery—and more recently, bigotry, greed, injustice and discrimination. From the individual's point of view, the story has often been a tragic and, at times, a seemingly pointless one. From history's perspective, however, the development of life has been a rich and multi-layered story.

Some scientists argue that, if God were the force behind evolution, He would not have chosen such a slow and inefficient process nor would he have used it to conceal His own role.[128] That view betrays science's pragmatic, analytic bias and overlooks the artistic aspect in creation. If God were solely an Engineer, it is true that a messy, ambiguous process like mutations—one that leads to frequent blind alleys and that includes more failures than successes—would likely have been unacceptable. But for a God who values art as much as science, and for whom the long, meandering journey of creation itself may be as important as reaching the final destination, mutations seem an ideal solution. God, after all, is not constrained, as human engineers are, by time or budget limitations. Mutations, too, allow God to remain in the background and, like a human artist, let His work speak for itself.

Mutations as God's Creative Tool

A mutation happens when a tiny piece of DNA—the genetic code–changes inside a cell. The result can be a change, large or small, in how the organism develops or functions. Kenneth Miller describes the importance of mutations in evolution as follows:

> Mutations are a continuing and inexhaustible source of variation, and they provide the raw material that is shaped by natural selection. Since mutations can duplicate, invert, delete and rewrite any part of the genetic system in any organism, they can produce any change that evolution has documented.[129]

In addition to the spontaneous mutations referred to above in which the cell's machinery makes a mistake copying DNA, mutations can come about through external causes such as radiation or chemical influences. Whatever the immediate cause of a mutation, the body's built-in mechanism for changing itself is designed to make God a part of the process. Those who can see and read the body's energies have begun to sketch a portrait of how God can influence body processes through the life energy system.

In Chapter 5 I referred to Barbara Brennan's work in tracing the structure of what she calls the Human Energy Field or HEF, commonly known as the aura. Brennan perceives seven layers in the aura that correspond to every aspect of human life—physical, mental, emotional and spiritual. The layers of the aura which are connected to the upper chakras are heavily imbued with spiritual energies. Those linked to the lower chakras contain, among other things, a kind of energy template for the body and its activities. Brennan describes one of the template layers, known as the Etheric Body, as follows:

> The etheric body consists of a definite structure of lines of force, or energy matrix, upon which the physical matter of the body tissues is shaped and anchored. The physical tissues exist as such only because of the vital [energy] field behind them; that is, the field is prior to, not a result of, the physical body. This relationship has been supported in the observations of plant growth by Dr. John Pierrakos and myself. Through the use of High Sense Perception, we observed that an energy field matrix n the shape of a leaf is projected by the plant prior to the growth of a leaf, and then the leaf grows into that already existing form.[130]

Brennan's comment that the energy field exists "prior to, not because of, the physical body," is especially telling. Her image of a leaf existing in energy form before it appears physically recalls the principle of Eastern and Western philosophy that mind precedes matter. If, as I argue in Chapter 3, the Unconscious is an energy brain that mirrors and underlies the physical brain, the instructions that tell the energy leaf to form come from that invisible energy brain. The physical part of reality—the green leaf and the DNA that tells it how and when to grow—are like echoes of a deeper, more unified reality within the energy system.

Within that system, as we have seen, are spiritual energies that come ultimately from God. The energy matrix thus represents a connection between human life and Spirit through which God can influence the life, health or consciousness of any living thing—and through which He can guide the processes of evolution.

The apparently random mutations that drive evolution only seem random, I argue, because we are unaware of the spiritual unity that underlies all of life. That unity requires that everything, including all biological processes—and all mutations, the useful and the useless alike—be orchestrated by the same presiding Intelligence. Contrary to the views of some scientists, God does not interfere with or manipulate natural processes to influence evolution—God *is* the process of evolution itself since the energies that guide it come from Him. All of the evidence cited in this chapter points toward that conclusion: the weakness of the materialist view; the insights of philosophers and mystics from both East and West; the evidence of both Engineering and Aesthetic Design; the perceptions of medical intuitives; and Western science's own understanding of the Big Bang and the Observer Effect.

The Universe as God's Body

Writers sometimes describe material creation as God's body, suggesting that God, like human beings, has both consciousness and physical form. If God guides evolution through the life energies that power mutations, Her mind and body, like ours, are connected through life energies. This is yet another example of the truth of Genesis 1:27— that human beings are made in the image of God.

The conventional Darwinian idea that God is a remote figure uninvolved in everyday life recalls the discussion in Chapter 3 of the schizoid personality pattern. In human beings, emotional health depends in part on the integration of mind and body energies. At the far end of the spectrum are unhealthy conditions in which a person loses contact with many of his or her body energies.

If God is, by definition, all-knowing and all-powerful, then She must be completely in touch with Her own body—the material universe—and with everything in it, including all the intricate workings of every human body. For God to guide evolution through the energies that drive mutations is thus a completely natural and healthy thing for Her to do. To do any less would mean that God is neither all-knowing nor all-powerful.

The Real Missing Link

In the early days of Darwinism, the search for the "Missing Link"—the half-ape, half-man whose fossil remains would prove humans were descended from the beasts—was a popular media story. It fascinated the public for years but no definitive link was ever found. Instead, scientists discovered a series of fossils that showed a gradual progression from the ape-type bone structure to the human form. The search for the Missing Link was finally abandoned.

The real Missing Link, I argue, is not an ape but an idea. It does not connect our ancestors with us—it connects us with our Creator. Life energy, the force through which God acts in evolution, unites mind, matter and Spirit and creates, bit by bit, the magnificent tapestry that makes up the world of living things. Evolution is thus both a natural and a divine process. Just as there is no conflict between nature and God, there is none between science and faith.

PART 5. FREE WILL AND GOD'S WILL

Chance as an Illusion

The unity that underlies life suggests that the conventional view of mutations is just one example of the erroneous belief that random-ness and chance govern everyday events. If God is always present and active and if life unfolds according to Her plan, chance ulti-mately has no meaning. Even events that seem on the surface random and unpredictable—flipping a coin, playing the lottery, predicting the weather a year from today—can all be predicted in principle because they are all based on a finite number of factors that can be known. If God is aware of every factor, and has an unlimited capacity to calculate their influences, it follows that God can, in principle, know and predict everything in advance.

Coincidence and Meaning

Apparent coincidences illustrate the collision between chance, or what appears to be chance, and the recurring feeling that there is a pattern or design in everyday life. Apparent coincidences link both small events and larger historical trends. A number of apparent coincidences in American history have hinted at the presence of an unseen Designer or Storyteller.

John Adams and Thomas Jefferson were two of America's Founding Fathers. Adams was the nation's second president and Jefferson the third. The two men had opposite temperaments and sharply conflicting political instincts, and they battled one another throughout their careers, promoting competing visions for the new American democracy. Though they were fierce rivals, they had deep respect and regard for one another.

Adams and Jefferson both died on July 4, 1826—exactly fifty years to the day after the signing of the Declaration of Independ-ence. On the day of his death, Adams' last words were said to have been, "Thomas Jefferson still lives!"

Another, more elaborate set of apparent coincidences connects the lives and careers of Abraham Lincoln and John F. Kennedy. Many of the parallels are trivial in themselves but there are so many of them, and they form such an uncanny pattern, that it seems almost unthinkable they could have been due to coincidence.

THE WISDOM OF ASIA

THE WISDOM OF ASIA 275

Abraham Lincoln was elected to Congress in 1846.
John F. Kennedy was elected to Congress in 1946.
Lincoln was elected President in 1860.
Kennedy was elected President in 1960.

Each man was particularly concerned with civil rights
while in office.
Each man lost a child while in office.
Both men were shot on a Friday, and both were
shot in the back of the head.

Lincoln was shot while sitting in Ford's Theatre.
Kennedy was shot while riding in a Ford automobile
(a Lincoln).

Both men were assassinated by Southerners; both were
succeeded by Southerners.
Both successors were named Johnson.
Andrew Johnson, who succeeded Lincoln, was born
in 1808.
Lyndon Johnson, who succeeded Kennedy, was born
in 1908.

John Wilkes Booth, who killed Lincoln, was known by
three names totaling fifteen letters.
Lee Harvey Oswald, who killed Kennedy, was known by
three names totaling fifteen letters.

In the Introduction I referred to another, more important parallel in
the lives of Lincoln and Kennedy and in the times when they governed. Each man presided over a period of great social upheaval
that foreshadowed a more enlightened era to come. The end of the
Civil War saw the beginning of a new and more inclusive American democracy. A century later, the 1960's saw the Vietnam War
abroad and civil unrest at home—but it marked, too, the beginning
of the Age of Aquarius, which may prove to be a more humane and

progressive period than the world has known before.

The less important but more eerie parallels in the lives of Lincoln and Kennedy could be taken as further evidence—a kind of cosmic hint—that the 1860's and 1960's are truly linked in some meaningful way. If so, the beginning of the Age of Aquarius is a milestone worthy of our attention.

Human Will and God's Will Converging

The Lincoln-Kennedy parallels connect events that happened over more than 150 years. The events were apparently unrelated and the people who participated in them were acting freely and with no sense of being part of a larger plan. Yet the pattern suggests there was such a plan, one that not only connects two important historical periods but that links a number of incidental details. Patterns like these suggest that the events of life both large and small come from a single unified source—that they are the product of both individual will and God's will.

The idea that human will and God's will converge is difficult for Westerners to accept because it violates our cherished notions of freedom, independence and autonomy. Those values have helped build Western society but in the process they have created a split in the Western understanding of Spirit and its connection to everyday life.

Free will is admittedly a tricky subject but it is possible to modify our conception of it somewhat without surrendering a basic sense of personal freedom. In fact, we can have what amounts to the best of both worlds—the knowledge that we are free to act according to our own thoughts, feelings and desires and the comfort of knowing that God is ever-present and that we are un-failing instruments of His will.

In Chapter 4, in discussing the relationship between crime and disease, I noted that we all behave as we do because of how we are made. The fact is that none of us decides, when we get up in the morning, what to think about or how to feel. Thoughts and feelings come into our awareness on their own and we pick up the thread and follow it from there. We believe, correctly, that we control our lives through the decisions we make both large and small. But if God presents the raw material to us in the form of thoughts, feelings, impulses and situations, He is always, in effect, one step ahead of us—creating the conditions in which we make those decisions. If God knows us well enough to predict what we will do in a given set of circumstances, our lives are ultimately an expression, not only of our own will, but of God's as well.

The view that free will and determinism are consistent with one another is known as compatibilism. One writer describes the compatibilist view as follows:

> Thus normal adult human beings in normal circumstances are able to act and choose freely. No one is holding a gun to their heads. They are not drugged, or in chains, or subject to a psychological compulsion. They are therefore wholly free to choose and act even if their whole physical and psychological make-up is entirely determined by things for which they are in no way ultimately responsible - starting with their genetic inheritance and early upbringing.[131]

According to this view, a person is free if she feels free—if she has the experience of making decisions based on her own beliefs, feelings and judgments. When freedom is defined in this way, a person is not any less free if her thoughts and feelings happen to come from God.

Our Role as God's Partners

Some people object to the idea that their lives are an expression of God's will, saying that it makes human beings into nothing more than puppets or marionettes. Puppets, of course, are unconscious objects that are manipulated without their knowledge. To the extent that human beings are puppets, it is only because they are unaware of their direct connection to Spirit. When we become aware that

A PROMISE OF EDEN

God acts through us, we become conscious partners in the unfolding of His plan—the opposite of puppets. Through our own free will, we have the power to decide how God's plan will manifest itself on earth. We can move ourselves, our relationships and society forward in more holistic directions, or we can choose a more narrow and, perhaps, more self-interested path.

In Chapter 7 I discuss some of the patterns of Western history, culture and religion that point toward a new and more spiritual age to come. Those patterns are reflections of the holistic blueprint that is part of the inner structure of each of us. Our awareness of that blueprint can make us more aware, in turn, of the importance of moving with, not against, our own nature and the flow of history— of becoming partners with God in bringing a more unified and enlightened world into being.

CHAPTER SEVEN
LIFE ENERGY, RELIGION AND SPIRITUALITY

Life energy's location at the intersection of mind, body and Spirit makes it a powerful tool for spiritual growth. In Part 1 below I describe the ancient Indian technique of *pranayama,* or life energy control. *Pranayama* promotes spiritual awareness by helping move life energies from ordinary energy pathways into spiritual channels along the spine.

In Chapter 1 I noted the symmetry of Chinese and Indian teachings and how the two traditions emphasize different but complementary parts of the energy blueprint. That symmetry can be a valuable aid in spiritual growth. India's knowledge of the chakras is a powerful tool for traveling the Vertical Pathway. To prepare for that experience, however, a person must first achieve a certain level of emotional development and maturity. For that preliminary part of the journey along what I call the Horizontal Pathway, the Chinese Five Elements can serve as an ideal guide. The Chinese and Indian systems, taken together, thus form a complete framework for personal growth.

A third system, the Kabbalistic Tree of Life, is unique in tracing the outlines of both the Horizontal and Vertical Pathways. I describe the Tree of Life below and how its energy centers, or sfirot, represent both meridian and chakra energies and their interactions. The Tree of Life is thus the most complete expression of the full life energy blueprint, and of the overall process of human growth, in any major spiritual tradition. For those drawn to its symbols and meanings, the Tree can serve many of the same purposes as the teachings of China and India combined.

The Tree of Life has another, broader meaning. It represents what I describe in Part 2 as the Horizontal and Vertical Pathways of History. The Horizontal Pathway corresponds to the two most recent astrological ages, to the early development of Judaism and Christianity and to the growth of Wood and Earth energies in individuals and society. The Vertical Pathway corresponds to the Age of Aquarius, which is now dawning, and which holds the prospect of a more enlightened and spiritual era to come.

PART 1. LIFE ENERGY AND INDIVIDUAL GROWTH

The Meridians and the Horizontal Pathway

All major schools of meditation teach that, before a person is ready for higher awareness, he or she must make a sincere effort at self-improvement. Within the energy system, the meridians, and the Controlling Cycle in particular, are the energy battlefield of daily life. It is there that decisions are made, challenges are met and personal growth occurs. Chapters 3 and 4 showed that the tensions between competing energies give shape to the personality and are a major influence on relationships and emotional health.

Energy balance is crucial to spiritual growth as well, since it reflects a person's attitudes, values and personal priorities as well as emotional strengths and weaknesses. The struggle between freedom and fear, kindness and self-interest, anger and compassion and other important values and impulses are all represented by the relationships of the Controlling Cycle. One can use that knowledge in a variety of ways. A first step might be to use energy therapies to help clear away some of the emotional debris that can build up over time, creating inertia and placing obstacles in the way of growth. Shiatsu, acupuncture, magnet therapies, massage and other techniques can help relieve emotional tension, reduce anger, dissipate fear and remove energy blocks that stifle love, empathy, will power, courage and compassion. The freeing effect of energy work can help create a more positive environment in which to move forward.

More generally, becoming aware of the natural connections between emotions can in itself be an important aid to growth. For a person who is vulnerable to anger, for example, knowing that the Wood energies of anger tend to smother and overwhelm the Earth energies of love and compassion is a potent reminder of how destructive anger can be, and of how important it is to control anger when it arises. Knowing that the Water energies of fear can be weakened or dissolved by the healing power of love and compassion is a reminder that talking about, and sharing, one's inner fears can be part of a strategy to overcome them.

The Five Elements can help, too, in broadening one's perspective and seeing the tangible connection between individual growth and the health and well being of society as whole. As we saw in Chapter 4, the same energies that shape individual personality, multiplied many times over, form the contours of civilization itself. That knowledge can help in seeing one's own growth as part of a much larger holistic pattern. In the language of Chinese philosophy, it can be a way of attuning oneself to the flow of Tao.

The Chakras and the Vertical Pathway

The Indian master Patanjali, who lived approximately 2,000 years ago, wrote a classic text known as the Yoga Sutras. Its 195 brief aphorisms address every aspect of spiritual growth, from moral and ethical development to meditation technique. The eight steps along Patanjali's path are as follows:

1. *Yama* (moral and ethical behavior)
2. *Niyama* (inner discipline and purity)
3. *Asana* (Hatha Yoga postures that prepare the body for meditation)
4. ***Pranayama* (control of *prana* or life energy)**
5. *Pratyahara* (withdrawal of attention from the senses)
6. *Dharana* (one-pointed concentration)
7. *Dhyana* (awareness of the vastness of God)
8. *Samadhi* (union with God/Enlightenment)

After the first three preparatory steps, *pranayama* begins the actual process of meditation. The transfer of life energies from the meridians to the spinal column sets the stage for withdrawing the attention from the everyday world into the inner world of consciousness. *Pranayama* is thus a central part of the meditation process.

There are many varieties of *pranayama* but most combine

some form of breath control with a mental technique that encourages energies to flow. Life energy responds to attention and will in meditation just as it does in shiatsu or Tai Chi. In one technique called Kriya Yoga, breath control combines with certain visualizations to stimulate the flow of energies along the spine. After a period of practice, one can begin to feel the energies flowing and even distinguish the cool *yin* energies from the warm *yang* energies. Kriya Yoga and similar techniques are regarded as ways of quickening human evolution and thus shortening the time before one is reunited with God.

The Tree of Life: the Horizontal and Vertical Pathways Meet

Judaism is the oldest of the three great Western faiths and, along with Islam, one of the religions most closely associated with the principle of one God. The "Shmah," one of the shortest and simplest of all Jewish prayers and a virtual symbol of Judaism, is repeated many times each day by observant Jews: "Hear O Israel, the Lord our God, the Lord is One."

It is ironic that a religion that places so much emphasis on God's unity has an ancient tradition that portrays God as a collection of different aspects, each of which has a different name. Kabbalah teaches not only that God is diverse but that reality itself has several levels, including one that corresponds to the life energy realm. Kabbalah's teachings include a strong current of belief in reincarnation and its most fundamental law—that right behavior has positive consequences and wrong behavior negative ones—is essentially identical to the Law of Karma.

Kabbalah is derived from the Hebrew verb "to receive" and is usually translated as Tradition. Its teachings have been handed down for centuries in both oral form and through a limited number of esoteric texts. Unlike yoga, Zen and other better known mystical teachings, Kabbalah has long been a semi-secret doctrine. One reason is that its basic texts, the *Zohar* (the Splendor) and the *Sefer Yitzirah* (the Book of Creation), are highly symbolic and their meanings are obscure and difficult to interpret. Another reason is that Kabbalistic practices are said to have great spiritual power and may not be appropriate, or even safe, for any but the most serious of seekers.

A third reason that Kabbalah has stayed on the fringes of Judaism has to do with the Jewish temperament itself. Kabbalah's mystical, holistic flavor feels somewhat foreign and exotic to the analytical, highly rational Jewish mind. Some Kabbalistic ideas, as I noted above, are uncomfortably close to those of Eastern faiths like Hinduism, which many Jews view as polytheistic. For all these reasons, many Jews, including many rabbis, have tended to avoid Kabbalah.

In recent years Kabbalah has become more well-known and popular, even fashionable, in some circles. Teachers and writers have begun to simplify its teachings and make them more accessible and relevant to everyday life. Some of the efforts to popularize Kabbalah have been more successful than others. Teachers who respect the integrity of the teachings perform an important service; others, who oversimplify the subject or have a strong commercial motive, may do more harm than good. Anyone interested in learning more about Kabbalah should be wary of teachers or groups who charge large fees or who market lines of "Kabbalistic products" to go with their lessons.

Kabbalah's Tree of Life is shown in Figure 44. It is composed of ten sfirot (sfeer-OHT), each of which corresponds to a divine quality or energy. As I noted in Chapter 5, the Tree is now believed to represent both divine and human energies and to express the truth of Genesis 1:27—that human beings are created in the image of God.

The first sfirah at the bottom of the Tree, Shekinah, is an energy that humans occasionally experience. Shekinah often appears in the Old Testament when God is said to descend and dwell among men.[132] Shekinah apparently corresponds more or less to the Holy Spirit in Christianity.[133]

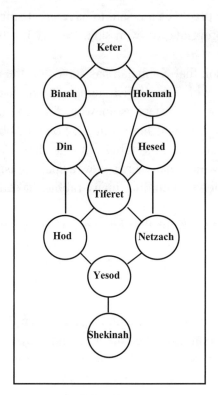

FIGURE 44.
THE KABBALISTIC TREE OF LIFE

The first sfirah may be related, too, to the human energy known as *shen*, or spirit, in Chinese medicine—the animating quality that gives life and sparkle to the personality and that is associated with the Fire energy of joy. One commentator on Shekinah describes its relationship to joy as follows:

> "but even for such [Shekinah] would not descend
> into an atmosphere of sadness (Shab. 30b and par-
> allel passages), since there can be no sorrow in the
> presence of God (☐ag. 5b); nor should one pray in
> a sorrowful frame of mind (Ber. 31a).[134]

At the opposite end of the Tree, the tenth and highest sfirah, Keter, represents the most abstract and inaccessible form of God: pure unmanifested Spirit. Keter is another clue that the Tree represents both divine and human energies. Keter, the Hebrew word for crown, is located at the top of the head, the location of the seventh or crown chakra. The opening of the crown chakra in meditation is the highest form of spiritual awareness, when one experiences God in Her purest form.

Although there are ten sfirot in the Tree, there are only seven vertical levels, the same number as the chakras. The right and left columns of the Tree are made up of three pairs of sfirot placed opposite one another. The divine qualities of these sfirot pairs correspond to human qualities and energies in natural tension in the Controlling Cycle. The correspondences are most clear in the sfirot pairs Netzach-Hod and Hesed-Din.

Netzach, Hod and the Courage to Be

The third and fourth sfirot, Hod (Majesty) and Netzach (Victory), are described as follows in one of Kabbalah's basic texts, the *Sefer Yitzirah* or Book of Creation:

> Three [the Third Sfirah]: Water and Breath. With it engrave and carve chaos and void, mire and clay. Engrave them like a garden plot, carve them like a wall, cover them like a ceiling.

> Four [the Fourth Sfirah]: Fire from Water. With it engrave and carve the Throne of Glory, Seraphim, Ophanim, holy Chayot, and Ministering Angels. From the three establish His dwelling, as it is written, "He makes His angels of breaths, His ministers from flaming fire" (Psalms 104:4).[135]

The divine energies identified in these passages—Water, Fire and Breath—almost certainly correspond to Water, Fire and Metal in the human energy system. Metal, the energy of the lungs and respiration in humans, is naturally associated with the cosmic Breath of

God. In the human body, Metal is the energy of structure and organization and it nourishes Water through the Nurturing Cycle. According to the above passage, God's Breath plays a similar role in creation. It takes the "chaos and void" of Water and "Engrave[s] them like a garden plot, carve[s] them like a wall, cover[s] them like a ceiling." The result is the order and structure of the physical universe.

In the fourth sfirah, the Fire of God is the divine counterpart to the human Fire energy of joy and inspiration. It embodies the "Throne of Glory, Seraphim, Ophanim, holy Chayot and Ministering Angels." A kind of cosmic *yang* to Water's *yin,* the dynamic, joyful energy of the fourth sfirah complements its polar opposite in the third, the energy of "mire and clay," and together the two bring the world of opposites into being.

On the human level, the struggle to overcome fear and confront life as a free human being—to have what the philosopher Paul Tillich called "the courage to be"—is one of life's basic challenges. The twin constraints on human freedom, as I noted in chapter 3, are represented by the natural tensions between Fire and its Controlling Cycle neighbors Water and Metal. These are the three energies of Hod and Netzach. Water represents fear and anxiety from within while Metal is the energy of society's rules and values that exert pressure to conform from without. A person's true state of freedom depends on how well-developed and balanced the three energies are.

A first major step in spiritual growth is therefore to find the best possible balance among Fire, Water and Metal: to resolve the conscious and unconscious fears and other conflicts at the level of Hod and Netzach. One commentator equates their energies with those of the lower chakras, and especially the second chakra, Svadhistana. He describes the challenge to personal growth as follows:

> Reaching Svadhisthana means that one is starting to penetrate the Hod-Nezach threshold of the unconscious. Usually one has to face the lowest

> manifestations first; there may be excessive fear
> (Hod) or sexual fantasies (Netzach)...in traditional
> symbolism the animal related to Swadhisthana is a
> crocodile. It is here that we encounter the dragon as
> described in mythology and fairy-stories, in other
> words the unconscious aspects of our psyche that
> are preventing us from evolving. "The way forward
> is keeping to the Path of Honesty...To get beyond
> Swadhisthana you must improve the general back-
> ground of your psychoemotional life."[136]

The above passage, with its images of crocodiles and dragons, suggests that growth at the Hod-Netzach level may be one of the more difficult steps along the spiritual path. The third sfirah's name, Netzach or Victory, hints at the significance of successfully completing that part of the journey.

Hesed and Din, Female and Male

The two sfirot Hesed (Kindness, Grace) and Din (Law, Judgment) represent, on the divine level, God's unconditional love tempered by the universal law of cause and effect or the Law of Karma. The tension between the two sfirot represents the balance between God's love for humankind and the discipline God imposes to maintain order and insure ultimate fairness over the course of many lifetimes.

On the human level, Din and Hesed represent the male and female energies of Wood and Earth. Din's alternate name, Gvurah, confirms its close association with male energies. The word gvurah (power, severity) is derived from gever, the Hebrew word for male.

The Tree of Life has traditional male and female sides but, strangely, Hesed, the sfirah of kindness, love and compassion, is on the right or male side while Din, the sfirah of strength, severity and judgment, is on the left or female side. The arrangement seems wrong on its face and, at least in human terms, contradicts everyday experience. Some commentators explain it by referring to dark or violent female energies at the level of Spirit (the goddess Kali might be a counterpart in Hinduism). Another explanation could be the longstanding male bias in Jewish thought and the desire of the men who designed the Tree of Life to create a more flattering portrait of men.

In everyday life, the universal tension between self-interest and personal ambition on the one hand and kindness, generosity and love on the other shows how important, and difficult, it can be to reconcile the energies of Hesed and Din. The goal in spiritual growth is to reach God's level: unconditional love combined with a discipline that comes, not from anger or a desire for punishment, but to set limits, maintain order and encourage strong personal values.

Tiferet and the Heart Chakra

When the energies of Hesed and Din are fully developed and completely balanced, they are integrated at the level of Tiferet or Beauty.[137] Tiferet (Tih-FERRET) is the midpoint of the Tree of Life and a major dividing line between everyday awareness and the realm of Spirit. Tiferet corresponds to the fourth chakra, or heart chakra, and the meeting of Hesed and Din at Tiferet is equivalent to the opening of the heart chakra.

Tiferet's location at the center of the Tree of Life recalls the placement of Earth at the center of the original Five Elements diagram (Figure 2). When Tiferet flowers, love truly becomes the center of one's being. The polarities of daily life fall away, including the perennial conflict between male and female energies.

The Higher Sfirot

The flowering of Tiferet apparently represents the successful integration of all five basic energies—Water, Fire and Metal at Hod-Netzach and Earth and Wood at Hesed-Din. At that point, a person is ready to experience Spirit, either as unconditional love or in some other form embodied by one of the higher sfirot.

On the level of the Divine, the eighth and ninth sfirot—Binah

(Understanding) and Hochmah (Wisdom)—represent the female and male aspects of God. They are sometimes likened to the Divine Mother and Divine Father in Hindu thought. Yoga masters teach that these feminine and masculine faces of God are concrete realities that one can experience in meditation.[138]

On the human level, the integration of Binah and Hochmah is said to correspond to the opening of the Third Eye or eye of intuitive perception. This is the sixth chakra, or Ajna Chakra, located between the eyebrows. One commentator describes this level of awareness as follows:

> Ajna Chakra (The Third Eye); Binah-Hokhmah Ajna is the chakra of higher intellect. Ajna is the witnessing centre where one becomes the detached observer of all events, including those within the body and mind. Here the level of awareness is developed whereby one begins to 'see' the hidden essence underlying all visible appearances. When Ajna is awakened, the meaning and significance of symbols flashes into one's conscious perception and intuitive knowledge arises effortlessly.[139]

The lines connecting Binah and Hochmah with the sfirot directly below them suggest that one can experience these higher levels of awareness without necessarily passing through Tiferet. If one is a Head type, for example, and more attuned to thinking than feeling, it may be more natural to rise directly from Hesed or Din to the intuitive level of Binah or Hochmah. The Book of Creation discusses the "32 Wondrous Paths of Wisdom" which correspond to 16 individual connections between sfirot. There are Kabbalistic meditation techniques for activating each of the connections. Some of them involve the use of symbols such as numbers, colors or letters of the Hebrew alphabet.

The tenth and highest sfirah, Keter, represents pure unmanifested Spirit. A person experiences it when the crown chakra has opened completely. The highest form of enlightenment is known in yoga as nirbikalpa samadhi and is reached only by the most highly advanced yogis.

Hegel, Marx and Dialectical Spirituality

The play of opposites and their eventual integration is not unknown to Western thinkers. G.W.F. Hegel, a major 18th century German philosopher, wrote that human progress depends on what he called dialectic—an ongoing competition between opposing ideas that ultimately resolves itself at a higher level. There are three parts to the process—thesis, antithesis and synthesis—and they repeat over and over again, steadily moving civilization and human consciousness forward. Hegel believed that dialectic represented a slow and gradual ascent toward knowledge of the Absolute or God.

Although Hegel was a man of faith, not all of his followers shared his beliefs. They split into two camps, left-wing and right-wing Hegelians. One writer describes the two groups as follows:

> Theologically and politically the right-wing Hegelians offered a conservative interpretation of his work. They emphasised the compatibility between Hegel's philosophy and Christianity. Politically, they were orthodox. The left-wing Hegelians eventually moved to an atheistic position. In politics, many of them became revolutionaries. This historically important left-wing group included Ludwig Feuerbach, Bruno Bauer, Friedrich Engels, and Karl Marx.[140]

Engels and Marx, of course, went on to inspire a new political movement called Communism. They incorporated Hegel's teaching of the dialectic but rejected the idea that Spirit had any role in human development. The philosophy underlying Communism thus came to be known as Dialectical Materialism.

If Marx and Engels had studied the energy teachings of China and India, they might have reconsidered their materialist views. The interplay of meridian and chakra energies strongly suggests that Hegel's view—that the dialectic is essentially a spiritual process—is the correct one. The unseen influence of Spirit appears to be the active principle in growth at every level. The teachings of ancient Asia might have persuaded Marx and Engels to rename their theory Dialectical Spirituality.

PART 2. JUDAISM, CHRISTIANITY AND BEYOND: THE HORIZONTAL AND VERTICAL PATHWAYS OF HISTORY

Chinese medicine teaches that a balance between Wood and Earth energies is essential to both physical and emotional health. The Tree of Life expands on that principle to show the central role of Wood and Earth in spiritual growth. At every level, the growth and integration of traditional male and female energies is an important part of human development.

The interplay of Wood and Earth can be seen in the larger patterns of history as well. The two most recent astrological ages, and the two great Western faiths whose birth and early development coincided with them, embody the qualities of Wood and Earth in certain fundamental ways. The evolution of Western society and religion is, in fact, a cosmic symbol of the growth process that occurs in every individual. And just as Wood and Earth are ultimately integrated at a higher level in the individual, society as a whole is beginning a transition from the Horizontal to the Vertical Pathway of Growth. For that reason I refer to the period from the birth of Judaism to the present day as the Horizontal Pathway of History.

JUDAISM, CHRISTIANITY AND THE HORIZONTAL PATHWAY

Judaism and the Age of Aries

When Christianity was born, Judaism was already 2,000 years old. Judaism's early development came at a time when civilization was young and survival was at a premium. There were frequent wars among the nomadic tribes of the Middle East, and the early

Hebrews fought the Canaanites, the Hittites, the Jebusites and others to avoid extinction. The Jews were conquered and enslaved by both the Egyptians and the Babylonians. It was a tough, unforgiving time when only the strong survived. The flavor of the era is captured by the spirit of Aries, the astrological age that coincided with the birth and early development of Judaism.

A new astrological age begins every 2,000 years. The Age of Aries began about 2,000 B.C., the time of Abraham and the other Jewish patriarchs, and ended around the time of Jesus. The Age of Pisces began in Jesus' time and is now ending. The Age of Aquarius is now beginning and will last until about the year 4,000.

Aries, the first of the twelve signs, is named after the Greek god of war. Aries' ruling planet, Mars, is named after the Roman god of war. Aries, as we saw in chapter 4, is the closest thing to a pure Wood sign among the twelve signs of the Zodiac. It is associated with all of the familiar *yang* qualities of Wood energy— strength, courage, intensity, ambition, egotism and anger—and at the far end of the spectrum, violence, cruelty and the desire for punishment and revenge.

The symbol of Aries, the ram, is an important symbol in Judaism. At High Holy Day services on Rosh HaShanah, the ritual blowing of the shofar, the ram's horn, is repeated several times as a way of ushering in the new year.

The God of the Old Testament is a stern, angry, vindictive and often violent God. The Bible is filled with examples of God's wrath, which he visits both on Israel's enemies and on the Israelites themselves. In the Book of Exodus, God frees the Hebrews by bringing twelve plagues upon Egypt, including blood, lice, boils, locusts and hail, and culminating in the slaying of the firstborn child of every Egyptian. God later drowns the Egyptian armies in the Red Sea after Moses has led the people through to safety.

God is equally harsh with the Israelites themselves. After handing down the Ten Commandments to Moses, God warns the people of the consequences of being unfaithful to His teachings:

For I the Lord thy God am a jealous God, visiting

> the iniquity of the fathers upon the children unto
> the third and fourth generation of them that hate me.
> Exodus 20:5

The prophets often remind the people of God's anger and its consequences:

> Who can stand before His indignation? And who
> can abide in the fierceness of His anger? His fury
> is poured out like fire, and the rocks are broken
> asunder before Him. Nahum 1:6

When the Israelites fail to heed the prophets' warnings, God makes
good on His threats. When Korah and his followers rebel against
Moses' authority, God's response is swift and fierce:

> And it came to pass, as [Moses] had made an e n d
> of speaking all these words, that the ground clave
> asunder that was under them: And the earth opened
> her mouth, and swallowed them   up,   and   their
> houses, and all the men that appertained unto
> Korah, and all their goods. They, and all that apper-
> tained to them, went down alive into the pit, and
> the earth closed upon them: and they perished from
> among the congregation...And there came out a
> fire from   the LORD, and consumed the two hun-
> dred and fifty men that offered incense. Numbers
> 16:31-35

God then resumes His support of the Israelites, helping them attack
and kill their enemies:

> And the LORD hearkened to the voice of Israel,
> and delivered up the Canaanites; and they utterly
> destroyed them and their cities: and he called the
> name of the place Hormah. Numbers 21:3

But no sooner do the Israelites triumph than they rebel again, and

God responds much the same as He did before:

> And the people spake against God, and against
> Moses, Wherefore have ye brought us up out of
> Egypt to die in the wilderness? for there is no
> bread, neither is there any water; and our soul
> loatheth this light bread. And the LORD sent fiery
> serpents among the people, and they bit the people;
> and much people of Israel died. Numbers 21:5,6

The same violent theme repeats itself again and again in the Old
Testament: God helps the people, then reminds them of their covenant with Him and exhorts them to be faithful. But before long, the
people go astray again and God punishes them. In the end, God
concludes that the people have broken their covenant and must be
exiled for their lack of faith. As the prophet Zechariah relates:

> But they refused to hearken, and pulled away the
> shoulder, and stopped their ears, that they should
> not hear. Yea, they made their hearts as an adamant
> stone, lest they should hear the law, and the words
> which the LORD of hosts hath sent in his spirit by
> the former prophets: therefore came a great wrath
> from the LORD of hosts...But I scattered them with
> a whirlwind among all the nations whom they knew
> not. Thus the land was desolate after them, that no
> man passed through nor returned: for they laid the
> pleasant land desolate. Zechariah 7:11-14

The destruction of the Second Temple in Jerusalem around 60 A.D.
marked the final defeat of the ancient Israelites and the beginning
of a 2,000 year exile. Thus the Age of Aries was bounded on one
side by the birth of Judaism and on the other by the Jews'
expulsion from their ancestral homeland. In the interim, Judaism
developed against a backdrop of almost continual conflict. Early
Judaism is thus an historic symbol of the Age of Aries and of
dominant Wood energies.

Christianity and the Age of Pisces

Aries is the first sign of the Zodiac and Pisces the last. Although the two constellations, the Ram and the Fish, adjoin each other in the heavens, the qualities they represent are virtual polar opposites. Aries is *yang* and very much concerned with the things of this world—action, power and accomplishment—while Pisces is *yin* and is a sign of gentleness, humility and the things of the next world. The houses that correspond to the two signs, the First and the Twelfth, straddle the horizon, a kind of symbolic dividing line between the everyday world and the realm of Spirit.

Early Judaism is at home in the First House because, as first-born among the Western faiths, it began the process of incorporating God into the daily struggle for existence. Early Christianity, which built upon the foundation that Judaism had established, was more radical. It encouraged the faithful to give up their homes, families and everyday lives to pursue a spiritual ideal. If early Judaism is an historic symbol of the Age of Aries and of dominant Wood energies, Christianity is its complementary opposite—a symbol of the Age of Pisces and of dominant Earth energies.

Jesus as the Embodiment of Pisces

Jesus was in many ways as different from traditional Judaism as Pisces is from Aries. His teachings were often at odds, not only with traditional Jewish values, but with the words of the Bible itself. The Old Testament, in Deuteronomy 19:19-21, lays down the law of retribution in no uncertain terms:

> Then shall ye do unto him, as he had thought to have done unto his brother: so shalt thou put the evil away from among you. And those which remain shall hear, and fear, and shall henceforth commit no more any such evil among you. And thine eye shall not pity; but life shall go for life, eye for eye, tooth for tooth, hand for hand, foot for foot.

Jesus, of course, established an entirely different principle, and one more in keeping with the Piscean spirit:

> Ye have heard that it hath been said, An eye for an eye, and a tooth for a tooth. But I say unto you, that ye resist not evil: but whosoever shall smite thee on thy right cheek, turn to him the other also. Matthew 5:38

In announcing a new spiritual law that directly contradicted the teachings of the Old Testament, Jesus might as well have said to his disciples, "The Age of Aries is ending; the Age of Pisces has begun."

Many who lived during the Age of Pisces would have laughed at the notion that the world was entering a new era of love and good feeling. War and oppression did not end, and for many they probably only seemed to be growing worse. In the first centuries after Jesus, the world's preeminent military power, the Roman Empire, became if anything even more cruel and bloodthirsty than before. Ironically, the early Christians were among the Romans' primary victims. Many were thrown into the Roman Coliseum and other arenas where they were killed and eaten by lions and tigers while crowds watched and cheered. Even today, 2,000 years later, an aura of death and horror hangs over the Coliseum, one of the most potent ancient symbols of an era of violence and brutality.

The Roman Empire, in fact, is the truest symbol of the Age of Aries. In its vast scope, its obsession with power and conquest, and its cruelty and sadism, it often expressed the darkest side of Wood energies and of human nature. The Romans' crucifixion of Jesus and their persecution of the early Christians was an especially cruel irony. It represented the destruction of spirituality and innocence by a force personifying violence and aggression—the symbolic meeting of the Ages of Aries and Pisces.

By comparison with Rome, early Judaism's link to the Age of Aries was more symbolic than real, particularly since Jewish culture went on to become one of the most civilized, educated and non-violent in the world. Meanwhile, the dominant Christian culture, after being persecuted for three centuries by the Romans, itself became the aggressor, and often at the expense of the Jews. The Crusades, the Inquisition and, worst of all, the Holocaust were grotesque twists in the relationship between Wood and Earth, Aries and Pisces, Judaism and Christianity.

Almost 2,000 years after the Age of Aries ended, and at the very cusp of the Age of Aquarius, a horrible echo of Aries and its Roman connection returned to the world for a short time. The Nazis under Adolf Hitler perfected a system of war and bestiality on a scale that far exceeded anything the Romans had done. Hitler not only acknowledged his link to ancient Rome, he reveled in it. He called the Nazi regime the Third Reich, or Third Empire, seeing it as a successor to both the Holy Roman Empire and the 19th century German Empire under Bismarck. Like the Romans before them, the Nazis reserved their most virulent hatred for a minority religious group—in this case the Jews. And whether intentionally or not, Hitler adopted a name for his people—the Aryan race—that chillingly recalled the age to which he and his henchmen belonged.

Hesed, Din and the Full Symbolism of the Tree of Life

There are no neat dividing lines between astrological ages. The warlike energies of Aries did not suddenly dry up and disappear when the Age of Pisces arrived. Today, 2,000 years later, they are still a force to be reckoned with. But the Age of Pisces was more than just a symbol of Earth energies and their peaceful influences. It was a critical time for civilization—when the values of caring, compassion and community began to flourish in the world. Much of that progress came toward the end of the Age and represented a kind of belated flowering of Earth energies. Today, as the Age of Aquarius begins, there is hope for a qualitatively different kind of society sometime during the next 2,000 years.

The Tree of Life, as we have seen, represents both divine and human energies, and the sfirot Din and Hesed represent Wood and Earth respectively. The correlation of those energies with Judaism and Christianity suggests that the Tree's symbolism may be even

broader than is generally believed. Din and Hesed, I argue, represent more than just the characteristic energies of Judaism and
Christianity—they are symbols of the two faiths themselves.

Din: the People of the Book

The sfirah Din, as I noted earlier, represents, on the divine level,
the cosmic law of justice or Law of Karma. On the human level it
represents, among other things, discipline and firmness and
suggests a tendency to view life from the perspective of law, order
and justice.[141]

The Jewish people, whose faith is based on close adherence to
the Torah, the first five books of the Old Testament, are often
referred to as the People of the Book. They might be described
even more precisely as the People of the Law. Every observant Jew
is expected to honor no less than 613 separate *mitzvoht*, or divine
commandments, based not only on the words of the Bible itself but
on centuries of later interpretation. The Talmud, the great compila-
tion of Jewish wisdom and learning, is on one level an extremely
long and detailed legal discussion. Talmudic scholars are legendary
for their ability to find insight and meaning in the most exhaustive
analyses of the fine points of Jewish law.

Judaism, too, gave Western society its first written code of
human conduct—the Ten Commandments. Many of Judaism's
most revered figures, such as Rashi and Maimonides, are remembered as much for their scholarship as for their holiness. The great
Jews of the past, it is true, have included prophets and seers and
Kabbalah is evidence of a strong current of mysticism in the Jewish soul. On balance, however, Judaism's most distinguishing feature has always been its unusual love of learning and understanding, together with its emphasis on obedience to God's commandments. Din, or Law, is a fitting symbol for Judaism, and the sfirah
Din, I argue, is a symbol of Judaism in the Tree of Life. Din may
be seen, too, as a symbol of the Age of Aries when Judaism was
born and began to develop.

Hesed and the Essence of Compassion

If Din is Judaism's natural home in the Tree of Life, Hesed plays a corresponding role for Christianity. On the divine level, Hesed represents God's unconditional love. In Christianity, love, compassion and generosity were the essence of Jesus' teachings. By giving literally everything he had for others, he set an absolute standard of human conduct. Law and justice were not unknown to Jesus—he set down standards of behavior of his own—but unlike the God of the Old Testament, Jesus' judgments were not motivated by anger or a desire for punishment. His love was unconditional and his message was entirely positive and for the benefit of others.

Christianity and Christians, of course, have not always been motivated by the Earth energies of love and compassion—history makes that abundantly clear. Judaism is, too, in certain respects a remarkably Earth-centered religion. Family, friends, caring and community are exceptionally important in Jewish culture. But historically at least, the teachings of Christianity have placed a special emphasis on the Earth qualities of love and compassion. Just as Din is a symbol of Judaism in the Tree of Life, Hesed, I argue, is a symbol of Christianity, and of the Age of Pisces when Christianity was born.

Tiferet and the Promise of Reconciliation

The Tree of Life is, above all, a blueprint for wholeness. In the individual, the energies of Din and Hesed ultimately meet at Tiferet where they are integrated at a higher level. The presence of Judaism and Christianity in the Tree points to a similar reconciliation of the two faiths. Tiferet, the meeting place of Din and Hesed, is, I argue, a symbol of that coming reconciliation, and of the Age of Aquarius when it will occur.

Tiferet's integrating power suggests that the meeting of Judaism and Christianity will be more than just an accommodation between two conflicting religious systems. The structure of the Tree of Life suggests that, like *yin* and *yang,* the two faiths are complementary halves of an organic whole.

Since the most obvious point of disagreement between Judaism and Christianity is over the identity of Jesus, the Tree's symbolism, I argue, points toward Jesus as the Messiah prophesied by Isaiah in the Old Testament. Today, with the ingathering of the Jewish people having occurred at the very dawning of the Age of Aquarius, it is important to reconsider the evidence as to who Jesus really was.

Adam, Eve and the Flesh of Judaism

The Tree of Life is not the earliest symbol of the underlying unity of Judaism and Christianity. That symbolism begins in the very first books of the Old and New Testaments. The Book of Genesis introduces the theme of male and female that links the two faiths. God creates Adam and places him in the Garden of Eden. He then creates Eve, not from the dust as with Adam, but from Adam's own flesh:

> And the LORD God caused a deep sleep to fall upon Adam, and he slept: and he took one of his ribs, and closed up the flesh instead thereof; And the rib, which the LORD God had taken from man, made he a woman, and brought her unto the man. And Adam said, This is now bone of my bones, and flesh of my flesh: she shall be called Woman, because she was taken out of Man. Genesis 2:21-23

In Matthew, the first book of the New Testament, God symbolically repeats His creation of woman from man. He creates Christianity, a religion of Earth (female) energies, from the literal flesh of Judaism—from Jesus, a Jewish man. Just as woman "was taken out of man" in the Garden of Eden, the Earth-centered faith of Christianity was taken out of the Wood-centered faith of Judaism. The implication is that the two faiths, like husband and wife, are an organic whole: "flesh of [each other's] flesh, bone of [each other's] bones."[142]

The Passover and the Passion

The stories and symbols of Passover and Easter further develop the theme of unity between the two faiths. Although Passover and Easter come at the same time of year, most Jews see the timing as nothing more than coincidence. The fact that Jesus came to Jerusalem on Passover, and that his Last Supper was apparently a traditional Seder dinner, is not seen to have any particular importance. In fact, there is a deep and meaningful connection between the symbols of the Passover and the Passion.

Passover is the story of the Israelites' bondage in Egypt and of their liberation through God's intervention under the leadership of Moses. After inflicting plague after plague on the Egyptians but without persuading Pharaoh to release the children of Israel, God sends a final plague—the slaying of the first-born. God instructs Moses as follows:

> Speak ye unto all the congregation of Israel, saying, In the tenth day of this month they shall take to them every man a lamb, according to the house of their fathers...and the whole assembly of the congregation of Israel shall kill it in the evening. And they shall take of the blood, and strike it on the two side posts and on the upper door post of the houses wherein they shall eat it...and ye shall eat it in haste: it is the LORD's passover. For I will pass through the land of Egypt this night, and will smite all the firstborn in the land of Egypt, both man and beast; and against all the gods of Egypt I will execute judgment: And the blood shall be to you for a token upon the houses where ye are: and when I see the blood, I will pass over you, and the plague shall not be upon you to destroy you, when I smite the land of Egypt. Exodus 12:3-13

The blood of the lamb is thus a primary symbol, not only of the Passover, but of God's grace in sparing the Jewish people and freeing them from slavery.

The symbolism of Jesus' life and death resonates powerfully with the symbols of Passover. In the New Testament, Jesus is often referred to as "the Lamb" or "the Lamb of God." The Book of John speaks of him as follows: "Behold the Lamb of God, which taketh away the sin of the world!" The Book of Revelation uses the same image:

> And I looked, and, lo, a Lamb stood on the mount Sion and with Him an hundred forty and four thousand, having His Father's name written in their foreheads. These are they which follow the Lamb whithersoever He goeth. These were redeemed from among men, being the firstfruits unto God and to the Lamb. Revelation 14:1-6

When Jesus was crucified, the blood of the Lamb was shed to help atone for the sins of the world. In both the Passover and the Passion, the blood of the lamb protects human beings from death. In Egypt it saved the Jewish people from physical death; for Christians it saves them from spiritual death through the promise of eternal life.

During Jesus' last Passover Seder, he explicitly links the Passover to his own imminent death through the Jewish blessings over the bread and wine:

> When the hour came, Jesus and his apostles reclined at the table. And he said to them, "I have eagerly desired to eat this Passover with you before I suffer...And he took bread, gave thanks and broke it, and gave it to them, saying, "This is my body given for you; do this in remembrance of me." In the same way, after the supper he took the cup, saying, "This cup is the new covenant in my blood, which is poured out for you." Luke 22:14-20

The ceremony that Jesus created, of course, became the Christian sacrament of communion. In linking two of the Seder prayers with his own suffering to come, Jesus created a direct connection between the Lamb of God and the sacrificial lamb of Passover.

Isaiah's Prophecy

The parallels between the Passover and the Passion, although striking, are only persuasive if one believes in both the Old and New Testaments. Christians, who believe in both, are not in need of persuasion. Jews, who tend to ignore the New Testament, have little interest in exploring parallels. Given some of the prophecies in the Book of Isaiah, however, that lack of interest is one of the most remarkable ironies in the history of Judaism, a religion of great ironies. Isaiah contains references which, by any reasonable interpretation, point directly to Jesus as the promised Messiah. Probably the best known is in Isaiah 7:14:

> Therefore the Lord himself shall give you a sign;
> Behold, a [Hebrew word *almah*] shall conceive,
> and bear a son, and shall call his name Immanuel.

Much has been written about the use of the word *almah* in the above verse. Christian versions of the Bible invariably translate it as "virgin" while Jewish translations render it as "young girl." The more standard meaning, according to Strong's Concordance, is "maiden," which can suggest either a virgin, a girl of marriageable age or one newly married.

The meaning of *almah* is clear from the context in which Isaiah uses it. When he says that "the Lord himself shall give you a sign," he is suggesting that something extraordinary, or at least unusual, will happen that will catch people's attention. The pregnancy of a virgin would certainly qualify, but the pregnancy of a young married woman would not be a sign of anything. Therefore Isaiah must have been referring to a virgin pregnancy.[143]

Isaiah's prophecies in Chapter 53 are further evidence that Jesus is indeed the promised Messiah. Isaiah refers to at least seven major events or themes in Jesus' life or to symbols associated with him:

1. That he will be rejected by his own people.
2. That he will be imprisoned and judged guilty.
3. That he will be wounded and whipped.
4. That he will suffer and die.
5. That he will die as a sacrificial lamb.
6. That he will die with others who were wicked.
7. That he will bear the sins of many.

The text of the verses in which Isaiah makes these references is as follows:

> 3 He is despised and rejected of men; a man of sorrows and acquainted with grief: and we hid as it were our faces from him; he was despised, and we esteemed him not. 4 Surely he hath borne our griefs, and carried our sorrows: yet we did esteem him stricken, smitten of God, and afflicted. 5 But he *was* wounded for our transgressions, *he was* bruised for our iniquities: the chastisement of our peace *was* upon him; and with his stripes we are healed. 6 All we like sheep have gone astray; we have turned every one to his own way; and the LORD hath laid on him the iniquity of us all. 7 He was oppressed, and he was afflicted, yet he opened not his mouth: he is brought as a lamb to the slaughter, and as a sheep before her shearers is dumb, so he openeth not his mouth. 8 He was taken from prison and from judgment: and who shall declare his generation? for he was cut off out of the land of the living: for the transgression of my people was he stricken. 9 And he made his grave with the wicked, and with the rich in his death; because he had done no violence, neither *was any* deceit in his mouth…11 He shall see of the travail of his soul, *and* shall be satisfied: by his knowledge shall my righteous servant justify many; for he shall bear their iniquities. 12 Therefore will I divide him *a*

> *portion* with the great, and he shall divide the spoil
> with the strong; because he hath poured out his soul
> unto death: and he was numbered with the trans-
> gressors; and he bare the sin of many, and made
> intercession for the transgressors.

These are the words, not of the New Testament, but of the Old Testament—the word of God according to the tenets of Judaism. If
Jesus is not the promised Messiah, the Jewish people must be waiting for another figure who will be brought "as a lamb to the
slaughter" and who will be rejected by his own people before being
finally accepted.

"And God Hardened [the Jewish People's] Heart"

In a final parallel between the Passover and the Passion, the Jewish
people's rejection of Jesus is foreshadowed by Pharaoh's earlier
treatment of the Jews. The Book of Exodus contains no less than
nine references to Pharaoh's stubborn refusal to hear the word of
God and let the Jewish people go free. It begins even before Moses
arrives in Egypt:

> And the LORD said unto Moses, When thou goest
> to return into Egypt, see that thou do all those won-
> ders before Pharaoh, which I have put in thine
> hand: but I will harden his heart, that he shall not
> let the people go. Exodus 4:21

Later, after God sends several plagues, including pestilence, boils,
hail, thunder and lightning, Pharaoh finally sees the greatness of
God and agrees to let the people go. But afterwards, he changes his
mind:

> And when Pharaoh saw that the rain and the hail
> and the thunders were ceased, he sinned yet more,
> and hardened his heart, he and his servants. And
> the heart of Pharaoh was hardened, neither would

he let the children of Israel go; as the LORD had
spoken by Moses. Exodus 9:34-35

In the end, after the firstborn of Egypt are slain, Pharaoh finally
lets the people go—but he then changes his mind one last time and
sends his chariots to pursue them:

And the LORD hardened the heart of Pharaoh king
of Egypt, and he pursued after the children of Israel. Exodus 14:8

The story ends only when God parts the waters of the Red Sea,
letting the children of Israel pass, then brings the waters together,
destroying the Egyptians' chariots and drowning them in the sea.

The Jewish people's failure to heed the prophecies of Isaiah
were like Pharaoh sending his chariots into the Red Sea. It was
only the last in a long series of refusals to hear the word of God—
and it had equally disastrous results. Within thirty years after
Jesus' death, the Jews would be scattered among the nations in an
exile that would last 2,000 years. It happened, as Zechariah relates,
because the Jews "made their hearts as an adamant stone, lest they
should hear the law, and the words which the LORD of hosts hath
sent in his spirit…"

The Challenge for the Jewish People

Many Jews reject Jesus without ever having seriously considered
the evidence. Like people the world over, Jews are strongly influenced by early conditioning. Jewish children are told by their
parents, "We don't believe in Jesus," and in most cases that settles
the question. Even those young Jews who might want to explore
the subject further are discouraged from doing so by subtle but
powerful pressures within the Jewish community.

The question of who Jesus is is too important to be settled once
and for all in childhood. Whatever one's ultimate conclusion, every
Jew owes it to himself or herself to consider the question carefully

at least once in a lifetime and to make a thoughtful, informed adult decision.

The challenge is a hard one for several reasons. Christianity has had a 2,000 year head start on Judaism in defining Jesus. Although he was a Jew, both Jesus' personality and teachings have come to be associated with a whole range of symbols, customs, rituals and beliefs that are, on an emotional level, decidedly un-Jewish. Jesus therefore feels like a stranger to most Jews.

Jews often assume incorrectly that accepting Jesus as their spiritual guide would mean becoming Christian. On the contrary, Judaism will surely develop its own customs, rituals and traditions that will effectively incorporate him and his teachings into Judaism. The job of reclaiming Jesus as a Jewish figure might start with simple steps, like calling him by his Hebrew name rather than his Christian name. Jesus is a translation from the Greek, but Yeshua (YEH-shoo-uh), or "God Saves," is the Hebrew equivalent of Jesus' original name in Aramaic.

Jesus and Monotheism

For many Jews, the ultimate objection to Jesus is that, at least as Christianity portrays him, he is a uniquely divine being, the only Son of God. For many Jews, their monotheistic faith cannot accept the idea that divinity can be split up into parts. But we have seen that, in Judaism's own Tree of Life, God's energies are represented in ten different forms and on seven different levels. Although in the deepest sense God may ultimately be One, mystical teachings from many traditions agree that Spirit can take a variety of forms and can be experienced in a wide range of different ways.

As interest in Kabbalah and other mystical teachings grows, it will probably become easier for Jews to see Jesus as a divine being in the same sense that Asian peoples regard illumined yogis and other spiritual masters as divine. As spiritual practice evolves, the Messiah may come to be seen less as a compelling human personality with a remarkable life story, and more as an invisible spiritual guide or presence—a kind of guru.

The gradual acceptance of Jesus, or Yeshua, by the Jewish people, and the development of uniquely Jewish ways of understanding him will have an important added benefit. It will show that, although one can use a variety of names, symbols and practices to commune with Spirit, God's essence ultimately lies beyond those things. Jews and Christians may come to view the Messiah, by whatever name he is called, as a kind of metaphor for the spiritual unity that underlies all faiths. When that happens, the two faiths will be well on their way to becoming the organic whole symbolized in the Tree of Life.

THE AGE OF AQUARIUS AND
THE VERTICAL PATHWAY

The coming of a new era, at least in its early stages, can be hard to detect and may seem more symbolic than real. When the Age of Pisces dawned 2,000 years ago, early Christians expected to see the Kingdom of God manifested on earth in their own lifetimes. They were surely disappointed and would have been shocked to know that today, 2,000 years later, it still has not arrived.

The current age, like the one that preceded it, began with hopes for great and fundamental change in both individuals and society. Those changes have not yet materialized and, on the surface at least, society seems to be in worse condition today than it was fifty years ago. In a world where terrorism is fueled by religious polarization; where politics and public discourse have been cheapened and demeaned; where violence explodes on every TV and movie screen; where schools and churches have become dangerous places for children; and where life is driven increasingly by consumption, competition, self-interest and the profit motive, the notion of a new and higher civilization may seem as unrealistic to us as it did to the early Christians 2,000 years ago.

In certain important ways, however, reality has begun to catch up with the promise of a new era. Democracy and human rights are on the march around the world. Globalization, despite the pain it inflicts on many workers, has the potential to unify and raise the standard of living of the world as a whole. Religious belief and spiritual practice continue to develop in spite of the many forces pulling in the opposite direction.

Recent historical events add weight to the argument that we are entering a new era. The ingathering of the Jewish people and the rebirth of Israel are often overlooked because the tragedy of the Palestinian conflict is so much more immediate and compelling. But in spite of Israel's tragic failure to be more compassionate toward a minority in its midst, those events foresee the eventual fulfillment of God's covenant with the Jewish people as prophesied in the Old Testament. The gradual acceptance by Jews of Jesus, or Yeshua, and the eventual reconciliation of Judaism and Christianity will, I believe, be important parts of that overall process.

All of these external events, although significant, will be secondary to a quieter and more private inner revolution. The real message of Aquarius is that spiritual understanding lies within every human heart. Thanks to the progress of the last 4,000 years, increasing numbers of people are, or soon will be, ready to begin experiencing that truth directly through the teachings of Hinduism, Taoism, Kabbalah and the world's other great mystical faiths and traditions. As a new era begins to unfold, there are signs that that process of inner discovery has already begun.

Belief and Beyond

The trend toward direct spiritual experience in the U.S. began, appropriately enough, in the 1960's when excitement over the coming of a New Age was at its peak. Although that excitement ultimately faded, the underlying holistic trend in spirituality has continued. The growing popularity of meditation-based practices has been paralleled by another important development: a decline in rigid, authoritarian religious teachings and institutions that seek to control their follower' personal behavior and, in some cases, even their political beliefs.

Recent discoveries in archeology are fueling a more holistic view of religion and spirituality even within the scholarly commu-

nity. Elaine Pagels is a professor of religion at Princeton University and author of *Beyond Belief: the Secret Gospel of Thomas.* The
title refers to a text, discovered in 1945 in Egypt, and attributed to
Jesus' disciple Thomas. Pagels points out some important differences between Jesus' message as reported in the four Gospels of
the New Testament and the Gospel of Thomas.

The most important difference is that, in the Gospels, and especially in the Book of John, Jesus describes himself as a unique
being, the only Son of God and the only means of salvation for
human beings. Thomas, however, suggests that Jesus portrayed
himself quite differently—as an example of spiritual perfection that
others could emulate through their own efforts. Pagels quotes Thomas, and Jesus, as follows:

> The Kingdom is inside you, and outside you.
> When you come to know yourselves, then you will
> be known, and you will see that it is you who are
> the children of the living Father.[144]

In another passage, Pagels says, "Jesus tells his disciples that not
only he comes forth from divine light but so do we all:"

> If they say to you, "where did you come from?" say
> to them, "we came from the light, the place where
> the light came into being by itself and was revealed
> through their image." If they say to you, "who are
> you?" say, "We are its children, the chosen of the
> living Father."[145]

Pagels describes a struggle within early Christianity between the
supporters of Thomas' description of Jesus' teachings and those
who subscribed to John's more conventional, faith-based version.
In the end John won, the Gospel of Thomas was discarded, and the
New Testament came into being as we know it today. In the struggle between belief and direct experience, belief won out, at least
temporarily. But as the Age of Aquarius begins, there is increasing
evidence that Thomas' interpretation may be a deeper and more

enduring statement of Jesus' teachings than the traditional Gospels.

Jesus through the Eyes of a Yogi

Eastern religions teach that every person has the capacity to experience the Spirit within and that many illumined beings throughout history have guided souls to God. In Hinduism, the greatest of these masters, the avatars or divine incarnations, include Krishna, who is regarded as Indian's greatest prophet and is sometimes seen as a kind of Asian counterpart to Jesus.

In Buddhism, the Bodhisattva or "Awakened Being" has many of the attributes of Jesus, and vice versa. The Bodhisattva is described as follows:

> [The Bodhisattva] cycles through rebirths to help liberate beings from suffering and further establish the Dharma [cosmic law] in the world...The *bodhisattva's* most distinctive feature is the motivation of compassion to forsake one's own immediate liberation to further the Buddhist teachings.[146]

Paramahansa Yogananda, in his book *Autobiography of a Yogi*, portrays Jesus as a kind of Bodhisattva who has taken on various human forms throughout history in order to further human evolution. According to Yogananda, Jesus has had a companion in the journey and the two have traveled together in a guru-disciple relationship. They appear first in the Old Testament as the prophets Elijah and Elisha. Later they reappear in the New Testament as John the Baptist and Jesus. Yogananda describes his understanding of their roles as follows:

> From a reverent study of the Bible from an Oriental viewpoint, and from intuitional perception, I am convinced that John the Baptist was, in past lives, the guru of Christ. Numerous passages in the Bible imply that John and Jesus in their last incarnations were, respectively, Elijah and his disciple Elisha....

The very end of the Old Testament is a prediction
of the reincarnation of Elijah and Elisha: "Behold, I
will send you Elijah the prophet before the coming
of the great and dreadful day of the Lord." (citing
Malachi 4:5)[147]

As evidence that John was indeed Elijah (or Elias, as he is known
in the New Testament), Yogananda cites the Book of Luke, where
an angel appears to John's father Zacharias:

But the angel said unto him Fear not, Zacharias: for
thy prayer is heard; and thy wife Elizabeth shall
bear thee a son, and thou shalt call his name John...
And many of the children of Israel shall he turn to
the Lord their God. And he shall go before him *in
the spirit and power of Elias,* to turn the hearts of
the fathers to the children, and the disobedient to
the wisdom of the just...[148]

Yogananda points out that Jesus himself twice identifies John as
Elijah. In Matthew 7:12-13 he says, "Elias is come already and
they knew him not...Then the disciples understood that he spake
unto them of John the Baptist." And in Matthew 11:13-14 Jesus
says, "For all the prophets and the law prophesied until John. And
if ye will receive it, this is Elias, which was for to come." When
Jesus washes the feet of John, his comment suggests that he is discharging the duty of a chela, or spiritual disciple, toward his guru:
"For thus it becometh us to fulfill all righteousness."

John's denial, in John 1:21, that he was Elijah is explained by
Yogananda as follows.

...he meant that in the humble garb of John he came
no longer in the outward elevation of Elijah the
great guru. In his former incarnation he had given
the "mantle" of his glory and his spiritual wealth to
his disciple Elisha. "And Elisha said, I pray thee,
let a double portion of thy spirit be upon me, And

he said, Thou hast asked a hard thing: nevertheless, if thou see me when I am taken from thee, it shall be so unto thee...And he took the mantle of Elijah that fell from him." [citing 2 Kings 2:9-14]...The roles became reversed, because Elijah-John was no longer needed to be the ostensible guru of Elisha-Jesus, now divinely perfected.[149]

The relationship between Jesus and Elijah has a contemporary importance that goes beyond Bible history or scholarship. Many people of faith today, including many Jews, are awaiting the coming of Elijah as a precursor to the Messiah. Their expectation is based, in part, on the words of Malachi quoted above: "Behold, I will send you Elijah the prophet before the coming of the great and dreadful day of the Lord." Yogananda's linkage of Jesus and Elijah supports the Christian view that Elijah, if he appears, will herald the Second Coming of Christ.

The Second Coming as an Inner Experience

Yogananda, like Elaine Pagels, argues that Jesus' true teaching is that the divine light exists within every person. According to Yogananda, Jesus himself hinted that the gateway to that light is none other than the chakra system itself. Yogananda cites the following verse from Luke in which, he says, Jesus refers to the opening of the sixth chakra—the Third or Spiritual Eye—at the point between the eyebrows:

> "The light of the body is the eye: therefore when thine eye is single, thy whole body also is full of light."[150]

Because Yogananda viewed Jesus as one of the greatest of all avatars, he refers to the sixth chakra as the Christ Consciousness Center. He thus identifies Jesus with the highest level of spiritual energy within the created universe ("the Son" or "the Word") second only to God Himself: absolute, unmanifested Spirit ("the

Father") which corresponds to the seventh, or crown, chakra.

A prayer offered during Self Realization Fellowship services, and recommended for devotees, captures both the universality of Yogananda's teachings and the special place Jesus holds in them. The names recited in the prayer, after Jesus and Krishna, make up the modern line of gurus from whom Yogananda is descended:

> O God, Jesus Christ, Bhagavan Krishna, Mahavatar Babaji, Lahiri Mahasaya, Swami Sri Yukteswarji, Gurudeva Paramahansa Yogananda, Saints and Sages of all religions, I humbly bow to you all.

As the prayer suggests, Yogananda regarded Jesus as a great spiritual force but as only one of many guides and pathways through which God can be known. Yogananda's special relationship with Jesus was unusual for an Asian master. In his *Autobiography*, he recounts a vision he had while working on an interpretation of the New Testament:

> One night while I was engaged in silent prayer, my sitting room in the Encinitas hermitage became filled with an opal-blue light. I beheld the radiant form of the blessed Lord Jesus. A young man, he seemed, of about twenty-five, with a sparse beard and moustache; his long black hair, parted in the middle, was haloed by a shimmering gold.

> His eyes were eternally wondrous; as I gazed, they were infinitely changing. With each divine transition in their expression, I intuitively understood the wisdom conveyed. In his glorious gaze I felt the power that upholds the myriad worlds. A Holy Grail appeared at his mouth; it came down to my lips and then returned to Jesus. After a few moments he uttered beautiful words, so personal in their nature that I keep them in my heart.[151]

In 2004, fifty-two years after the passing of Paramahansa

Yogananda, a number of his teachings and writings were compiled and published as a two volume work entitled *The Second Coming of Christ*. It is an interpretation of the hidden mystical meaning of Jesus' words, gained, according to Yogananda, from direct communion with Christ himself. The overall message is that the Second Coming refers, not to a physical appearance, but to the inner realization of truth that every person can gain through deep meditation. This recalls the words of Luke 17:20-21:

> The kingdom is not coming with signs that can be observed...the kingdom of God is within you.

Jewish Mysticism and the Fulfillment of the Covenant

In the Merkavah tradition of early Jewish mysticism, seekers had to travel through seven palaces before arriving at the throne of God. Later, in the Tree of Life, God's energies were depicted on seven vertical levels. Jewish mystical tradition thus strongly suggests that meditation on the chakras—the Vertical Pathway—will play a major role in the fulfillment of Jewish destiny.

Since the Tree of Life includes both chakra and meridian influences, many Jews will surely use the teachings of their own faith as a path to deeper awareness. The traditional symbols of Kabbalah may play a role, too, in helping Jews incorporate Yeshua into Judaism. As a spiritual force second only to God Himself, Yeshua is naturally associated with the sixth level of the Tree of Life, the sfiroth Binah and Hochmah. Through meditation on those sfirot and related symbols, Jews may find the spiritual connection that represents, for them, the true meaning of the Messiah.

The *yin-yang* structure of the Tree of Life—the Horizontal Pathway—has important implications for the future of Judaism as well. It anticipates the coming of an era whose spirit of love, compassion and forgiveness will complement the law, order and discipline of traditional Judaism. This is perhaps the final symbolism of the Tree of Life—as a vision of God's covenant with Israel fulfilled. When the Jewish people, represented by the sfirah Din, embrace their promised Messiah represented by the sfirah Hesed, Judaism will have its ultimate flowering at Tiferet. The heart chakra of the Jewish people will open and Israel will at last be ready to fulfill Isaiah's prophecy as a Light unto the Nations. The tensions between Judaism and Christianity, Aries and Pisces, Wood and Earth will have resolved themselves into a new paradigm of strength, gentleness, conciliation and peace. In the words of Isaiah 11:6:

> The wolf also shall dwell with the lamb, and the leopard shall lie down with the kid; and the calf and the young lion and the fatling together; and a little child shall lead them.

CONCLUSION

Astrological ages come and go. A new age begins every 2,000 years and a new cycle of ages every 24,000. The pattern has repeated itself countless times over the millennia, in most cases with no particular meaning for individual human beings or for the world as a whole.

The pattern this time is different. The Ages of Aries and Pisces corresponded to, and symbolized, the birth and early development of two great world religions. The Age of Aries coincided, too, with the appearance of a violent and aggressive European empire whose gradual decline signaled the coming of a new and more civilized era. The meeting of the Roman Empire and early Christianity was a dramatic, and tragic, symbol of a clash between two very different historical periods—and of a basic conflict within every human heart.

The coming of the Age of Aquarius, too, is filled with important symbolism, and with events that are making that symbolism real. Its dawning coincided with the end of World War II, the ingathering of the Jewish people and the rebirth of Israel, creating continuity with the events of the Old and New Testaments and the ages they represented. The structure of the Tree of Life mirrors the two ages past and the one now beginning and foresees a new kind of human society in centuries to come. The pattern is already manifesting itself in the accelerating world movement toward globalization, in the slow but steady growth in holistic understandings, and in the growing trend toward direct spiritual experience. All of these developments suggest that cosmic symbols and earthly events are converging in a way that has never happened before.

Yin, Yang and Planet Earth

The interplay of *yin* and *yang* is usually shown as a circle whose two interconnecting halves flow into, complement and help create one another (Figure 45). If the *yin-yang* circle is seen as a sphere or globe, it becomes a picture of planet Earth itself. Although human beings long ago divided the world into two parts—Orient and Occident, East and West—they probably never anticipated that the two hemispheres would evolve as complementary halves of an organic whole. Recent patterns make it clear that there is an ongoing two-way flow of *yin* and *yang* energies—*yin* from the East and *yang* from the West—that is making the world both more balanced and more complete.

FIGURE 45.
THE *YIN-YANG* CIRCLE

The flow of *yang* energies from the West has been going on for over 200 years. The West has led the way since at least the 18th century in bringing the tools of modern civilization to the world. Some of the highlights have been the Industrial Revolution that began in England in the 1700's; the French and American Revolutions that gave the world modern democracy; and the development of free market economic principles which have helped raise the standard of living for millions around the globe. Those principles are now beginning to bring wealth and prosperity to Asia's two largest and most populous nations—China and India.

The dawning awareness in the West of the life energy realm, the theme of this book, is the second half of that *yin-yang* exchange. The knowledge in the West that there is a deeper and more subtle dimension of reality—one that bridges the gap between mind and body and that can serve as a gateway to Spirit—represents a flow of *yin* energies from East to West. Life energy understandings have the potential to transform Western society in ways that are unimaginable today. In the end they will likely improve the spiritual lives of Westerners as much as Western ideas have improved the material lives of Easterners.

The Message in God's Art

In Chapter 6 I argued that God's art—the beautiful connections between human energies and the natural world, and between our own personalities and the heavens above—is evidence of an underlying unity in all of creation. We can see further evidence of that unity in the patterns that link Western society and religion with the passage of astrological ages, and in the diversity of human development that makes the earth itself a great symbol of the interplay of *yin* and *yang*.

Art as we understand it is intended for the enjoyment, and sometimes the education, of an audience. Who the intended audience is for God's art is an open question. Is it God Himself? Is it an unseen collection of living beings in other realms? Or could it be, at least in part, us?

People have been enjoying God's art since time began. The beauty of a sunset, the stillness of a summer morning, the charm of a baby's smile are universal human pleasures. The message in God's art—the lessons it contains—can be more elusive. On rare occasions a series of patterns converges and the message comes into clearer focus. As the 21st century begins, four separate holistic patterns are coming together: the growth of Western society and religion, the passage of astrological ages, the exchange of material and spiritual information across the hemispheres, and the blueprint for wholeness that mirrors those processes in every human body. All are pointing in the same direction—toward a collective vision of reconciliation and unity. The message in God's art is clear: we are embarking on an exceptionally important period in human history.

The important question for each of us is whether we will hear that holistic message and act on it—for the benefit of ourselves, our communities and the world as a whole. If we do, we may be rewarded one day with a chance to meet the Artist Himself.

ACKNOWLEDGEMENTS

This book was made possible by my shiatsu teacher, Kiku Miyazaki, and her staff at the Boston Shiatsu School who introduced me to the world of energy healing. I received further instruction, support and encouragement from many members of the greater Boston holistic healing community. Special thanks to Patricia Carusone and her staff at the Charles River Shiatsu School; to Rich Byrne and Herb Pearce for sharing their knowledge of the Enneagram; and to Henry Oliveras for teaching me Tai Chi.

For generously giving of their time to read and comment on the manuscript, my thanks to Joan Klagsbrun, Susan Lennox, Sarah James and Lonny Jarrett. For sharing her knowledge of astrology, reading and commenting on portions of the manuscript, and providing birth data for astrological charts, my thanks to Pat Taglilatello and Astrodatabank.com. Thanks to Daniel Will-Harris for his cover design and for his valuable guidance in choosing a title.

My sincere thanks to the staff at the Medford and Arlington, Massachusetts public libraries, and to the Minuteman Library Network, for being so helpful, courteous and efficient.

Finally, thanks beyond words to my mother, Ruth Lewin, for her complete and unconditional love and support, now and always, and to my partner, Kay Chambers, for her love, support and keen editorial eye.

NOTES

1. Those who argue today for a completely new kind of spirituality are recreating, in a slightly different form, the same belief in society's instant transformation as their counterparts of forty years ago. Some of these spiritual revolutionaries were members of the 60's generation themselves.

2. In China, life energy is known as *chi*; in India, *prana*; in Japan, *ki*; and in Korea, *dahn*.

3. Gia-Fu Feng and Jane English translators, *Tao te Ching*. New York: Vintage Books, 1972, Verse 1.

4. Ibid, Verse 42.

5. The four Fire meridians are heart, pericardium, small intestine and triple heater. Triple heater is the only one of the twelve primary meridians that is not named for a bodily organ. It governs, among other things, the body's heat regulating mechanism which in Chinese medicine is divided into upper, middle and lower parts—hence the name triple heater.

6. Giovanni Maciocia, *Foundations of Chinese Medicine*. Edinburgh: Churchill Livingstone, 1989, p. 19.

7. Lonny S. Jarrett, *Nourishing Destiny: The Inner Tradition of Chinese Medicine*. Stockbridge, MA: Spirit Path Press, 1998, p. 278.

8. *The Yellow Emperor's Classic of Medicine*, Maoshin Ni, Ph.D., translator. Boston: Shambhala Books, 1995, p. 116.

9. The lower and higher chakras overlap in many of their functions. The lower chakras carry some of the energies of love, compassion, creativity and other higher qualities. Upper chakras are responsible for everyday activities including thinking and talking. See, for example, the discussion of the chakras and intuition in chapter 5.

10. Caroline Myss, in her book *Anatomy of the Spirit: the Seven Stages of Power and Healing,* sees a triple parallel that includes the Tree of Life, the chakras and the seven Christian sacraments. All of these symbols, she says, are based on the same underlying truth, which can be experienced using whatever symbols or ideas are most meaningful to the individual.

11. www.healthandage.com/html/res/com/ConsModalities/ AnIntroductionToCAMcm.html.

12. "Complementary and Alternative Medical Therapies: Implications for Medical Education." Miriam S. Wetzel, Ph.D.; Ted J. Kaptchuk, OMD; Aviad Haramati, Ph.D.; and David M. Eisenberg, M.D., *Annals of Internal Medicine*, Vol. 138, Issue 3, Feb. 4, 2003, pp. 191-196. www.annals.org/cgi/content/abstract/138/3/191.

13. M. Irwin, M. Daniels M, S.C. Risch, E. Bloom and H. Weiner, "Plasma Cortisol and Natural Killer Cell Activity During Bereavement." *Biological Psychiatry*. 24: 173-78. 1988.

14. Daniel W. Foster, "Diabetes Mellitus," from *Harrison's Principles of Internal Medicine.* New York: McGraw-Hill, 1998.

15. Ibid.

16. Einstein later showed, in his theory of relativity and his equation $E=MC^2$, that matter and energy are interdependent and can be transformed into one another. In an analogous way, matter is seen in Asian philosophy as a kind of condensed life energy.

17. Barbara Ann Brennan, *Hands of Light: a Guide to Healing Through the Human Energy Field.* New York: Bantam Books, 1988, p. 42.

18. From "Sigmund Freud," www.iep.utm.edu/f/freud.htm#SH6b.

19. Leon Hammer, M.D., *Dragon Rises, Red Bird Flies.* Barrytown, NY: Station Hill Press, 1990, p. 226.

20. An excellent book on the Enneagram and spiritual growth is *Facets of Unity: The Enneagram of Holy Ideas* by A.H. Almaas. Berkeley, CA: Diamond Books, 1998.

21. Don Richard Riso with Russ Hudson, *Personality Types: Using the Enneagram for Self-Discovery.* Boston: Houghton Mifflin, 1996, p 331.

22. Candace Pert, Ph.D., *The Molecules of Emotion—Why You Feel The Way You Feel.* New York: Scribner's, 1997, p. 307.

23. "Examination of Brain Serotonin Receptors in Patients with Mood Disorders," www.clinical trials.gov/ct/gui/show/nct00026832.

24. C.W. Leadbeater, *The Chakras*, Wheaton, Il: Theosophical Publishing House, 1927, p.42.

25. Ibid.

26. James Morrison, *DSM-IV Made Easy: the Clinician's Guide to Diagnosis*. New York: Guilford Press, 1995, p. 265.

27. Ibid.

28. Ibid, p. 474.

29. The Germans' Wood dominance is undeniable, not only from their work ethic but from their recent history. Wood, as we have seen, is the energy of anger and aggression and World Wars I and II are ample evidence that, in the past at least, the Germans have been a strongly Wood-dominant people. The same can be said for the Japanese, who were aggressors in World War II and whose powerful work ethic has made their relatively small country into one of the world's largest economies.

As for the United States, Americans have an unusual combination of powerful Wood and Earth which have been struggling for dominance for over two centuries. I discuss that topic in Chapter 4.

30. Lonny S. Jarrett, *Nourishing Destiny: The Inner Tradition of Chinese Medicine*. Stockbridge, MA: Spirit Path Press, 1998.

31. Harriet Beinfield and Efrem Korngold, *Between Heaven and Earth*. New York: Ballantine Books, 1991.

32. Leon Hammer, M.D., *Dragon Rises, Red Bird Flies*. Barrytown, NY: Station Hill Press, 1990, p. 226.

33. Lonny S. Jarrett, *Nourishing Destiny: The Inner Tradition of Chinese Medicine*. Stockbridge, MA: Spirit Path Press, 1998, p. 278.

34. Harriet Beinfield and Efrem Korngold, *Between Heaven and Earth*. New York: Ballantine Books, 1991, p. 203.

35. Leon Hammer, M.D. *Dragon Rises, Red Bird Flies*. Barrytown, NY: Station Hill Press, 1990, p. 226.

36. http://Psychology.about.com/library/weekly/aa022000a.htm.

37. Donna Eden, *Energy Medicine*. New York: Jeremy P. Tarcher/Putnam, 1998, p. 245.

38. Ibid, p. 246.

39. Leon Hammer, M.D. *Dragon Rises, Red Bird Flies*. Barrytown, NY: Station Hill Press, 1990, p. 182.

326 NOTES

40. Barbara Ann Brennan, *Hands of Light: A Guide to Healing Through the Human Energy Field.* New York: Bantam Books 1987, p. 102.

41. Ibid, p. 82.

42. Richard S. Beaser, M.D., Phillip Levy, M.D., John A. Newcomer, M.D., "Schizophrenia, Bipolar Disorders and Diabetes: Interrelationships and Interventions," www.Medscape.com/viewprogram/2779.

43. The authorities are divided as to whether anxiety is mainly a Water or Metal disturbance. See for example *Manifesto for a New Medicine* by James S. Gordon, M.D. Reading, MA: Addison-Wesley Publishing, 1996, p. 194. But whether Earth fails to nourish Metal or to control Water, Earth's connecting power may play a role in either case.

44. Gary Yontef, "Introduction to Gestalt Therapy," www.gestalt.org. Excerpted from *Awareness, Dialogue and Process* by Gary Yontef. Highland, NY: Gestalt Journal Press, 1983.

45. Martin S. Fiebert, "Stages in a Gestalt Therapy Session and an Examination of Counselor Interventions." www.csulb.edu/~mfiebert/gestalt.htm.

46. Eugene T. Gendlin, Ph.D., *Focusing.* New York: Bantam New Age Books, 1978, p. xi (from the Introduction by Marilyn Ferguson).

47. Ibid, p. 165.

48. Ibid, p. xi.

49. Derek and Julia Parker, *The New Compleat Astrologer.* New York: Harmony Books, 1984, p. 12.

50. Ibid, p. 16.

51. Paramahansa Yogananda, *Autobiography of a Yogi.* Los Angeles: Self-Realization Fellowship Press, 1997, p. 187 (quoting Sri Yukteswar Giri).

52. Western astrology has four elements, not five, because Western astrology is derived from the Greek system, which recognizes only four elements.

53. There is a debate among astrologers as to whether the stars and planets actively influence personality and human life or whether they are merely passive symbols. Energy principles suggest there is a causal influence. On the other hand, if the arrangement of the planets is not in some sense symbolic, it would be hard to explain why the moment of birth is so much more important

than any other time in determining a person's makeup.

54. Chinese energy principles can help explain the connection between Air and Metal. In Chinese medicine Metal is the energy of the lung meridian and of the lungs, the organs of respiration. The relationship between Metal and breathing helps confirm, too, that in the Kabbalalistic Tree of Life, the cosmic Breath of God corresponds to Metal energy in the human body (see Chapter 7).

55. Aries is the third traditional Fire sign but, because its dominant energy is Wood, not Fire, I treat Aries as a Wood sign and discuss it in the section on Wood energies.

56. Birth data courtesy of AstroDatabank.com. Rodden Rating A.

57. Derek and Julia Parker, *The New Compleat Astrologer*. New York: Harmony Books, 1984, p. 141.

58. Birth data courtesy of AstroDatabank.com. Rodden Rating B.

59. Birth data courtesy of AstroDatabank.com. Rodden Rating A.

60. Birth data courtesy of AstroDatabank.com. Rodden Rating A.

61. Birth data courtesy of AstroDatabank.com. Rodden Rating DD (conflicting/unverified).

62. Birth data courtesy of AstroDatabank.com. Rodden Rating AA.

63. Birth data courtesy of AstroDatabank.com. Rodden Rating B.

64. Birth data courtesy of AstroDatabank.com. Rodden Rating A.

65. Birth data courtesy of AstroDatabank.com. Rodden Rating DD (conflicting/unverified).

66. Birth data courtesy of AstroDatabank.com. Rodden Rating DD (conflicting/unverified).

67. From "Thomas Jefferson," http://en.wikipedia.org/wiki / Thomas_ Jeffer-son.

68. Derek and Julia Parker, *The New Compleat Astrologer*. New York: Harmony Books, 1984, p. 124.

69. Birth data courtesy of AstroDatabank.com. Rodden Rating AA.

70. Derek and Julia Parker, *The New Compleat Astrologer.* New York: Harmony Books, 1984. p. 137.

71. Ibid, p. 145.

72. I am a member of Self Realization Fellowship and Paramahansa Yogananda is my guru.

73. Birth data courtesy of AstroDatabank.com. Rodden Rating A.

74. Birth data courtesy of AstroDatabank.com. Rodden Rating DD (conflicting/unverified).

75 .www.vatican.va/news_services/liturgy/saints.

76. Birth data courtesy of AstroDatabank.com. Rodden Rating B.

77. John Gray, Ph.D., *Men are from Mars, Women are from Venus.* New York: HarperCollins, 1992, p. 16.

78. Ibid, p. 18.

79. There are, of course, many ways of understanding society and the forces that shape it other than through life energies. Just as in studying personality, non-energy based models have their own unique value and insights. The advantage of a Five Elements approach is that the five energies are basic building blocks of every human being. Therefore, whether in the study of individual personality or society, an energy model is primary rather than derivative.

To compare, see for example "The Never-Ending Quest: An Interview with Dr. Don Beck" by Jessica Roemischer in *What is Enlightenment? Spirituality for the 21st Century,* Fall-Winter 2002. The model discussed there, Spiral Dynamics, is composed of what are called memes, each of which represents a stage of human development. Each of the eight memes is given a color ("the red meme," the "green meme" and so on). The descriptions of the memes make it clear that each corresponds roughly to a chakra or to one or more Five Elements energies. The red meme, for example, which arose about 10,000 years ago, represents the "raw, egocentric self" and "conquers, outfoxes and dominates other aggressive characters." The red meme is another name for Wood energy dominance and—not surprisingly, since it is the third of eight memes—it embodies the energies of the third or power chakra.

The blue meme illustrates the hybrid quality of memes and how, as with astrological signs, knowing the combinations of energies that make them up can give greater understanding. The blue meme, which appeared around the

time of the Old Testament, represents, according to Don Beck, the clash between the desires of the personal ego, a search for unity and transcendence
and a developing sense of law, order and justice. That conflict is embodied in
the universal tension between Wood energy and its Controlling Cycle
neighbors, Metal and Earth. It is portrayed graphically on page 101, Figure
18 where I describe it as a portrait of civilization.

80. From "Types of Governments," http://users.erols.com/, mwhite28/20c-govt.htm.

81. Harriet Beinfield and Efrem Korngold, *Between Heaven and Earth.* New
York: Ballantine Books, 1991, p. 140.

82. *Bhagavad Gita*, Edwin Arnold translation, Chapter 1.

83. David G. Myers, *Intuition: Its Powers and Perils.* New Haven: Yale University Press, 2002, P. 1.

84. Barbara Ann Brennan, *Hands of Light: A Guide to Healing Through the
Human Energy Field.* New York: Bantam Books 1987, p. 5.

85. Ibid, p. 153.

86. Ibid, p. 43.

87. Ibid, p. 7.

88. Ibid, p. 10.

89. Ibid, p. 7.

90. Ibid,. p. 10.

91. Caroline Myss, *Anatomy of the Spirit: the Seven Stages of Power and
Healing.* New York: Three Rivers Press, 1996, p. 33.

92. Ibid, p. 33-34.

93. Ibid, p. 3.

94. Paramahansa Yogananda, *Self-Realization Fellowship Lessons.* Los
Angeles: Self-Realization Press, S-1, P-25, p. 6, quoting Sri Yukteswar Giri.

95. "The 60's Peace Symbol," http://en.wikipedia.org/wiki/Peace_Symbol.

96. Anodea Judith, *Wheels of Life, a User's Guide to the Chakra System*. St. Paul, MN: Llewelyn Publications, 2001, pp. 114, 117. 157, 201.

97. Donna Eden, *Energy Medicine*. New York: Jeremy P. Tarcher/Putnam, 1998. p. 148.

98. Ibid, p. 151-2.

99. Anodea Judith, *Wheels of Life, a User's Guide to the Chakra System*. St. Paul, MN: Llewelyn Publications, 2001, p. 112.

100. Ibid, p. 193.

101. Caroline Myss, *Anatomy of the Spirit: the Seven Stages of Power and Healing*. New York: Three Rivers Press, 1996, p. 39.

102. Davidine Siaw-Voon Sim and David Gaffney, *Chen Style Taijiquan: the Source of Taiji Boxing*. Berkeley, CA: North Atlantic Books, 2002, p. 49.

103. Ibid, p. 101.

104. Ibid, p. 61-62.

105. Donna Eden, *Energy Medicine*. New York: Jeremy P. Tarcher/Putnam, 1998, p. 150.

106. Gia-Fu Feng and Jane English, translators, *Tao te Ching*. New York: Vintage Books, 1972, Verse 1.

107. Daniel Dennett, *Consciousness Explained*. New York: Little, Brown & Co., 1991, p. 40.

108. Ibid, p. 35.

109. Ibid,. p. 25.

110. Ibid, p. 431.

111. Paul Davies, *God and the New Physics*. New York: Simon and Schuster, 1983, p. 141.

112. Sri Yukteswar Giri, *The Holy Science*. Los Angeles: Self-Realization Press, 1990, p. 47.

113. Gia-Fu Feng and Jane English, translators, *Tao te Ching*. New York:

Vintage Books, 1972, Verse 1.

114. Some individuals and groups today use the term Intelligent Design as a euphemism for creationism, and as a tactic for introducing a creationist world view into public education and the debate over evolution. I believe the universe was intelligently designed but am not a believer in creationism.

115. Ho, M.W. and Saunders, P.T., "Beyond Neo-Darwinism—an Epigenetic Approach to Evolution," *Journal of Theoretical Biology*, 78, 589 (1979) (Source: Michael J. Behe, *Darwin's Black Box*. New York: Touchstone Books, 1996, p. 28).

116. Michael J. Behe, *Darwin's Black Box*. New York: Touchstone Books, 1996, p. 65.

117. Ibid, p. 187.

118. William Paley, *Natural Theology*. New York: American Tract Society, pp. 9-10. (Source: Michael J. Behe, *Darwin's Black Box*. New York: Touchstone Books, 1996 p. 211).

119. Ibid, p. 212.

120. Richard Dawkins, *The Blind Watchmaker*. New York: Norton, 1986, p. 112.

121. Ibid, p. 141.

122. Ibid, p. 6.

123. Kenneth R. Miller, *Finding Darwin's God*. New York: Cliff Street Books, 1999, p. 236.

124. Charles Darwin, *The Origin of Species*, Chapter 1.

125. From "The Life and Letters of Charles Darwin" dated May 22, 1860. (Source: Kenneth R. Miller, *Finding Darwin's God*. New York: Cliff Street Books, 1999, p. 312).

126. In his letter to Asa Gray, Darwin said the following: "There seems to me too much misery in the world. I cannot persuade myself that a beneficent and omnipotent God would have designedly created the Ichneumonidae [wasps] with the express intention of their [larvae] feeding within the living bodies of Caterpillars, or that a cat should play with mice."

127. The laws of quantum mechanics apparently play a role in events at the molecular level where mutations occur. This suggests that mutations, like the behavior of matter at the quantum level, may be, at least for us, inherently unpredictable. Unpredictability, however, is not the same as chance. See for example "Chance from a Theistic Perspective" by Loren Haarsma. www. talkorigins.org/faqs/chance/chance-theistic.html.

128. Kenneth R. Miller, *Finding Darwin's God.* New York: Cliff Street Books, 1999, p 233.

129. Ibid, p. 49.

130. Barbara Ann Brennan, *Hands of Light: A Guide to Healing Through the Human Energy Field.* New York: Bantam Books,1987, p 49.

131. from "Free Will," www.rep.routledge.com/article/V014.

132. From "Kabbalah," www.jewish encyclopedia .com/kabbalah.

133. Ibid.

134. Ibid.

135. G. Scholem, translator, *Sefer Yitzirah*, Chapter 1, Verses 11-12. www. psyche.com/psyche/txt/scholem_sy.html.

136. Rebeka Kenton, "A Kabbalistic View of the Chakras*,"* www.kabbalah society.org/chakras.htm, 1997 (quoting in part from *Kundalini Tantra* by Swami Satyananda Saraswati).

137. In the Tree of Life, Hesed and Din are one level above Tiferet, suggesting that their energies may be superior to Tiferet even though they ultimately merge there. Since that is not how personal growth works, the diagram, like most simple models of complex systems, may simply be inaccurate on certain points.

138. Paramahansa Yogananda commented that a person could experience God either as Male or Female, and that the latter was easier because "The Mother is closer than the Father."

139. Rebeka Kenton, "A Kabbalistic View of the Chakras." www.Kabbalah society.org/chakras.htm, 1997.

140. From "G.W.F. Hegel (1770-1831)," www.marxists.org/reference/ archive/hegel/help/hegelbio.htm.

141. Din is the Hebrew word for law. A lawyer is an Orech Din (Arranger of Law). Since Metal is the energy of laws and structures, Din has an important Metal component. Seen as a symbol of Judaism, Din represents a blending of values and judgment (Metal) with the strength and firmness needed to enforce those values and judgments (Wood). Din's alternate name, Gvurah (Strength or Power), underscores the important Wood component in the sfirah Din.

142. More generally, the story of the Garden of Eden is the story of *yin* and *yang* themselves. The Tree of the Knowledge of Good and Evil is a symbol of life's duality. Before they succumb to temptation and eat from the Tree, Adam and Eve's energies, like God's, are integrated; they live in a state of grace and wholeness. The Fall represents the transition of Spirit into a human body where it must navigate through a world of pleasure and pain, freedom and fear, love and hate. The Tree in the Garden, in fact, is the Kabbalistic Tree of Life itself.

143. If Isaiah had wanted to be absolutely clear, he could have used the word *btulah*, the Hebrew word for virgin. But if he had done that, the Jewish people might have accepted Jesus 2,000 years ago and Christianity as we know it might never have come into existence.

When Isaiah says that the Messiah "shall be called Immanuel" ("God is With Us"), he is apparently referring, not to the Messiah's name, but to his spiritual elevation.

144. Elaine Pagels, *Beyond Belief: the Secret Gospel of Thomas.* New York: Random House, 2005, p. 54, citing Gospel of Thomas 3, in NHL 118.

145. Ibid, pp. 55-56, citing Gospel of Thomas 50, in NHL 123.

146. From "A Glossary of Buddhist Terms," http://villa.lakes.com/cdpatton/Dharma/Canon/glossary.html.

147. Paramahansa Yogananda, *Autobiography of a Yogi.* Los Angeles: Self-Realization Fellowship Press, 1997, pp. 370-71.

148. Ibid, p. 371, citing Luke 1:13-17.

149. Ibid, pp. 371-2.

150. Ibid, p. 194, citing Luke 11:34-35.

151. Ibid, p. 551.

BIBLIOGRAPHY

Almaas, A.H., *Facets of Unity: the Enneagram of Holy Ideas*. Berkeley, CA: Diamond Books, 1998.

Behe, Michael J., *Darwin's Black Box*. New York: Touchstone Books, 1996.

Beinfield, Harriet and Korngold, Efrem, *Between Heaven and Earth*. NY: Ballantine Books, 1991.

Brennan, Barbara Ann, *Hands of Light: A Guide to Healing Through the Human Energy Field*. New York: Bantam New Age Books, 1987.

Brill, Dr. A.A., *The Basic Writings of Sigmund Freud*. New York: Modern Library, 1938.

Burns, E., M.D. and Leventhal, E., Ph.D., M.D., "Aging, Immunity and Cancer," *Cancer Control: Journal of the Moffitt Cancer Center,* 7 (6), 2000, pp. 513-522.

Clark, Ronald W., *Freud: the Man and the Cause: a Biography*. New York: Random House, 1980.

Davies, Paul, *God and the New Physics*. New York: Simon and Schuster, 1983.

Darwin, Charles, *The Origin of Species,* 1859.

Dawkins, Richard, *The Blind Watchmaker*. New York: Norton & Company, 1986.

Dennett, D.C., *Consciousness Explained*. New York: Little, Brown & Co., 1991.

Eden, Donna, *Energy Medicine*. New York: Jeremy P. Tarcher/ Putnam, 1998.

Felten, David L., M.D., "Chronic Depression and Cancer," Klsdesign. com/anti-ox/healthy-mind-depression.htm.

Feng, Gia-Fu and English, Jane translators, *Tao te Ching*. New York: Random House/Vintage Books, 1972.

Freud, Sigmund, *The Interpretation of Dreams*. Cutchogue, NY: Buccaneer Books, 1985.

Gallacher, Sweetnam et al, "Is Type A Behavior Really a Trigger for Heart Disease Events?" *Psychosomatic Medicine*, 65(3), May 2003.

Gendlin, Eugene T., Ph.D., *Focusing*. New York: Bantam New Age Books, 1981.

Gordon, James S., M.D., *Manifesto for a New Medicine*. Reading, MA: Addison-Wesley Publishing, 1996.

Gray, John, Ph.D. , *Men are from Mars, Women are from Venus*. NY: HarperCollins, 1992.

Haarsma, Loren, "Chance from a Theistic Perspective," www.talk origins.org/faqs/chance/chance-theistic.html.

Hammer, Leon, M.D., *Dragon Rises, Red Bird Flies*. Barrytown, NY: Station Hill Press, 1990.

Harris, William S. and Calvert, John H., "Intelligent Design: the Scientific Alternative to Evolution," *The National Catholic Bioethics Quarterly*, Autumn 2003.

Haynes, S., Feinleib, M. et al, "The Relationship of Psychosocial Factors to Coronary Heart Disease in the Framingham Study," Studies II and III, *American Journal of Epidemiology*. Vol. 107, 1978, pp. 387-402, and Vol. 111, 1980, pp. 37-58.

Jarrett, Lonny S., *Nourishing Destiny: The Inner Tradition of Chinese Medicine*. Stockbridge, MA: Spirit Path Press, 1998.

Judith, Anodea, *Wheels of Life: A User's Guide to the Chakra System*. St. Paul, MN: Llewelyn Publications, 2001.

Kaptchuk, Ted J., O.M.D., *The Web That Has No Weaver*. Chicago: Congdon and Weed, 1983.

Leadbeater, C.W., *The Chakras*. Wheaton, IL: Theosophical Publishing House, 1927.

Lowen, Alexander, M.D., *Bioenergetics*. New York: Penguin Books, 1975.

Lundberg, Paul, *The Book of Shiatsu*. New York: Simon and Schuster, 1992.

Maciocia, Giovanni, *Foundations of Chinese Medicine*. Edinburgh: Churchill Livingstone, 1989.

Masunaga, Shizuto with Ohashi, Wataru, *Zen Shiatsu: How to Harmonize Yin and Yang for Better Health*. Tokyo: Japan Publications Inc., 1977.

Miller, Kenneth R., *Finding Darwin's God*. New York: Cliff Street Books, 1999.

Morrison, James, *DSM-IV Made Easy: the Clinician's Guide to Diagnosis*. New York: Guilford Press, 1995-2001.

Myss, Caroline, Ph.D., *Anatomy of the Spirit: the Seven Stages of Power and Healing*. New York: Three Rivers Press, 1996.

Ni, Maoshing, Ph.D., translator, *The Yellow Emperor's Classic of Medicine*. Boston: Shambhala Books, 1995.

O'Connor, John and Bensky, Dan, translators and editors, *Acupuncture: a Comprehensive Text,* Shanghai College of Traditional Medicine. Seattle: Eastland Press, 1981.

Osborne, Arthur, *Ramana Maharshi and the Path of Self-Knowledge*. York Beach, ME: Samuel Weiser, Inc., 1970.

Pagels, Elaine, *Beyond Belief: the Secret Gospel of Thomas*. New York: Random House, 2005.

Parker, Derek and Julia, *"The New Compleat Astrologer*. New York: Harmony Books, 1984.

Perls, Fritz, *The Gestalt Approach & Eyewitness to Therapy.* Palo Alto, CA: Science and Behavior Books, 1973.

Pert, Candace B. Ph.D., *Molecules of Emotion: Why you Feel the Way you Feel.* New York: Scribner's, 1997.

Riso, Don Richard with Hudson, Russ, *Personality Types: Using the Enneagram for Self-Discovery.* Boston: Houghton Mifflin, 1996.

Roemischer, Jessica, "The Never-Ending Quest: An Interview with Dr. Don Beck," from *What is Enlightenment? Spirituality for the 21st Century,* Fall-Winter 2002.

Scholem, Gershom, *Major Trends in Jewish Mysticism.* New York: Schocken Books, 1995.

———, *On the Kabbalah and Its Symbolism,* Ralph Manheim translator. New York: Schocken Books, 1965.

—— translator, *Sefer Yitzirah.* www.psyche.com/psyche/txt/scholem_sy.html.

Sim, Siaw-Voon and Gaffney, David, *Chen Style Taijiquan: the Source of Taiji Boxing.* New York: North Atlantic Books, 2002.

Wilber, Ken, *A Theory of Everything.* Boston: Shambhala Books, 2000.

Yogananda, Paramahansa, *Autobiography of a Yogi.* Los Angeles: Self Realization Fellowship, 1996.

———, *Self-Realization Fellowship Lessons Volumes 1 and 2.* Los Angeles: Self-Realization Fellowship, 1978.

Yukteswar, Swami Sri, *The Holy Science.* Los Angeles: Self- Realization Fellowship, 8th Edition 1990.

INDEX

Nazism, 297
Netzach, 285-87
Neuropeptides, 95
Nirvana, 254
Nixon, Richard, 173-76, 204
Nostradamus, 220
Nurturing and Controlling Cycles
 conflict, value of, 36
 correspondences, 35
 diagram, 34
 and emotional health, 83-121
 and energy homeostasis, 47-48
 and the Enneagram, 80-83
 and Freud's developmental stages,
 75-80
 and men and women, 185-91
 and physical health, 48-67
 and spiritual growth, 280-81, 285-
 88, 291
 and the Tree of Life, 285-88

Observer Effect, 251, 272
Obsessive-Compulsive Disorder, 99-
 100
Oral Stage, *See* Freud, Sigmund

Pagels, Elaine, 310-11
Palestinian conflict, 309
Paley, William, 255-57
Passion, the, 301-05
Passover, the, 301-03, 305-06
Peace symbol, '60's, 225-27
Perls, Fritz, 124-25
Pert, Candace, Ph.D., 95, 227
Phallic Stage, *See* Freud, Sigmund
Pisces, Age of, 295-98, 308, 316-17
 as symbol of Christianity, 159, 295-
 96
 symbol of in Tree of Life, 299
Pisces, sign of, 159-62
Poetry of the body, 34-35, 79, 264
Pranayama, 279, 281-82
Psyche, split in the American, 194-95
Puritans, 105

Quality and quantity of life energy,
 60-61

Reagan, Ronald, 179-80, 205-07
Reichian therapy, 123-124

Reiki, 121-22
Repressed emotion defined, 72
Republicans, 203-05
Rising sign defined, 140-41
Robber Barons, 199-200
Roman Empire, 296-97, 317
Romantic temperament, 89
Roosevelt, Franklin D., 201-03
Roosevelt, Teddy, 199-200
Rousseau, Jean Jacques, 192-94, 202-04

Sadness, 31, 56, 88-89, 97, 166
Sagittarius, sign of, 142-45, 179-80, 207
Saturn as planet of limitation, 153-54, 265
Schizoid pattern, 115-18, 192-93, 273
Scorpio, sign of, 148-53
Seasonal Affective Disorder, 97-99
Second Coming, 313-15
Sefer Yitzirah, 282, 285-86
Serotonin, 95-97
Shekinah, 284
Shiatsu, 54, 68
Shen, 84, 284
Social Contract, 192-94
Spleen energy, 66-67, 111-12
Sports and body energies, 236-41
SSRI's, 96
Stomach energy, 64-66, 107-08, 117-18
Subjective Idealism, 250-51

Tai Chi, 99, 234-237, 240-41
Tao, 26-27, 198, 241, 253, 281
Tao te Ching. 26-27, 241, 253
 existence before the Big Bang, 26
 origin of *yin* and *yang*, 27
Taoism, 26-27, 253
Taurus, sign of, 172, 182-84
Teresa, Mother, 179-82
Third Eye, 232-33, 289
Thomas, Gospel of, 310-11
Tiferet, 288, 299-300, 316
Tillich, Paul, 286
Toxic energies, 61-62
Tree of Life, 23, 40-41, 279-80,
 282-90, 297-300, 307-08, 315-16
Tumor formation, 59-61
Type A behavior, 48-55

Unconscious, the, 20, 72-74, 233-34, 240,
 245, 249, 272